Student Teacher to Master Teacher

MICHAEL S. ROSENBERG
THE JOHNS HOPKINS UNIVERSITY

LAWRENCE J. O'SHEA
FLORIDA ATLANTIC UNIVERSITY

DOROTHY J. O'SHEA
FLORIDA ATLANTIC UNIVERSITY

Student Teacher to Master Teacher

A Handbook for Preservice and Beginning Teachers of Students with Mild and Moderate Handicaps

MACMILLAN PUBLISHING COMPANY
NEW YORK
COLLIER MACMILLAN CANADA
TORONTO

Editor: Robert Miller
Production Supervisor: Betsy Keefer
Text Designer: Robert Freese
Cover Designer: Natasha Sylvester

This book was set in 10/12 Baskerville by V & M Graphics, printed and bound by R.R. Donnelly & Sons. The cover was printed by Phoenix Color Corp.

Macmillan Publishing Company
866 Third Avenue, New York, New York 10022

Collier Macmillan Canada
1200 Eglinton Ave, E.
Don Mills, Ontario M3C 3N1

LIBRARY OF CONGRESS CATALOGING-IN-PUBLICATION DATA

Rosenberg, Michael S.
    Student teacher to master teacher : a handbook for preservice and beginning teachers of students with mild and moderate handicaps Michael S. Rosenberg, Lawrence J. O'Shea, Dorothy J. O'Shea.
        p.   cm.
    ISBN 0-02-403650-1
    1. Handicapped children — Education — Handbooks, manuals, etc.
2. Special education — Handbooks, manuals, etc.   3. Teachers of handicapped children — Training of — Handbooks, manuals, etc.
I. O'Shea, Lawrence J.   II. O'Shea, Dorothy.   III. Title.
LC4015.R664   1991
371.9 — dc20   90-30606
                                                              CIP

Printing: 1 2 3 4 5 6 7   Year: 1 2 3 4 5 6 7

To Irene and Daniel — so much!
                          MSR

*To Lindsay and Chris — For the love,
devotion, and patience.*
                          LJO
                          DJO

Foreword

I have been a special education teacher and teacher of special education teachers for more than twenty years. During much of that time, sometimes four times a year, students have appeared at the end of their final quarter or semester of study ready to "quit teaching." Confronted with the possibility of making the transition from school to the real world, many very well-trained people seem to have serious doubts about their competence. At those times, I usually point out the significant number of hours of professional credits they have, the fine reputation of the faculty who have taught them, and the wonderful reputation of their department and college. Usually, those speeches don't make much difference in how the students feel or in their apparent willingness to actually start teaching. That's when I always fall back on some inane, equally innocuous advice: "Don't worry. Be happy. Nobody knows what they're doing when they leave undergraduate (graduate) school." It's times like those that I often wished I had a book to recommend or give to these students—a book to hand to them and say, "Things will work out."

Mike Rosenberg and Larry and Doris O'Shea have written such a book. Grounded in the idea that successful field-based experiences are central to effective and efficient development of teachers, *Student Teacher to Master Teacher* is a textbook that neophyte and experienced teachers will find very useful. Taking the perspective that good teachers plan, deliver, and manage instruction, Rosenberg, O'Shea, and O'Shea have prepared a comprehensive resource for teachers, teachers-in-training, and teacher trainers. Based largely on the premise that most students in special education classes are mildly handicapped, *Student Teacher to Master Teacher* is full of practical suggestions for what to do when teaching them in self-contained classes and resource rooms.

It is clear from reading this book that the authors have been successful teachers and teachers of teachers. The examples of worksheets and forms as well as the clear organization and writing style are just the kinds of information prospective beginning (or experienced) teachers need. I am pleased to have had an opportunity to contribute to this book; I encourage you to read it and to share it often with students and friends.

Bob Algozzine, Ph.D.
University of North Carolina at Charlotte

Preface

The basic purpose of *Student Teacher to Master Teacher: A Handbook for Preservice and Beginning Teachers of Students with Mild and Moderate Handicaps* is to provide a written text intended primarily for use during a supervised special education student teaching experience or graduate practicum. New teachers using the handbook will be involved with students with mild and moderate mental retardation, learning disabilities, and/or behavior disorders. The field experience of new teachers usually is listed as the terminal requirement for teacher certification sequences at both undergraduate and graduate levels. It is often described as the single most important component of the preservice level training program. In terms of approach and content, the handbook may also be an appropriate choice for other preservice settings such as methods or laboratory courses, as well as a variety of inservice activities specifically designed for teachers new to the field of special education.

The approach used in this handbook is based on two interrelated assumptions. First, we believe student teaching and initial practicum experiences should be rigorous and as realistic as possible. They should be developed to insure the preservice level teacher enters the professional job market with the skills needed for both survival and success. Few teacher educators would question this view, and many may regard it as an obvious, somewhat pious statement of fact. Interpretation and actual field implementation of this view appear to vary considerable, however, affecting the validity of the basic assumption in reference to specific teacher training programs. In the absence of structure and purposeful activities or requirements, there may be no valid criteria for assessing easily delineated teaching skills across varied settings. In fact, the apparent discrepancy between theory and successful application may significantly reduce program credibility.

Our second assumption is that special education field experiences should incorporate a variety of structured requirements and activities that collectively "bridge the gap" between methods and/or laboratory courses and actual independent, professional teaching. We recognize the need for more structured, reality-based, and relevant preservice experiences. Prior to the handbook's development, we noted the paucity of information available to developing teachers on links between offerings of tertiary trainings and actual classroom happenings. What we found when observing, supervising, managing, and evaluating preservice and beginning teachers often was a progressive problem of linking preservice training and practicum requirements to real teaching skills and actual on-the-job activities. Topics of this handbook were chosen because we believe these represent many of the most pertinent issues new teachers will face when they begin their initial practicum experiences or when they manage their first classrooms on their own.

Throughout the development of the handbook and through our own experiences as classroom teachers and supervisors of developing teachers, we also realized the needs of college supervisors. We believe these individuals involved with the supervision of student teachers and practicum students often are the forgotten souls, desperately trying to promote tertiary practices while perceiving problems of logistics, timing, and realities of modern schools. These often are individuals who must face experienced teachers' claims to novice teachers that "it can't be done like that" or "theory is only relevant in textbooks and it will never work here" to the university instructors' calls for "increased best practices" in classrooms. We believe college supervisors will welcome a commercially prepared resource to aid them in their roles. The handbook was developed to reduce the amount of time needed by supervisory faculty and staff in the review and possible remediation of key concepts associated with successful teaching. We hope the use of the handbook will allow more time for the important job of observing and providing feedback to preservice teachers and in supervisors' roles as liaisons to classroom teachers and administrators, university faculty, and preservice teachers.

In summary, throughout this handbook we provide to new and beginning teachers tips and insights to help them grow professionally with their chosen career over time, starting during their practicum and continuing through their beginning years in teaching. We recognize the enormous amount of information teachers new to special education must obtain and be able to demonstrate during their initial work with students with mild and moderate handicaps. The handbook is meant to help new teachers' transitions from the role of student at the preservice level to professional at the inservice level. Each of the topics in the handbook has been judged a pertinent topic for new teachers and we believe will remain relevant to them as their experience grows.

Chapter 1 of the text is written to provide an introduction to the student teaching experience and an overview of the field of working with students with mild and moderate handicaps. The chapter provides a discussion on the typical fears and concerns of student teachers and beginning special education teachers. It also introduces ethical and professionals standards of teachers that will be highlighted throughout the proceeding chapters. Tips to use diplomacy in the workplace and an emphasis on maximizing people skills underscore our call for both effective interpersonal communication and teaching skills necessary to become "master teachers." As do all chapters, Chapter 1 ends with a summary of related resources for the interested reader.

Chapter 2 is provided to give the novice teacher an understanding of the legal bases for assessment and programming to students with handicaps. Pertinent legislation and litigation of the last three decades are presented as the foundation of legal challenges teachers today will face. Major components of federal mandates for school-aged students and infants and toddlers are summarized as are tips for working within the system to solve potential legal problems faced by teachers. Assumptions underlying successful mediation attempts with students, family members, and professionals are discussed as means to avoid unnecessary litigation.

Chapter 3 deals with the "nuts and bolts" of actual instructional themes of the classroom. Tips to organize and manage instructional time with an emphasis on effectiveness and consistency are presented. Ways of setting up and maintaining effective scheduling procedures are discussed. A system for the development of classroom rules and procedures, as well as other management strategies (e.g., planning for group size, arranging the physical environment) are provided. Available resources at the new teacher's disposal and tips for beginning the school year are included.

Chapter 4 is meant to stress the need for effective planning as a catalyst to appropriate instruction. Successfully planned lessons are illustrated to include the relationship of instructional objectives to students' individualized education plans (IEP), the teacher's preparation for and demonstration of understanding of prerequisite skills of students, task analyses and learning sequences, the need for concise descriptions of instructional activities and materials linked to predetermined objectives, systematic methods to evaluate lessons, and anticipation of problems that might occur anywhere along the implementation phase of the instructional delivery to students. A section on lesson plan follow-up with tips to remediate and/or prevent actual problems observed during lessons, a review of instructional techniques used in varied lesson formats, and tips for lesson appraisal so new teachers can practice self-evaluation are embedded within the chapter.

Chapter 5 is organized to stress the importance of delivery of instruction. The concept of effective teacher behaviors is discussed along the dimensions of a structured academic focus, specific teaching of academic concepts, and a planned instructional sequence that is based on environmental variables and needs of students. Dimensions of direct instruction and the guided discovery approach are identified with numerous examples of these teaching approaches throughout the chapter.

The information in Chapter 6 is provided to encourage classroom management by the new teacher from the beginning of his or her involvement with students. The chapter is written to underscore the importance of the dimensions of promoting discipline by teachers and the development of self-control in students. A brief review of behavioral principles and rules governing classroom behavior is provided to highlight teachers' use of strategies to increase and/or maintain appropriate student behaviors and to decrease or eliminate inappropriate student behaviors. Tips to identifying, observing, recording, and illustrating problem behaviors are explained. Logistical concerns in developing large group management and means of designing individual behavior change programs and reports are discussed. Finally, the chapter is structured to provide some practical strategies to teachers to facilitate and promote self-control strategies of their students.

Chapter 7 is written to provide developing and beginning teachers a summary of paperwork involved in special education and the documentation necessary in the referral process of special education. The chapter begins with the prereferral steps of helping students with problem behaviors or learning difficulties to remain in the least restrictive environment before calling for changes in students' educational placements. New teachers are provided the steps of working with other professionals and parents to document precisely the need for all changes in educational decisions. Tips for working with parents, administrators, regular educators, and others involved in educational planning teams are pinpointed. Additionally, IEPs and IEP meetings are discussed, stressing the IEP as a legal plan parents and professionals develop together. The chapter is ended with suggestions provided to help developing and beginning teachers write reports to others of students' progress and to promote continuous methods of communication with parents and significant professionals to students with mild and moderate handicaps.

Chapters 8 and 9 are written to provide insights into methods of collaborative consultation new teachers will use when working with professionals and parents in school-based activities and educational meetings. The role of teaming is stressed throughout the handbook as an important strategy to encourage effective educational decision making for all students. Chapter 8 is intended to build a case for the necessity of strong interpersonal communication skills of teachers including colleague relationships stressing positive regard, empathy, and warmth toward peers. Tips on consulting services, especially when interacting with supervisory personnel, accepting constructive criticism from supervisors and administrators, and working as consultants with peers are discussed. Chapter 9 also is written to provide insights into working collaboratively with other professionals and paraprofessionals from the teaming dimension. Stresses involved when teachers apply increased teaming strategies are sources of conflict to many new teachers (e.g., in their roles as managers of volunteers and paraprofessionals; in their responsibilities as student advocates to parents, peers and other professionals; and in their efforts to uphold professional ethics often in the face of unseemingly large risks and impossible odds). Teacher burnout issues that may impede the master teacher process and means of recognizing and managing stress are presented in Chapter 9. Finally, the chapter is ended with suggestions to plan for continued employment or advancement within the field and to maintain the status of master teacher through involvement in professional organizations, active participation in recertification and inservice programs, and commitment to advocacy groups.

By designing the handbook as an easy-to-use resource, we hope the use of the text will not end once the practicum/student teaching or first year of teaching ends. We believe the chapters of the book reflect concerns typically faced by many teachers as they continue to grow as special educators. The handbook was written with the hopes of assisting beginning special education teachers to become and maintain their status as master teachers throughout their teaching careers.

We wish to express our gratitude to the following individuals who devoted a great deal of personal and professional time to the task of helping us complete this book. The faculty and staff in the Division of Education at The Johns Hopkins University, the Schonell Special Education Resource Centre of the University of Queensland, the University of Florida, and Florida Atlantic University provided much support and encouragement throughout all phases of this project. In particular, we acknowledge the artistic contributions of Ruth Roberts and Sharon Lampkin and the overall assistance of Shirley Belz and Ellen Noel. Pam Tupe helped to type the original manuscript. We also gratefully acknowledge the many contributions of the experienced teachers we have worked with who continually remind us that there is a vast number of master special education teachers. We also appreciate the efforts of the numerous developing teachers we have supervised over the past ten years. They have inspired us to focus on their needs for survival and success. We appreciate the efforts of significant individuals who served as role models to us including Bob Algozzine, Bill Reid, Paul Sindelar, and James Van Tassel. We also wish to express our appreciation to Robert Miller at Macmillan and to Betsy Keefer, who kept us "on task" and "on-time" as well as the reviewers of the earlier drafts of our chapters including John R. Beattie, University of North Carolina at Charlotte; Sandra B. Cohen, University of Virginia; Stewart Ehly, University of Iowa; Janet Lerner, Northeastern Illinois University; Terry M. McLeod, North Georgia College; and Virginia Trumble, Keene State College.

Finally, we wish to express our love and appreciation to our families in providing us with the support, encouragement, and patience to finish our task.

MSR
LJO
DJO

Contents

CHAPTER 3

Setting Up for Instruction   *62*

Planning for Instruction   87

Delivering Instruction   119

CHAPTER 6

Classroom Management: Promoting Discipline and Self-Control   *165*

CHAPTER 7
The Paperwork

199

*Student Teacher
to Master Teacher*

CHAPTER 1

Field Experiences with Students Who Possess Mild and Moderate Handicaps

Field experiences are among the most important components in the professional development of quality teachers. As is the case with a variety of other human service professions (e.g., medicine, social work, counseling), supervised field experiences provide appropriately trained candidates with opportunities to apply freshly acquired skills within nurturing and supportive environments. In most teacher-training programs, field experiences are viewed as critical transition activities. Experiences are designed to link the knowledge base presented in the college classroom to the independent activities expected of beginning teachers. In sharp comparison to the unidirectional and vicarious nature of textbooks, journal articles, university lectures, and classroom simulations, field experiences bring emotion and immediacy to the teacher-education process. With a built-in network of support, developing teachers are (a) placed in real-world situations that allow for the constructive discovery of strengths and weaknesses, (b) given ample numbers of opportunities to improve on their assessed deficiencies, and (c) encouraged to enhance creatively their areas of strength. Working with students, parents, and colleagues, developing teachers experience the daily rewards and, at times, many of the challenges and frustrations inherent in their chosen profession.

In comparison to those of the past, today's teacher-training programs allocate increased amounts of time to field experiences. Developing teachers and their university supervisors are spending more of their time in direct contact with students and school personnel. Local education agencies (LEAs) and institutions of higher education are forming partnerships to ensure that developing and beginning teachers are provided with the opportunities to become effective in today's schools. Recognizing the importance of field experiences, state lawmakers and the varied professional organizations involved in the education of teachers (e.g., American Association of Colleges for Teacher Education) are advocating that field experiences be expanded and improved even more. For example, it has been recommended that clinical experiences include greater opportunities for analytical problem-solving activities and fewer tasks that merely require imitation (Case, Lanier, & Miskel, 1986). Such activities would produce reflective professionals who could apply their knowledge and skills to a range of challenges and, more importantly, use the results of their experiences to form new approaches to the education of the children in their charge.

In this introductory chapter, we will address a wide range of issues faced by developing teachers who are placed in field-based practicum experiences with students identified as having mild and moderate handicaps. First, we will describe briefly the characteristics of students with mild and moderate handicaps. Special attention will be given to issues surrounding the categorical and noncategorical descriptions of this heterogeneous population of students. Second, we will explore the variety of systems for delivering special education services and discuss how these systems may change in years to come. Third, we will explore the roles of the key individuals involved in field-based practicum activities including the university supervisor, the cooperating teacher, and the practicum student. We will conclude this chapter with a series of strategies that can help the practicum student understand the social reality of schools. We believe that these "sensible tips" can assist developing teachers in becoming effective participants in their field experiences.

Students with Mild and Moderate Handicaps: Definitions and Characteristics

When developing teachers first enter the setting for students with mild and moderate handicaps, it becomes obvious that the children look like most other children. There is no strange or alien quality to their outward appearance; the layman's conceptualization of what it means to be handicapped doesn't seem to apply. From initial contacts, it seems nearly impossible to distinguish the students with handicaps from students considered normal. However, as the developing teacher spends more and time in the classroom, learning and behavioral problems do become apparent, and students identified as having mild and moderate handicaps function with lower levels of success on academic tasks and have more difficulty in social situations than do their nonhandicapped peers.

In most cases, students with mild and moderate handicaps are not identified until they enter school. Two major reasons exist for the lack of success in the early detection of mild and moderate handicaps. First, many children display slight developmental difficulties that are virtually unnoticeable to the untrained eye. Even in cases where these difficulties are noted during the preschool years, there is no guarantee that these problems persist into later developmental periods. Second, for many behaviors there are no clear delineations as to what constitutes normal and abnormal functioning. In regard to hyperactivity or attention problems, for example, objective behavioral criteria that could assist in differentiating normal and problem preschoolers are virtually nonexistent. Thus, it is extremely difficult to differentiate a vigorous, unrestrained, and capricious 3-year-old child considered age-appropriate from another 3-year-old child who is overactive, inattentive, and impulsive to a clinically significant degree (Campbell, 1985). The beginning of school, however, is a time when professional educators first evaluate children's abilities in meeting age- and grade-appropriate expectations. Children who violate the norms of their school or grade level in terms of behavior, academic performance, acquisition of spoken and written language, motivation, and aspirations for achievement are those most often identified as having mild or moderate handicaps.

The definitions and descriptions of students' educational problems tend to vary according to the specific philosophies and policies of individual state education agencies (SEAs) and local education agencies (LEAs). As a result of this interstate and intrastate variation, developing and beginning teachers will experience a variety of nomenclature and administrative arrangements used to describe students with mild and moderate handicaps. For the most part, the variety of arrangements can be reduced into two broad approaches: the use of categorical referents and category-free clusters of characteristics. In the sections that follow we will (a) define the categories associated with mild and moderate handicaps and (b) describe the category-free cluster approach to problem identification.

Categories of Mild and Moderate Handicaps

The categories of exceptionality used most frequently to define students experiencing mild to moderate learning and behavior problems are **learning disabilities, emotional disturbance** or **behavior disorders**, and **mild/moderate mental retardation**. Students identified as belonging to any one of these categories are presumed to share a specific behavior or pattern of behaviors. In recent years, the validity of this presumption has been the topic of considerable controversy.

LEARNING DISABILITIES   The vast majority of children having mild and moderate handicaps are considered to be learning disabled. Central to the diagnosis of learning disabilities, the newest category in the field of special education, are problems in academic achievement. The disorder is defined by Public Law (PL) 94–142:

> a disorder in one or more of the basic psychological processes involved in understanding or in using language, spoken or written, which may manifest itself in an imperfect ability to listen, think, speak, read, write, spell, or do math calculations. The term includes such conditions as perceptual motor handicaps, brain injury, minimal brain dysfunction, dyslexia, and developmental aphasia. The term does not include children who have learning problems which are primarily the result of visual, hearing, or motor handicaps, or emotional disturbance, or of environmental, cultural, or economic disadvantage (U.S. Office of Education, 1977, p. 42478).

Most students identified as having a learning disability have average to above average intellectual ability as measured by intelligence tests. However, on measures of achievement, these students do not perform to levels commensurate to their assessed intellectual abilities. These differences between a student's intelligence test scores and achievement test scores are typically referred to as discrepancies between intellectual ability and educational performance. If there is a **severe discrepancy** between the intellectual abilities and actual achievement of the student, he may be considered learning disabled. Unfortunately, there is no clear consensus as to what level of discrepancy between ability and achievement constitutes a severe discrepancy.

The federal definition of learning disabilities has been criticized widely and continues to spark emotional debates among professionals in the field. Some critics (e.g., Hallahan & Kauffman, 1982) have argued that the definition of learning disabilities needs to be broadened so that any child not achieving up to potential can receive special education services. Such a definition would not rely on causal explanations nor exclude children who may be suffering from other handicapping conditions along with their learning disability. Others (e.g., Council for Learning Disabilities, 1986; Kirk & Gallagher, 1986) have tried to narrow the definition of learning disabilities and have remained steadfast in their view that all underachieving students are not learning disabled. In fact, these professionals view the excessive incidence of students with learning disabilities as a direct result of the inclusion of students whose low achievement or underachievement are reflections of factors other than specific learning disabilities (e.g., depressed intellectual functioning, motivational problems, inadequate instruction, and so forth). These professionals see learning disabilities as just one possible cause of under-achievement and believe that specific interventions geared to the specific learning disabilities can enhance remedial efforts. Underachievement stemming from extrinsic sources, such as poor environmental conditions, would be better served if we could change their living and learning environments.

EMOTIONAL DISTURBANCE OR BEHAVIOR DISORDERS   As with learning disabilities, it is difficult to identify and define formally the emotional and behavioral problems of school-aged children. A major source of the difficulty is that a variety of terms are used to refer to problem behaviors. For example, professionals involved in the education and treatment of students with problem behaviors do not even agree on what generic name most appropriately captures the category. Under the provisions of PL 94–142, children who are handicapped by their behavior have been referred to as seriously emotionally disturbed. While this term is commonly used, many professionals (e.g., Council for Children with Behavior Disorders [CCBD]) believe that it is neither accurate nor beneficial to the educational process. The official position statement of CCBD (Huntze, 1985), lists seven reasons supporting the use of the term **behavioral disorder** over the traditional referent **emotional disturbance**. These seven reasons are highlighted in Reference Box 1.1

In PL 94-142, the Bower (1969) definition of emotional disturbance is used for identifying students who may need special education services. Briefly, an emotionally disturbed student exhibits one or more of the following characteristics to a marked extent and for a prolonged period of time: (a) an inability to learn that cannot be explained by intellectual, sensory, or health factors, (b) an inability to build or maintain satisfactory relationships with peers and teachers, (c) inappropriate types of behavior or feelings under normal circumstances, (d) a general pervasive mood of unhappiness or depression, or (e) a tendency to develop physical symptoms or fears associated with personal or school problems. The federal categorical definition of emotional disturbance does embrace children who may be schizophrenic or autistic but does not include those who are socially maladjusted unless it is determined that they are seriously emotionally disturbed.

As with the definition of learning disabilities, the PL 94–142 definition of emotional disturbance has been the subject of widespread criticism. The major problem with the definition is that it contains many vague and nebulous terms. Key terms and phrases are not defined, quantified, or operationalized. For example, the initial qualifying terms, *to a marked extent* or *for a prolonged period of time,* are not quantified and are open to subjective interpretation. Similarly, the phrase "satisfactory interpersonal relationships" is much too general for precise decision making. Other problems with the definition include (a) its failure to consider

BOX 1.1

Seriously Emotionally Disturbed or Behaviorally Disordered?

In a recent position paper, The Council for Children with Behavioral Disorders (CCBD) advocated replacing the term *seriously emotionally disturbed* with the term *behaviorally disordered* as a descriptor for children and youth who are handicapped by their behavior.

Listed below are seven reasons for their support of this change. Detailed explanations for each component of the rationale are available in Huntze (1985).

- The term *behaviorally disordered* has far greater utility for education than does the term *seriously emotionally disturbed*.
- The term *behaviorally disordered* is not associated exclusively with any particular theory of causation and therefore with any particular set of intervention techniques.
- The term *behaviorally disordered* affords a more comprehensive assessment of the population.
- The term *behaviorally disordered* is less stigmatizing than the term *seriously emotionally disturbed*.
- The term *behaviorally disordered* is more representative of the students who are handicapped by their behavior and currently served under PL 94–142.
- The professional judgment of the field, generally, appears to be moving in the direction of the term *behaviorally disordered*.
- The change in terminology is representative of a focus on the educational responsibility delineated in the statute and is descriptive of the population currently served.

problem behaviors as existing within a social context (Sindelar, 1983) and (b) the seemingly incongruous inclusionary and exclusionary caveats regarding autism, schizophrenia, and social maladjustment. As observed by Kauffman (1981), the five criteria within the definition indicate that autistic and schizophrenic children *must be included* and the socially maladjusted children *cannot be excluded* from any conceptualization of emotional disturbance or behavior disorder.

Unfortunately, there is no clear answer to the problems related to the identification of students with emotional disturbance. Many of us believe that we know problem behaviors or indicators of emotional disturbance when we see them. The quantification of emotional disturbance under the present definition, however, is severely limited by a lack of quantitative measures for determining eligibility of services. This state of affairs has not limited the number of students referred as emotionally disturbed. In most school districts, emotional disturbance is defined socially by the relatively imprecise tolerance levels of teachers, administrators, and parents. Consequently, students identified as emotionally disturbed are a heterogenous population that vary in behavioral characteristics both within and between individual classrooms, school buildings, and LEAs.

MILD MENTAL RETARDATION   For a student to be considered mentally retarded, he or she must have two specific deficits: (a) below-average intellectual functioning as measured by standardized tests of intelligence, and (b) deficits in adaptive behavior — those everyday behaviors believed to be necessary for survival in our society (Grossman, 1977). The majority of students with mental retardation fall within what is considered the **educable** or **mild range** of retardation. According to the criteria set by the American Association on Mental Deficiency (AAMD), students with mild mental retardation score between 55 and 69 on standardized intelligence tests and can learn academic skills up to approximately the sixth grade level. These students, however, have limited ability to think abstractly, and their interest patterns and conceptualizations of world events tend to be childlike and concrete (Madle, 1983). Students with mild retardation develop social and communication skills and can acquire the vocational skills necessary for self-support. In most cases, mild retardation is not discovered until the early elementary school years.

Even though the AAMD definition of mental retardation requires that students have deficiencies in both intellectual functioning and adaptive behavior, the primary mechanism used by LEAs for identifying students with mild retardation remains the IQ test. Two reasons exist for this emphasis on the IQ dimension rather than the adaptive behavior component. First, in terms of interpretation, the IQ dimension of the AAMD mental retardation classification system is simple and straightforward; to qualify for services, students must score below 70 on the Wechsler Intelligence Scale for Children — Revised (WISC-R) standardized intelligence test. Second, the practice of assessing adaptive behavior lacks the simplicity and reliability of intelligence testing. Because most adaptive behavior scales are completed by individuals familiar with the person being evaluated, the scales are inherently at risk for rater biases.

The use of mild mental retardation as a categorical referent, along with its heavy emphasis on IQ score eligibility, is not without criticism. It has been argued (e.g., Edgar & Hayden, 1985) that mild retardation is related more closely to variables such as socioeconomic status, family education level, and literacy than to IQ scores. In fact, there are data to support the view that children from poor families and minority groups tend to be overrepresented among the rosters of students identified with mild mental retardation. While critics have noted that such students are questionable candidates for inclusion in the category of mild mental retardation, these children are undoubtedly in need of some type of special intervention if they are to have success in school. The question, as posed by Edgar and Hayden, remains — How can these students best be served?

Category-Free Descriptions

While the use of categorical referents is the traditional approach to the description of students with mild and moderate handicaps, many educators have found that it is more beneficial to adopt an alternative conceptualization — a category-free classification system. This category-free approach, often referred to as a noncategorical or cross-categorical perspective, puts greater emphasis on variables related to students' **behavioral functioning** than on the specific factors used either to include or exclude a student from a particular category. Operationally defined, behavioral functioning refers to the overt behaviors of students and their relationship to the environment. These are learned, often situation-specific behaviors that occur in response to the demands of different environmental settings (Gloecker & Simpson, 1988). Most importantly, students' levels of behavioral functioning are viewed as being, in part, modifiable through classroom intervention.

In general, the problem behaviors most typical of students with mild and moderate handicaps fall into several generic domains: academic underachievement, sensory and perceptual processing problems, perceptual-motor difficulties, attention deficit problems, long- and short-term memory deficits, receptive and expressive language disorders, hyperactivity, impulsivity, poor peer relationships, and deficient social/emotional skills. It should be remembered, however, that while students with mild and moderate handicaps as a group exhibit problem behaviors across all of these domains, no one student actually experiences difficulties in all domains.

Proponents of the noncategorical perspective cite three major reasons for advocating their position. First, the categorical approach to the description of students with mild and moderate handicaps implies that there is homogeneity within each of the categories. This is not the case. In fact, there is such heterogeneity of characteristics among students within each of the categories that there is a resultant blurring of categorical boundaries. The overlap between the traditional categories is most often noted in a sharing of common behavioral features including (but not limited to) deficient academic functioning, poor social skills, memory problems, impulsivity, and problems in the generalization and maintenance of newly acquired skills.

The second argument forwarded by proponents of the noncategorical orientation involves instructional procedures typical of most special education settings. In short, traditional methods of labeling or defining students with learning and behavioral problems are basically administrative procedures that have little impact on how to best teach students. In contrast, the **precise definition** of assessed problems constitutes the first step in providing appropriate instructional interventions. Because many of the criteria used to determine categorical eligibility include generic references to traits and etiological considerations, there is often little instructional relevance to a categorical label. Instruction based on strict categorical consideration has not been very successful (Hallahan, Kauffman, & Lloyd, 1985; Smith, Price, & Marsh, 1986).

A third reason forwarded by advocates for noncategorical programming is that the use of traditional categories promotes the faulty assumption that learning and behavioral difficulties can be attributed exclusively to the labeled student. Clearly, learning and behavior problems are not solely student-based, but are often the result of a myriad of interacting ecological factors including classroom setting, teacher behavior, community characteristics, and the entry level behavior of a student (Blankenship & Lilly, 1981).

How Special Education Services Are Delivered

One of the first concepts presented to college students interested in pursuing a career in special education is the **cascade of educational services**. This cascade system, originally outlined by Reynolds (1962) and expanded upon by Deno (1970), suggests that the delivery of educational services to all students is best viewed as a continuum. As illustrated in Figure 1.1 and Box 1.2, the continuum ranges in both degree and type of special services required for an individual learner. Several assumptions are inherent in the cascade conceptualization of available educational services. First, the model assumes that a variety of service delivery options should be available to meet the specific educational needs of individual students. Rather than focusing on classifications or labels, the ultimate goal is to tailor instructional programs and settings to meet the needs of students. Second, the triangular shape of the model indicates that the majority of students, those with handicaps and without handicaps, are appropriately placed in least restrictive settings. Third, the cascade assumes that placement within a particular setting is not permanent. Students should be able to move between levels of services based on their educational performance. The greatest emphasis should

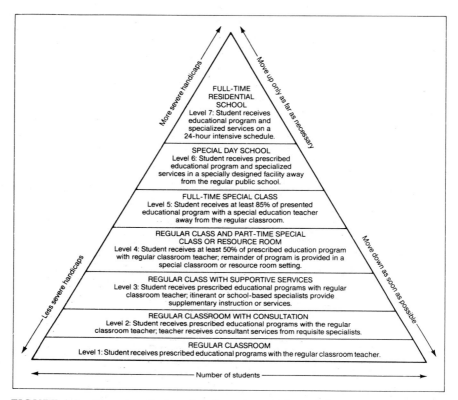

FIGURE 1.1   Cascade of educational services. (Adapted from Deno, E. (1970). Special education as developmental capital. *Exceptional Children, 37,* 235; and Reynolds, M.C. (1962). A framework for considering some issues in special education. *Exceptional Children, 28,* 368.)

be on returning students to less restrictive environments (LRE); movement to more restrictive settings should occur only when necessary.

Regardless of their categorical designation, most students with mild and moderate handicaps typically receive educational services within the regular school environment. Therefore, most developing and beginning teachers find that they will be teaching in the traditional special education settings of full-time special classrooms, part-time special settings, or resource rooms. However, with the movement toward the increased integration of students with mild and moderate handicaps into regular classroom settings, it is also possible that developing and beginning teachers will find themselves working in nontraditional service delivery roles — as consulting teachers or as itinerant learning specialists in integrated classroom settings.

While many practicum students will be in regular school environments, it is possible that some will sense an unusual estrangement from their

BOX 1.2

Levels of the Cascade: Examples of Students Receiving Services

1. *Full-time residential school:* Educational services are provided directly to the student in his place of residence on hospital or institutional grounds.

   Example: John has been diagnosed as severely mentally handicapped, is deaf-blind, and requires full-time medical assistance. The LRE for John may be the Maryhurt Residential School and Treatment Center.

2. *Special day school:* Students with handicaps are educated in a special school with similar students.

   Example: Mary has been found to be functioning at a profound level of cognitive functioning. She requires the assistance of a wheelchair and feeding tubes during lunch. The LRE for Mary may be the Fanley Special Day Care Center.

3. *Full-time special class:* Students with handicaps are educated in a special class located on the grounds of a regular school.

   Example: Tara functions at a profound level of functioning although she displays no major problems with self-help skills or motor skills. She displays no medical difficulties. The LRE for Tara may be a full-time special class at Flanigan Middle School.

4. *Part-time regular class and part-time special class:* Students with handicaps spend some part of the instructional week with regular peers.

   Example: Tommy displays problem behaviors, specifically inattention to a task during academic instruction. However, he displays excellent motor skills and is especially proficient in rhythm activities during music class. The LRE for Tommy may be a part-time special class in which he divides his time between instruction with regular students and instruction with students with handicaps at Santa Rosa High School.

5. *Regular class with supportive instructional services:* The majority of the student's classwork is provided during regular class scheduling, but, for a portion of the time, education is provided in a resource-room setting.

   Example: Bill displays excellent reading and spelling skills but requires assistance by the teacher in the resource room for mathematics. Bill functions effectively in all the aspects of the school curriculum. The LRE for him may be the resource-room model at Tandy Elementary. His special education teacher may work on a consulting basis with the regular class teacher to monitor Bill's progress in the mainstream.

(continued)

BOX 1.2 (continued)

6. *Regular class with consulting services for regular class teacher:* Resource room teachers and itinerant teachers consult with regular class teachers about modifications in the regular curriculum. Prereferral strategies may be implemented for students who can profit by instruction with regular class peers.

   Example: Ellen demonstrates adequate comprehension skills but has trouble reading the text. Teachers at Taylor School have consulted about the use of a tape-recorded text for her regular class reading program. When she is allowed to hear stories read from the tape, Ellen demonstrates no difficulty following the written discourse. The LRE for Ellen may be the regular class with consulting services. Use of the tape recorder may be monitored by her teachers through prereferral conferences.

7. *Regular classroom:* The LRE for education of all students is the regular class.

   Example: Sara requires speech therapy for a diagnosed articulation problem although she displays no educational difficulties other than an articulation problem. Sara is 5 years old, and her LRE is the regular class at Public School #16.

regular education colleagues. This feeling of separation is typically the result of a host of factors but is caused to a great degree by the lack of coordination between the special education and regular education systems of educating students with problems. The significant growth and progress of the special education delivery system have resulted in one major deleterious by-product—a barrier between regular and special educators as to who is responsible for the education of students identified as being handicapped. The growth of special education has resulted in a dual system of education—one for nonhandicapped youngsters and another for those with learning and behavioral difficulties. In settings where a dual system of education is institutionalized, many administrators and regular classroom teachers feel that they are no longer involved in the education of students with handicaps. Many regular classroom teachers feel that they lack the specialized training that could enable them to teach the other 25 to 30 students in their classrooms along with the students with handicaps. By virtue of identifying students as handicapped, the education of these problem students is viewed as the exclusive professional responsibility of a specialist—the special educator. Unfortunately, these attitudes do little to promote the reintegration and mainstreaming of students with handicaps and often put barriers between special and regular educators.

By the time they enter the school environment, developing and beginning teachers are keenly aware that the success of students with mild and moderate handicaps depends on the collaborative efforts of regular and special educators. This need to bring together regular and special educators has been approached in a number of ways and with varying degrees of intensity. Several special educators have advocated a complete merging of special and regular education efforts into a single unified system. Such restructuring would radically change how students with handicaps would be identified and served in their local communities. As observed by Stainback and Stainback (1984), the adoption of a unified system of education for all students would have an impact on many facets of special education. Possible impact areas are summarized in Table 1.1.

TABLE 1.1   Comparative Effects of Dual Versus Unified Systems of Education on Selected Areas of Concern

Concern	Dual System	Unified System
1. Student characteristics	Dichotomizes student into special and regular	Recognizes continuum among all students of intellectual, physical, and psychological characteristics
2. Individualization	Stresses individualization for students labeled special	Stresses individualization for all students
3. Instructional strategies	Seeks to use special strategies for special students	Selects from range of available strategies according to each student's learning needs
4. Type of educational services	Eligibility generally based on category affiliation	Eligibility based on each student's individual learning needs
5. Diagnostics	Large expenditures on identification of categorical affiliation	Emphasis on identifying the specific instructional needs of all students
6. Professional relationships	Establishes artificial barriers among educators that promote competition and alienation	Promotes cooperation through sharing resources, expertise, and advocacy responsibilities
7. Curriculum	Options available to each student are limited by categorical affiliation	All options available to every student as needed
8. Focus	Student must fit regular education program or be referred to special education	Regular education program is adjusted to meet all student's needs

SOURCE   From Stainback, W., & Stainback, S. (1984). A rationale for the merger of regular and special education. *Exceptional Children, 51*, 107. Copyright 1984 by The Council for Exceptional Children. Reprinted by permission.

These service delivery issues remain controversial within all levels of the teaching profession. Whether referred to as the **regular education initiative**, **general education initiative**, or simply a **merger between regular and special education systems**, it is heartening to see that we are continuing to seek more effective ways of delivering special education services to those students who need them. Currently, there are several efforts underway to evaluate the utilization of alternative service delivery systems on the education of students with and without handicaps. There is little doubt that these investigations will provide us with better strategies for coordinating the efforts of all educators in delivering specialized educational services to those students in need.

Whether or not individual LEAs decide to restructure their systems of identifying and educating students with handicaps, cooperation between regular and special educators still comes down to individuals and their interactions. Cooperation and collaboration involve people skills and mutual respect. Developing and beginning teachers of students with mild and moderate handicaps should avoid the "us versus them" mind-set when working with their regular education colleagues and should instead actively seek to develop collaborative relationships. As with the many obstacles we face in our personal lives, diplomacy is the key to achieving good working relationships and positive outcomes.

Roles and Responsibilities

We have limited our discussions to the definitions and characteristics of students with mild and moderate handicaps and descriptions of the various educational settings in which they are served. In the remaining sections, we will focus on the developing teacher and describe the roles and responsibilities of the individuals who are influential in determining the success of field-based practicum experiences. For developing teachers of students with mild and moderate handicaps to derive the maximum benefit from field-based practicum experiences, a well-planned team effort must be initiated and maintained. The primary members of this team are the **university supervisor**, the **cooperating classroom teacher**, and most importantly, the **practicum student**.

University Supervisor

The university supervisor assumes primary responsibility for the success of practicum students' field experiences. The supervisor is the direct representative of the university and serves as the liaison between the best interests of the practicum student and the requirements of the school or LEA. The university supervisor should foster professional development, provide honest performance feedback, and constructively smooth over possible rough spots during the teaching experience.

In addition to their liaison responsibilities, university supervisors typically assume four responsibilities in their development of preservice special educators. First, the university supervisor arranges for the most appropriate placement for the practicum student. This entails the careful analysis of the practicum student's entry-level skills and the type of setting in which the student anticipates teaching (e.g., level of service, age or grade level, severity of handicap, and so forth). Factors also considered include the availability of both quality instructional settings and cooperating teachers within reasonable commuting distance of the practicum student and university supervisor.

Second, the university supervisor monitors the progress of the practicum student throughout the field experience. This typically involves the direct observation of lessons, meetings with the cooperating teacher and principal, and critiquing of lesson plans, unit projects, and behavior change efforts. A critical component of this monitoring process is the delivery of feedback. The university supervisor accentuates the strengths of the developing teacher and identifies weaknesses for the purpose of improving performance. Feedback, in many cases, will be specific to the lessons observed and suggestions for improving student achievement should be offered. The supervisor is also the link between the practicum student's university-inspired idealism and the real-world pressures of our schools. The supervisor can serve as the buffer between the way-things-ought-to-be approach typical of college classrooms and the complex, less-than-ideal realities of school settings. Some practicum students observe that some of their cooperating teachers' behaviors are not consistent with many of the principles of effective teaching covered in methods classes. The supervisor should clarify such inconsistencies and mediate diplomatically any disagreements between the practicum student and the cooperating teacher.

Cooperating Teacher

The cooperating teacher will have the greatest amount of direct contact with the practicum student. In the best of situations, a mentor relationship is forged between the cooperating teacher and the practicum student. Cooperating teachers are to (a) be models of effective instructional procedures and paragons of tempered professional practice, (b) be well-schooled in the ability to share their instincts of teaching, (c) be able to prepare their environment to maximize opportunities for novice teachers to succeed and learn from their errors, (d) be able to observe and evaluate practicum student performance while ensuring that little damage is occurring to the often fragile self-concept of the novice teacher, and (e) set the pace for the integration of the practicum student into classroom activities, allowing gradually increased levels of responsibility. Box 1.3 lists the more commonly cited competencies desired of cooperating teachers. While much is expected of cooperating teachers, it must be remembered that their first responsibility is to their students, ensuring that instruction of an appropriate quantity and quality is delivered consistently.

Practicum Student

For most practicum students, the transition from the role of university student to professional teacher is completed with little difficulty. Nonetheless, the rigors and responsibilities of practicum experiences are considerable and should never be underestimated. How these responsibilities are met by practicum students will have dramatic effects on the success of the experience itself as well as the individual's future career in teaching. It is best to conceptualize the many responsibilities of the practicum student as falling into five specific domains of responsibilities:

1. Students and their parents.
2. The cooperating teacher.
3. The university.
4. Personal professional growth.
5. The profession.

RESPONSIBILITIES TO STUDENTS AND THEIR PARENTS   Practicum students must realize that the instruction they deliver is of vital importance to the students in their classes. Every moment of available instructional time is of extreme value, particularly for students with mild and moderate handicaps. With this in mind, it is important that practicum students come **prepared to teach effectively**. This preparation should include thorough lesson planning and the necessary consultations with the cooperating teacher and university supervisor. Students Individualized Education Plans (IEPs) and diagnostic test information should also be reviewed (see Chapters 3 and 4 for greater detail).

In general, students enjoy working with developing teachers. Their youth, vitality, and creativity are seen as welcome changes of pace. Practicum students should be aware, however, that students in their classes will depend on them to follow through with planned activities. Therefore, practicum students should avoid unnecessary absences, be prompt in following through on promised events, and avoid promising things that will not be delivered. Practicum students should be models of appropriate decorum and controlled in their responses to negative or frustrating events. Initial student enthusiasm toward working with the practicum student can be returned by becoming acquainted with the students and

BOX 1.3

Commonly Cited Competencies Desired of Cooperating Teachers

COMPETENCIES RELATED PRIMARILY TO THE WORKING RELATIONSHIP BETWEEN THE COOPERATING TEACHER AND THE PRACTICUM STUDENT

- The cooperating teacher is available for consultation and moral support when needed.
- Analyzes with the practicum student the value of experiences: helps her to discover which ones are most worthwhile.
- Helps the practicum student set her goals and formulate her educational philosophy.
- Shares in planning.
- Plans and teaches with another adult; originates and suggests new ideas without dominating the practicum student's thoughts and actions.
- Establishes a feeling of security for the practicum student by clarifying her responsibilities throughout the field experience.
- Offers criticism—continuous, specific, and constructive—in an empathic manner.
- Invites the practicum student to participate in the professional and social activities of the staff.
- Helps the practicum student to develop an understanding of her own strengths and weaknesses, and to build a healthy self-concept.
- Shows willingness to consider new and different techniques in an open-minded manner.

COMPETENCIES RELATED TO THE TRANSITION FROM THE OBSERVER STATUS OF THE PRACTICUM STUDENT TO HER ACTIVE TEACHING STATUS LATER IN THE FIELD EXPERIENCE

- Gradually lets the practicum student accept increasing responsibility until full teaching responsibility is assumed.
- Helps the practicum student to understand her job in relation to the entire school program.
- Helps the practicum student build teaching skills through observation of her own teaching.
- Helps the practicum student link theories to practice.

(continued)

BOX 1.3 (continued)

COMPETENCIES RELATED PRIMARILY TO INSTRUCTION,
CLASSROOM PROCEDURES, AND TECHNIQUES

- Gives suggestions in matters of discipline.
- Acquaints the practicum student with routine matters.
- Displays accuracy in keeping records.
- Creates a democratic setting for learning—one in which pupils share in some decision-making experiences.
- Assists the practicum student in setting reasonable standards of performance for her instructional group.
- Encourages creative thinking and planning by the practicum student.
- Models effective instructional procedures during his own teaching.

COMPETENCIES RELATED PRIMARILY TO PERSONAL
CHARACTERISTICS OR TRAITS OF THE SUPERVISING TEACHER
THAT MIGHT BE EMULATED BY THE PRACTICUM STUDENT

- Sets a good example for the practicum student in personal appearance, grooming, speech, and appropriate mannerisms.
- Makes rational judgments, takes appropriate action, and accepts responsibility for the consequences.
- Reflects a positive professional attitude and real liking and respect for teaching.
- Exhibits interest in continuous self-improvementr and educational advancement.
- Reflects a mature personality with enthusiasm and broad interests.

COMPETENCIES RELATED PRIMARILY TO DEVELOPING BROAD
PROFESSIONAL AND SCHOOL RESPONSIBILITIES

- Is an active participant in local and state teachers' organizations.
- Perceives the opportunity to work with future teachers as a professional responsibility.
- Actively participates with his colleagues in developing and enforcing standards fundamental to continuous improvement of his profession, and abides by those standards in his practice.
- Exhibits willingness to accept out-of-class responsibilities.
- Participates effectively in faculty meetings and the work of professional committees.
- Is acquainted with sources of current thinking—journals, conferences, yearbook, workshops.
- Exhibits a cooperative attitude in relationships with other members of the staff.

SOURCE Adapted from Ball State University. (1981). *Competencies of the supervising teacher*, Muncie, IN: Author.

interacting with them in a lively, interested fashion. Practicum students should be careful, however, not to become overly friendly and should always conduct themselves in a firm, controlled, and impartial manner.

Practicum students may have the opportunity to interact with the students' parents in their class. This may be a regularly scheduled IEP conference or the result of some critical incident requiring parental input. The practicum student must recognize parents as partners in the education process and, in concert with the cooperating teacher, must discuss constructively the behaviors of the student as they relate to the solution of the presenting problem.

RESPONSIBILITIES TOWARD THE COOPERATING TEACHER
Perhaps the most critical responsibility toward the cooperating teacher is the maintenance of clear communication. It is best to discuss situations in a direct, diplomatic manner without letting minor obstacles fester into major stumbling blocks. With the assistance of the university supervisor, the cooperating teacher should be made aware of the personal goals and aspirations of the practicum student, and a plan to achieve those goals within the context of the overall practicum experience should be developed and monitored. If questions about the methods used to pursue these goals arise, it is the responsibility of the practicum student to initiate requests for assistance. Finally, because the education of the students in the class is the ultimate responsibility of the cooperating teacher, practicum students should share activity or lesson plans well in advance of their implementation. This will allow the cooperating teacher to provide constructive feedback prior to the delivery of the lesson.

RESPONSIBILITIES TOWARD THE UNIVERSITY   As a practicum student in the local schools, the developing teacher is a representative of the sponsoring university. By placing a practicum student within a particular setting, the university is stating that the developing teacher is ready to assume the multifaceted responsibilities associated with teaching students with mild and moderate handicaps. Consequently, the behavior of each practicum student reflects on the institution that has provided training for that individual.

The best ways for practicum students to represent their institutions include (a) putting forth the maximum effort possible in all facets of the field experience, (b) being open to suggestions from various school-based personnel, (c) becoming involved in team-based solutions to problems, (d) doing a fair-share of the noninstructional and extracurricular duties required of teachers, (e) being enthusiastic and positive during instructional and noninstructional tasks, (f) facilitating the cooperative relationship between the visiting university supervisor and the school-based teachers and administrators, and (g) maintaining a professional and ethical demeanor when dealing with students' problem behaviors and confidential records. Practicum students should avoid falling into the trap of lounge gossip and must be careful whenever references to students, by name, are made during social situations away from the classroom.

RESPONSIBILITIES TOWARD PERSONAL PROFESSIONAL GROWTH
While many practicum situations represent the culmination of a set of experiences within a special education training program, they are actually the cornerstones for future professional development activities. Instructing and managing challenging students in busy classrooms tend to illuminate specific content or skill areas that require additional growth or refinement. This feeling will recur throughout one's professional development. As a rule, professionals seldom let their acquired skills stagnate. In special education, instructional technology is advancing much too quickly for any teacher to neglect personal professional development.

A number of mechanisms exist for developing teachers to fulfill their own need for professional growth. The most convenient method is to consult recent publications in the field. A variety of professional textbooks, curriculum resource guides, and journals are available in regional resource centers, teacher development centers, and university libraries. Box 1.4 lists the professional journals that would be of greatest interest to developing teachers of students with mild and moderate handicaps.

A second method for developing teachers to augment their skills is attendance at local, regional, or state conferences sponsored by professional organizations and advocacy groups involved in the education and treatment of students with handicaps. Information regarding the schedules of such events can be obtained directly from the professional organizations or from listings in professional journals and newsletters.

A third means of professional development are inservice and staff development workshops provided by local school districts. These activities are usually open to all personnel within the district and practicum students are typically urged to attend.

Finally, professional development can include taking additional courses in university settings. To begin considering the type of coursework or graduate programs that would most appropriately match professional development needs, practicum students can consult college catalogues. Most university libraries contain these catalogues in either hard-copy or microfiche formats.

RESPONSIBILITIES TOWARD THE PROFESSION   The most critical of responsibilities toward the profession of special education is to behave in both an ethical and professional manner throughout field experiences. The trademark of any quality profession is its willingness to establish

BOX 1.4

Professional Journals of Interest to Developing and Beginning Teachers of Students with Mild and Moderate Handicaps

Listed below are the titles of many of the more prominent journals that would be of interest to those involved in the education of students with mild and moderate handicaps. Most of these publications are available at major university libraries. To contact the journals directly, use the business addresses provided below.

- *Academic Therapy*
  PRO-ED
  5341 Industrial Oaks Boulevard
  Austin, TX 78735
- *American Journal of Mental Deficiency*
  American Association on
    Mental Deficiency
  5101 Wisconsin Avenue, N.W.
  Washington, DC 20016
- *Behavioral Disorders*
  Division for Children with
    Behavior Disorders
  The Council for Exceptional
    Children
  1920 Association Drive
  Reston, VA 22091
- *Career Development of Exceptional Individuals*
  Division of Career
    Development
  The Council for Exceptional
    Children
  1920 Association Drive
  Reston, VA 22091
- *Diagnostique*
  Council for Education
    Diagnostic Services
  The Council for Exceptional
    Children
  1920 Association Drive
  Reston, VA 22091

- *Education and Training of the Mentally Retarded*
  Mental Retardation Division
  The Council for Exceptional
    Children
  1920 Association Drive
  Reston, VA 22091
- *Education and Treatment of Children*
  Clinical Psychology Publishing
    Company
  4 Conant Square
  Brandon, VT 05733
- *Exceptional Children*
  The Council for Exceptional
    Children
  1920 Association Drive
  Reston, VA 22091
- *Exceptional Parent*
  20 Providence Street
  Boston, MA 03116
- *Focus on Exceptional Children*
  Love Publishing Company
  1777 S. Bellaire Street
  Denver, CO 80222
- *Journal of Applied Behavior Analysis*
  Department of Human
    Development
  University of Kansas
  Lawrence, KS 66045

(continued)

BOX 1.4 *(continued)*

- *Journal of Child and Adolescent Psychotherapy*
  Rivendell Foundation
  5100 Poplar Avenue
  Memphis, TN 38137
- *Journal of the Division of Early Childhood*
  Division of Early Childhood
  The Council for Exceptional Children
  1920 Association Drive
  Reston, VA 22091
- *Journal of Learning Disabilities*
  PRO-ED
  5341 Industrial Oaks Boulevard
  Austin, TX 78735
- *Journal of Special Education*
  PRO-ED
  5341 Industrial Oaks Boulevard
  Austin, TX 78735
- *Journal of Special Education Technology*
  Technology and Media Division
  The Council for Exceptional Children
  1920 Association Drive
  Reston, VA 22091
- *Learning Disabilities Focus*
  Division for Children with Learning Disabilities
  The Council for Exceptional Children
  1920 Association Drive
  Reston, VA 22091
- *Learning Disabilities Research*
  Division for Children with Learning Disabilities
  The Council for Exceptional Children
  1920 Association Drive
  Reston, VA 22091
- *Learning Disabilities Quarterly*
  Council for Learning Disabilities
  P.O. Box 40303
  Overland Park, KS 66204
- *Mental Retardation*
  American Association on Mental Deficiency
  5101 Wisconsin Avenue, N.W.
  Washington, DC 20016
- *Remedial and Special Education*
  PRO-ED
  5341 Industrial Oaks Boulevard
  Austin, TX 78735
- *Special Services Digest*
  Buttonwood Farms
  Neshaminy Plaza
  Bristol Pike and Street Road
  Bensalem, PA 19020
- *Teaching Exceptional Children*
  The Council for Exceptional Children
  1920 Association Drive
  Reston, VA 22091
- *Topics in Early Childhood Special Education*
  PRO-ED
  5341 Industrial Oaks Boulevard
  Austin, TX 78735

and abide by (a) a code of ethics and (b) corresponding standards that can provide a basis for evaluating professional practice related directly to a code of ethics (Heller, 1983). Whether or not special educators have reached the stage of true professionalism in the eyes of most members of our society is arguable. What cannot be denied, however, is that all involved in the education and treatment of students with handicaps must continue to operate in a professional fashion if we are to expect those outside of our profession to treat us as such.

In a major move toward the professionalization of special education, the Delegate Assembly of the Council for Exceptional Children (CEC) adopted in 1983 a code of ethics for educators of persons with exceptionalities. Responsibilities believed to form the basis of professional conduct in relation to three major areas, the exceptional student, the employer, and the profession, were formulated into a code of eight ethical principles. Correspondingly, this code of ethics was translated into a set of minimum standards of conduct called the Standards for Professional Practice. Together, both the code of ethics and the Standards of Professional Practice were viewed as providing guidelines for (a) professional etiquette, (b) effective interpersonal behavior, (c) resolution of ethical issues, and (d) making professional judgments concerning what constitutes competent practice. This CEC code of ethics is presented in Box 1.5. The complete set of standards is contained in Appendix A.

Preparing for a Successful Practicum Experience

In the previous sections of this chapter, we have discussed the behavioral characteristics of students with mild and moderate handicaps as well as the large number of responsibilities required of practicum students during their field-based experiences. In this final section, we offer a listing of sensible tips that, if addressed, can enable practicum students to cope with their increased responsibilities and maximize the benefits of their field experiences.

1. *Have the opportunity to succeed.* The demands placed on practicum students during their field experiences are considerable. The time and effort required of most practicum experiences equal or even exceed that which is typical of full-time teaching positions. Wherever possible, practicum students should limit the amount of time devoted to extracurricular activities, additional courses, and part-time jobs, and allow for the maximum opportunity of success. Plan to get some well-deserved rest; teaching students with mild and moderate handicaps is a challenging and demanding job!

2. *Visit the assigned field-based setting prior to beginning the practicum.* Much of the anxiety related to a practicum student's impending experiences is the result of nonspecific fears of the unknown. It is wise, therefore, to get an "advance organizer" or mind-set of what will be experienced when the practicum officially begins. In addition to relieving some

BOX 1.5

Council for Exceptional Children's Code of Ethics

We declare the following principles to be the Code of Ethics for educators of exceptional persons. Members of the special education profession are responsible for upholding and advancing these principles. Members of the Council for Exceptional Children agree to judge by them in accordance with the spirit and provisions of this Code.

I. Special education professionals are committed to developing the highest educational and quality of life potential of exceptional individuals.

II. Special education professionals promote and maintain a high level of competence and integrity in practicing their profession.

III. Special education professionals engage in professional activities which benefit exceptional individuals, their families, other colleagues, students, or research subjects.

IV. Special education professionals exercise objective professional judgment in the practice of their profession.

V. Special education professionals strive to advance their knowledge and skills regarding the education of exceptional individuals.

VI. Special education professionals work within the standards and policies of their profession.

VII. Special education professionals seek to uphold and improve where necessary the laws, regulations, and policies governing the delivery of special education and related services and the practice of their profession.

VIII. Special education professionals do not condone or participate in unethical or illegal acts, nor violate professional standards adopted by the Delegate Assembly of CEC.

SOURCE   From Council for Exceptional Children. (1983). Code of ethics and standards for professional practice. *Exceptional Children, 50*(3), 205.

of the jitters, this visit will (a) convey to the cooperating teacher a genuine interest in the practicum process, (b) allow for a brief introduction to the students, (c) provide important first impressions regarding the standards of protocol and comportment within the school, and (d) allow for the learning of school and classroom-specific policies.

3. *Present yourself appropriately.* Whether it is correct or not, people some-times judge others rather superficially — on the basis of their appear-ance, comportment, and surface behaviors. To heighten the chances of making a favorable first impression, it is important that the prac-ticum student be dressed and groomed appropriately. Moreover, the general tenor of how one expresses opinions and shares personal lifestyles needs to be checked. Although many facets of a person's individuality are important components in the motivation of students, some forms of personal expression conflict with local community standards (however they tend to be defined) and are best saved for environments other than the school (Behling, 1978).

4. *Monitor all written work.* Practicum students are judged on the quality of the written documents (applications, personal statements, and so forth) that are required for the field experience. Unfortunately, some developing teachers are identified as sloppy and careless merely be-cause they do not put the extra effort of good written expression or do not proofread their written products prior to submission. Written prod-ucts reflect directly on the author. Developing teachers should ensure that their written work contains correct punctuation and spelling, is grammatically correct, and possesses a logical sequence of ideas.

5. *Remain patient.* The assumption of instructional responsibilities by the practicum student is a gradual process. Although the practicum stu-dent may feel "all fired up and ready to take charge," a gradual integration into the flow of activities allows for observations of the cooperating teacher in action and for a general orientation to the operating procedures of the school. These observation periods also allow the students in the class to become accustomed to the new teacher in the environment. Also, be sure to get the approval of the cooperating teacher prior to making any changes in instructional procedures or behavior management programs. No matter how en-thusiastic you may feel about implementing a change for a student, it must be remembered that the cooperating teacher is responsible for all programming within the classroom.

6. *Remain diplomatic.* Being the new person in the school means that many veteran teachers are going to give you advice on any number of topics related to education (and life in general). While some of this real-world advice may be in sharp contrast with what you believe or have learned about education, it is best to treat these interactions with colleagues as valuable learning experiences, as opportunities to get others' perceptions of certain issues. During these interactions, practicum students should avoid arrogantly flaunting their knowledge of the **innovative instructional procedures** they heard about in their methods classes. Interaction should be kept on a professional level with efforts of mutual respect being initiated by the developing teacher.

6. *Maintain enthusiasm in the face of others' disillusionment.* As observed by

Behling (1978), it is not unusual for practicum students to meet teachers and administrators who appear worn out, disillusioned, and apathetic. While we anticipate that contacts with these individuals will be kept to a minimum, it is critical that developing teachers avoid falling into these highly contagious feelings of hopelessness and frustration. Even with the most challenging of students with handicaps, there is enough potential job satisfaction to merit enthusiasm.

7. *Think "team" rather than individual.* Practicum students face an overwhelming number of challenges related to the education and treatment of their students. An effort should be made to avoid trying to save the world singlehandedly. The problems faced by students in special education settings require collaboration and assistance from a variety of sectors within the school system. As is fully described in Chapters 8 and 9, successful efforts in meeting the challenges found in comprehensive special education programs typically require the enthusiasm and cooperation of a multidisciplinary team of professionals.

8. *Get to know the other professionals and paraprofessionals.* Each school has a number of people who contribute to the effective schooling of children and youth. It is wise to use the practicum experience to learn the various roles and responsibilities of the individuals who populate the school. Certainly, visits with the school psychologist and social worker would allow for alternative perspectives on the student with mild and moderate handicaps. Also, getting to know the administrators of the school building and system could help when seeking a first teaching position.

Summary

This chapter addressed a number of prerequisite issues associated with the initial field experiences of developing special education teachers. The chapter opened with a brief description of the characteristics of students with mild and moderate handicaps. Specific emphases were given to both categorical and noncategorical conceptualizations of these handicaps. This was followed by a discussion of the range of service delivery options that are typical of most LEA placements. Issues related to (a) the concept of least restrictive environment and (b) possible changes in how we deliver educational service to students with handicaps were highlighted. The bulk of the chapter was devoted to the many roles and responsibilities of the key individuals involved in field-based teaching experiences. Concerns related to communication maintenance, professionalism, and preparation were emphasized. The chapter concluded with a list of 8 "sensible tips" related directly to the practical aspects of field-based experiences.

References

BEHLING, H. (1978). *Some coping suggestions for student teachers* (Monograph No. 6). Annapolis, MD: Maryland Association of Teacher Educators.

BLANKENSHIP, C., & LILLY, M. S. (1981). *Mainstreaming students with learning and behavior problems*. New York: Holt, Rinehart, & Winston.

BOWER, E. M. (1969). *Early identification of emotionally handicapped children in school*. Springfield, IL: Charles C Thomas.

CAMPBELL, S. B. (1985). Hyperactivity in preschoolers: Correlates and prognostic implications. *Clinical Psychology Review, 51*, 401–408.

CASE, C. W., LANIER, J. E., & MISKEL, C. G. (1986). The Holmes Group report: Impetus for gaining professional status for teachers. *Journal of Teacher Education, 37*(4), 36–43.

COUNCIL FOR LEARNING DISABILITIES (1986). Inclusion of nonhandicapped low achievers and underachievers in learning disabilities programs: A position statement by the Board of Trustees of the Council for Learning Disabilities. *Learning Disability Quarterly, 9*(3), 246.

DENO, E. N. (1970). Special education as developmental capital. *Exceptional Children, 37*, 229–237.

EDGAR, E., & HAYDEN, A. H. (1985). Who are the children special education should serve and how many children are there? *Journal of Special Education, 18*, 523–539.

GLOECKER, T., & SIMPSON, C. (1988). *Exceptional students in regular classrooms: Challenges, services, and methods*. Mountain View, CA: Mayfield.

GROSSMAN, H. J. (1977). *Manual on terminology and classification in mental retardation* (7th ed.). Washington, DC: American Association on Mental Deficiency.

HALLAHAN, D. P., & KAUFFMAN, J. M. (1982). *Exceptional children: Introduction to special education* (2nd ed.). Englewood Cliffs, NJ: Prentice-Hall.

HALLAHAN, D. P., KAUFFMAN, J. M., & LLOYD, J. W. (1985). *Introduction to learning disabilities* (2nd ed.). Englewood Cliffs, NJ: Prentice-Hall.

HELLER, H. W. (1983). Special education professional standards: Need, value, and use. *Exceptional Children, 50*(3), 199–204.

HUNTZE, S. L. (1985). A position paper of the Council for Children with Behavioral Disorders. *Behavioral Disorders, 10*, 167–174.

KAUFFMAN, J. M. (1981). *Characteristics of children's behavior disorders* (2nd ed.). Columbus, OH: Merrill.

KIRK, S. A., & GALLAGHER, J. J. (1986). *Educating exceptional children* (5th ed.). Boston: Houghton Mifflin.

MADLE, R. A. (1983). Mental retardation. In R. Smith, J. Neisworth, & F. Hunt (Eds.), *The exceptional child: A functional approach* (pp. 332–337). New York: McGraw-Hill.

REYNOLDS, M. C. (1962). A framework for considering issues in special education. *Exceptional Children, 28*, 367–370.

SINDELAR, P. T. (1983). Emotional disturbance. In R. Smith, J. Neisworth, & F. Hunt (Eds.), *The exceptional child: A functional approach* (pp. 358–387). New York: McGraw-Hill.

SMITH, T. E. C., PRICE, B. J., & MARSH, G. E. (1986). *Mildly handicapped children and adults*. New York: West Publishing.
STAINBACK, W., & STAINBACK, S. (1984). A rationale for the merger of special and regular education. *Exceptional Children, 51*, 102–111.
UNITED STATES OFFICE OF EDUCATION (1977). Implementation of Part B of the Education of the Handicapped Act. *Federal Register, 42*, 42474–42518.

CHAPTER 2

Legal Aspects of Special Education: A Brief Review

In the past three decades, **legislation** (laws and regulations) and **litigation** (court cases) have influenced many innovations in special education and the interpretation of rights and responsibilities of participants of the educational process. Changes in public policy have posed new challenges to professionals. Preservice and beginning teachers who understand important laws and court cases may deal more effectively with the complex issues involved in providing a **free and appropriate public education (FAPE)** to students with handicaps. Awareness of legal issues may help developing teachers to (a) provide a sound rationale for current laws and regulations affecting their classrooms, (b) avoid past policy mistakes, and (c) ensure quality educational programming provided to the special-needs students they serve.

A brief discussion of special education legal issues is summarized in this chapter. Presented are legislation and litigation that have had an impact on the development of a free, appropriate public education to students with special needs. Major components of federal laws are discussed. Legal and professional responsibilities of developing teachers are illustrated to highlight the need for advocacy on the part of professionals.

The Legal Basis of Educational Rights for the Handicapped

Every teacher in a public school setting will come into contact with the **Education for All Handicapped Children's Act (EHA)** passed in 1975.

29

BOX 2.1

PL 94–142 Definitions and Types of Students Served

Special education: "Specially designed instruction, at no cost to the parent, to meet the unique needs of a handicapped child, including classroom instruction, instruction in physical education, home instruction, and instruction in hospitals and institutions" (34 C.F.R. §300.14 (a) (1)).

Related services: "Developmental, corrective, and other supportive services (which) are required to assist a handicapped child to benefit from special education" (34 C.F.R. §300.13 (a)).

The term includes such services as speech therapy, language development, physical and occupational therapy, recreation, social work services, counseling services, psychological services, and school health services.

Handicapping conditions warranting special education:

1. Mentally retarded
2. Learning disabled
3. Seriously emotionally disturbed
4. Multiple handicapped
5. Deaf-Blind
6. Hard of hearing
7. Deaf
8. Speech impaired
9. Visually handicapped
10. Orthopedically impaired
11. Other health impaired

This law, also referred to as **Public Law 94–142**, has changed the course of education of children with special needs. The political coalition of parents, concerned professionals, and advocates brought about the passage of this landmark legislation at a time when children were being excluded from schools, misclassified through biased testing procedures, or served inadequately across the country. Without a strong commitment from a variety of individuals challenging existing procedures, progress would have remained very slow, and services and programs would have continued to be inadequate and inconsistent from locality to locality. EHA defined special education and provided a structure through federal mandates to educate all students with handicaps. Box 2.1 describes the federal definition of special education and related services and names each group of students receiving specialized help.

New teachers are wise to recognize and implement innovative ways of assessing, programming, and evaluating progress of these students. It is hoped that beginning professionals will realize most innovations resulted from efforts of dedicated individuals who sought to change public policy through legal means.

Specific Legislation

Legislation entails the political processes by which elected members of the local, state, or federal government affect policy changes by proposing, debating, and passing laws. New laws and regulations evolve continually as policies are challenged and redefined, affecting the ever-changing field of special education. For the new teacher, this means that the job of the special educator is not static but changes with legal and educational evolutions.

Prior to the passage of EHA, some local and state statutes had guaranteed some degree of service to students in need of special help. While these statutes were minimal and provided limited monies for the education of students with handicaps, they provided some direction (e.g., the commitment of procedural safeguards, assurances in state plans, education to school-aged students residing in institutions, and expansions or initiations of local programs). These laws, passed between 1950 and 1975, eventually provided the basis for federal mandates to provide services to all students in need of special education and related services. Box 2.2 describes pertinent laws having a direct bearing on special education. Today's professionals familiar with these legal actions may prevent educational injustices similar to those occurring before these laws were passed.

Specific Litigation

Litigation entails court cases in which a judge and/or members of a jury examine data. A decision is rendered about a particular case based on the evidence provided by those seeking judicial interpretation. Through the litigation process, laws have been challenged and redefined, creating new laws and regulations (Weintraub, Abeson, Ballard, & La Vor, 1977). This has resulted in significant changes not only for children and teachers, but also for parents. Most legislative acts evolved because parents, educators, and advocates questioned, through legal channels, practices occurring within the educational system that, from their standpoint, violated rights of their children or others unable to defend themselves within the school setting.

BOX 2.2

Laws Influencing Special Education

- PL 83–531, The Cooperative Research Act (1954), was implemented to assist cooperative research in education. Of the $1
  million appropriations, $675,000 was earmarked for research
  with the mentally retarded.
- PL 85–926, Training of Professional Personnel (1958), expanded teaching of students with mental retardation and facilitated grants to state agencies and to tertiary institutions, establishing a model for support to teacher trainees in special education.
- PL 88–164, The Mental Retardation Facilities and Community
  Mental Health Center's Construction Act (1963), was a corner-
  stone legislative act for students with special needs. It brought
  together into one unit the "captioned film" program of PL 85–
  905 (1958), an expanded teacher-training program from PL
  85–926, and a new research program for the education of students with handicaps.
- PL 88–164, §301, Training Professional Personnel, amended PL
  85–926 to include a number of other handicapping conditions.
  Included in this legislation was funding of personnel training to
  teach students labeled "emotionally disturbed".
- PL 88–164, §302, Research and Demonstration Projects in Education of Handicapped Children, authorized the Commissioner
  of Education to make grants to various state and local agencies
  in order to educate students with handicaps. PL 89–105 later
  supplemented PL 88–164, §302, by allowing funds to be used
  for construction, equipment, and operation of facilities for research and training of research personnel.
- PL 89–10, Assistance to Children in Disadvantaged Areas
  (Elementary and Secondary Education Act, Title VI: [1965]),
  provided federal monies to initiate programs for schooling of
  children who were educationally deprived, especially children
  with handicaps in low-income families.
- PL 89–313 (1965) encouraged programs to educate children
  with handicaps residing in institutions and other similar state-
  operated or state-supported residential facilities.
- PL 89–105, Community Mental Health Centers Act Amendments (1965), provided additional traineeships and fellowships
  from original legislation developed by the 99th Congress and
  provided additional funds for research and demonstration projects in the education of students with special needs. It authorized construction of at least one research facility.

BOX 2.2 *(continued)*

- PL 89–750, Title VI, Education for Handicapped Children (1966), allowed grants to states through the Elementary and Secondary Education Act (ESEA) for special needs students. PL 89–750 was particularly important because the Division of Handicapped Children and Youth had been disbanded in 1965.
- PL 90–538, The Handicapped Children's Early Education Assistance Act (1968), was developed exclusively for children with handicaps and authorized the Commissioner of Education, acting through the Bureau of Education for the Handicapped, to negotiate grants and contracts with both private and public agencies to establish experimental preschool and early education programs for special needs students.
- PL 91–61, National Center of Educational Media and Materials for the Handicapped (1969), provided the authority to the Secretary of Health, Education, and Welfare to contract a university to develop, construct, and operate a national center of educational media and materials for persons with handicaps.
- PL 91–230, Elementary, Secondary, and Other Educational Amendments (1969), consolidated a number of previous provisions on serving children with handicaps and was divided into seven basic sections—Parts A through G—all of the categories of programs and services for educating children with special needs who receive federal assistance. Part B was intended to authorize grants for the initiation, expansion, and improvement of state and local educational programs for children requiring specialized help and was meant to specify the kind and amount of federal dollars to be provided to public agencies for special education.
- PL 92–424, The Economic Opportunity Amendments (1972), mandated a minimum of 10% of the nation's places in Head Start p rograms be made available to students with handicaps.
- PL 93–112, §504, 29 U.S.C. §794, The Rehabilitation Act (1973), specified no handicapped individual in the United States shall, solely by reason of his handicap, be excluded from the participation in, be denied the benefits of, or be subjected to discrimination under any program or activity receiving federal financial assistance.
- PL 93–380, The Education Amendments (1974), modified Part B to increase monies available to public agencies for the education of students with special needs and to expand the assurances in state plans for children's and parents' rights. Emanating from this law was the Family Educational Rights and Privacy Act of 1974, also referred to as the Buckley Act, which protected the confidentiality of school records and provided procedures to

(continued)

BOX 2.2 (continued)

challenge questionable information contained in the records. Title VI extended and revised the Adult Education Act, The Education of the Handicapped Act, The Indian Education Act, and The Emergency School Aid Act. It required states to locate and serve all children with handicaps. The state must protect the rights of handicapped children and their parents in making educational changes; it assured an education with one's peers, as possible; and it asked that evaluation materials be racially and culturally fair.

- PL 94–142, Education for All Handicapped Children Act (1975), included a comprehensive revision of Part B of the Education of the Handicapped Act increasing federal funding for the education of elementary and secondary programs for all special needs students. It has often been referred to as the Bill of Rights for children with handicaps.
- PL 98–199, Parent Training and Information Centers (1983), entailed the training and provision of information to parents and volunteers.
- PL 99–457, Education of the Handicapped Act Amendments (l986), mandated special education and related services beginning at age three and created a discretionary early intervention program to serve children from birth through age two. It provided monies to train early intervention teachers in clinical settings and preschools.

SOURCE   Based on Reinert, H.R., & Huang, A. (1988). *Children in Conflict* (3rd ed.). Columbus, OH: Merrill.

Recurring Legal Themes

The 14th Amendment to the United States Constitution, illustrated in Figure 2.1, forbids states from depriving anyone of life, liberty, or property without due process and equal protection of law. The equal protection clause and the due process clause of the 14th Amendment should be foremost in the developing teacher's mind. These components formed the basis of litigation resulting in the enactment of PL 94–142. Abeson and Zettel (1977), cited in Reinert and Huang (1988), described legal theories that hold today's professionals accountable for the manner in which educational treatment of students is carried out under the tenets of the 14th Amendment.

DUE PROCESS   Fair procedures must be followed before citizens can be denied certain interests. Due process entails **procedural due process** in which a person has the right to be heard and to protest if a government agency is about to take action affecting that person. Due process also

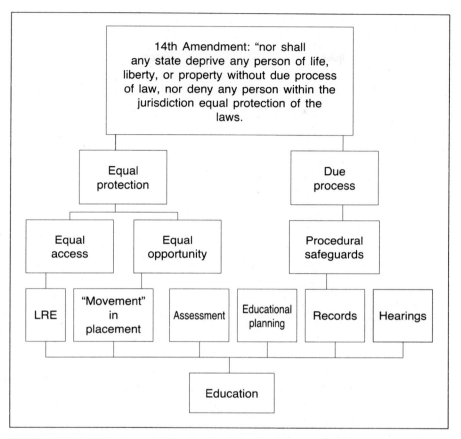

FIGURE 2.1 The conceptual structure of the 14th Amendment to the U.S. Constitution as it relates to provisions for the education of students with handicaps.

entails **substantive due process** such that certain rights are inviolate and cannot be taken away by any state agency.

An example of a violation of procedural due process by a first year teacher or other school official is a change in educational placement of a student without prior notice and without consulting the parents. The arbitrary institutionalization of a student by school officials is an illustration of a substantive due process claim.

EQUAL PROTECTION   The state must provide the same rights and benefits to individuals with handicaps as to persons without handicaps. They are guaranteed the opportunity or equal access to participate in programs. Any variance must be justified in court.

An example of equal protection entails the opportunity for students with handicaps to participate in sports programs if such programs are

TABLE 2.1.   Themes of Litigation Prior to the Passage of EHA in 1975

Litigation	Major Themes
Brown v. Board of Education (1954)	Separate But Not Equal a. Separated educational facilities for black students: violation of student rights. b. Unlawful to discriminate against a class of persons for an arbitrary or unjustifiable reason.
Hansen v. Hobson (1967)	Disproportionate Minorities a. Disproportionate number of minority students assigned to lower "tracks" in public school classes of Washington, DC, via biased testing. b. Unlawful to use student performance data of standardized aptitude and achievement tests to make grouping or placement decisions. Educational placements based on performance on standardized tests biased against whole classes of students.
Diana v. State Board of Education (1970)	Fair Practices a. Misclassification of minority and non-English speaking students based on biased assessment is unlawful. b. Must eliminate "unfair verbal items" from assessment and use standardized appropriate ability tests at all times. c. Every student's primary language must be used in testing situations.
PARC, Bowman, et al., v. Commonwealth of Pennsylvania (1971)	Exclusion of Students a. Exclusion from school of students with mental retardation violates equal protection and due process of law. b. Students with mental retardation have a right to FAPE and a right to notice in educational decision making.
Mills v. Board of Education (1972)	a. FAPE must be provided to all students with handicaps. b. Education funds must be used equally for all.

available for students without handicaps. Another example is the provision of funds for band uniforms for special needs students if all other students are provided the band uniforms. School officials would be asked to justify why some students warrant school-related uniforms while other students with handicaps do not.

Many participants in court decisions have relied on the constitutional basis to attack legal injustices occurring in public school settings (Turnbull & Turnbull, 1978). Accordingly, the benefits of an education are considered by the courts a property interest, and the reputation of an individual is considered a liberty interest. When students with handicaps are provided inadequate services, the denial of access to appropriate public education constitutes a deprivation of property. The negative effects of exclusion or labeling on their reputations are considered a deprivation of liberty. Consequently, teachers should be aware of constitutional guarantees protecting all students from unilateral decisions by school personnel to deny students access to FAPE.

Issues

Central themes or issues occurring within school litigation have affected the practices of school personnel during past years. These issues are considered to be unconstitutional and should be avoided actively by new teachers.

Court cases have been initiated by individuals who challenged unilateral decision making by school professionals. Among relevant issues in past litigation are separate but not equal standards; disproportionate number of minority children assigned to special education; fairness practices in referral, assessment, or placement; and exclusion of students from programs (Ballard, Ramirez, & Weintraub, 1982). These issues are described in Table 2.1.

After the passage of PL 94–142, court litigation followed a slightly different course. Litigation of the 1980s entailed the interpretation of federal laws and regulations at the state and local levels including: delivery of special education programs and services; definition of related services; denial and/or unavailability of special education programming and services; financial issues in providing FAPE; and expulsion/suspension of students with handicaps (*Education for the Handicapped Law Report*, 1977–1988). These issues are described in Table 2.2.

All of these issues are related to the federal laws mandating services for students with special needs. New teachers should be familiar with components of the federal laws that ensure fair educational practices to the students they serve.

Major Components of the Federal Law

PL 94–142 is the most important legislation passed in favor of educating children and youth with handicaps. It contains the framework from which students with special needs are educated today. Preservice and beginning teachers will be involved actively in implementing EHA standards no matter what type of class placement teachers direct. Mandated

TABLE 2.2.   Themes of Litigation after the Passage of EHA

Litigation	Major Themes
Larry P. v. Riles (1979)	Delivery of Special Education Services a. Special class placement of minority students is unlawful when based on biased assessment instruments. b. Disproportionate number of minority students have been placed in classes for the mentally retarded in California. c. Professionals must monitor number of black students assigned to programs for the mildly retarded.
Jose P. v. Ambach	a. Rights of students with handicaps must be maintained to be referred, evaluated, and placed in appropriate educational programs and services in a timely fashion. b. Urgent need of accessibility of facilities. c. Systematic monitoring of services includes consideration of time factors between screening and actual placement.
Board v. Rowley (1982)	Definitions of Related Services a. "Appropriate" in FAPE needs clarification. b. District should consider progress of the student relative to handicap and to IEP in determining need of interpreter.
Frederick L. v. Douglas (1978)	Denial of Special Education a. LEA failed to provide FAPE to students with learning disabilities. b. Programs must be available to match needs of students.
Lora v. NY City Board of Education (1978)	a. LEA failed to provide FAPE to students with emotional handicaps. b. LEA must evaluate, place, and monitor all students with emotional handicaps.
Luke S. and Hans S. v. Nix (1984)	a. Adequacy of special education? Massive backlog of students awaiting evaluations. b. Prereferral evaluations, curriculum-based assessment, and statewide inservice training of assessment personnel are mandated.
Howard v. Friendswood School District (1978)	Financial Issues a. Parents have a right to injunctive relief in order to provide FAPE. b. School district must contract for private educational services to reimburse parents for cost of private schooling.
Smith v. Robinson Burlington School (1984)	a. Reimbursement consideration of attorney's fees in PL 94–142's financial allotment.

TABLE 2.2 *(continued)*

	b. Reimbursement must be considered to parents for unilateral placement in private special education schools.
Stuart v. Nappi (1978)	Suspension/Expulsion
	a. LEA enjoined from expelling student with handicap because of student's history of learning and behavioral problems.
	b. LEA failed to provide district's own IEP.
	c. LEA failed to respond adequately to student's lack of special education participation.
	d. Expulsion prior to resolution of plaintiff's complaint is an EHA violation.
Doe v. Koger (1979)	a. LEA requirement: determine whether student's disruptive behavior is related to handicap.
	b. LEA accepting EHA funds prohibited from expelling students whose disruptive behavior is related to handicap.
	c. Suspensions cannot be indefinite.
	d. LRE must be identified for disruptive students.
S-1 v. Turlington (1981)	a. LEA: provision of expelled students with handicaps procedural safeguards/ educational services considered.
	b. "Trained and knowledgeable group" must decide whether a relationship exists between a student's handi- cap and misbehavior before expulsion.
	c. Expulsion: a change in placement.
	d. Expulsion: an appropriate form of discipline in some cases.
Honig v. Doe (1988)	a. LEA: all students with handicaps in placement designated on student's current IEP until it can be demonstrated to a court that placement must be changed ("stay-put" provision).
	b. Burden of proof to change placement is on school officials.
	c. LEA need not exhaust administrative remedies but may go directly to court.
	d. Expulsion: a "change in placement" under PL 94–142.
	e. Expulsion: used as a form of discipline.
	f. Cessation of all educational services is prohibited by law.

components of the law form the basis of what teachers do and where or how teachers operate in the class. Preservice-level teachers will be exposed to various aspects of the law as they progress in the student-teaching process. Beginning teachers may be expected to demonstrate knowledge of the federal law from the first day of school.

1. Teachers in training may be involved in implementing and monitoring objectives of the student's educational program under the guidance of the directing classroom teacher. They may be asked to observe a classroom in which a child is being considered for special education. Their data may be used to monitor a child's progress in the mainstreamed class.
2. Beginning teachers may be asked to attend conferences prior to the beginning of the school year and to begin implementing the special education program during the initial week of classes. First year teachers may be involved in the referral process or a student's exit from the special education program.

Four major components of the law have an impact on the developing teacher's roles with special needs students: (a) a full range of **services**, (b) guidelines for a specific **funding formula**, (c) steps in **referral, evaluation, and placement proceedings**, and (d) **procedural safeguards**.

Full Range of Services

Writers of PL 94–142 stipulated a continuum of special education placement options must be available to meet the needs of special students in the **least restrictive environment (LRE)**, the placement closest to the normal classroom environment. To ensure appropriate placements, school personnel must provide a continuum of alternative placements, including regular classrooms, special classes, special schools, home instruction, and education in residential facilities. (Chapter 1 illustrates the cascade of service delivery, one of the most common continua.) State officials are required to establish facilities so that children with handicaps have the opportunity to participate with others to the extent possible. New teachers may be assigned to instruct in regular classes, special classes, or separate schools. However, removal of children with special needs under the special education teacher's direction occurs only when the nature of the severity of the handicap is so great that servicing them in regular classes could not be achieved satisfactorily.

All special students have the right of access to supplementary services or aids. This may mean that the new teacher provides prosthetic devices, adaptive equipment, flexible scheduling, test modifications, and so forth, to make it possible for the student to remain in a regular class placement. Federal law also guarantees the right to placement in the school the child would have attended if nonhandicapped unless participants in the educational process agree to some other arrangement. If a school district does not have a particular placement option, it may contract for the needed services.

INCENTIVE FOR MAINSTREAMING   Currently there is a movement against the mass pull-out program of students with mild to moderate handicaps from regular class placements. Emphasis is on educating the student demonstrating less severe mental, learning, or social handicaps in the **mainstream** with normally functioning peers to the extent that the student can handle. The Regular Education Initiative (REI) is a recent movement to restructure special education so that mildly to moderately handicapped students can receive most of their education in general education classrooms (Maheady, 1988). A new direction of the mainstreaming incentive through the REI or other reform movements of service delivery (e.g., consulting services, prereferral strategies) may expand the role of the special education teacher. In addition to being a direct-service provider to students with handicaps, the new teacher may be asked to provide consulting help and assistance to regular classroom teachers. New teachers may offer a combination of direct services and consulting assistance to make the regular classroom setting more appropriate to a student's needs. New teachers may help to develop, maintain, and evaluate prereferral strategies that regular classroom teachers implement. One idea of prereferral is to allow special modifications in teaching strategies, materials, evaluation, or curricula implemented in the regular class, thus circumventing the need for a formal referral for special education. The added assistance in the regular class to overcome learning deficiencies and/or problem behaviors of the student is provided by a **multidisciplinary team** of professionals. The special education teacher is an important member of the team. Examples of direct services, consulting assistance, or prereferral strategy suggestions that developing teachers may help to develop within a team format include:

1. Identifying discrepancies in the student's progress within regular class subject areas.
2. Identifying effective assessment techniques for specific learning weaknesses and problem behaviors.
3. Observing and recording the success of prereferral strategies.
4. Designing with the regular class teacher appropriate instructional plans to ameliorate and prevent future deviations.
5. Modifying classroom academic materials and strategies to make it easier for the student to remain in grade level curricula.
6. Devising, implementing, and monitoring behavior management plans of regular class–special class contracts, or of home–school contingencies.

7. Providing resources/sufficient materials to aid in teaching students with handicaps in the regular class.
8. Monitoring the progress of mainstreamed students systematically in cooperation with the regular class teacher.
9. Facilitating the multidisciplinary team within the school.

Chapter 7 provides details of the prereferral process.

All of these suggestions are examples of roles new special education teachers may fulfill as they progress in their careers. The job of the new professional is not static but changes continually to meet the needs of students.

Funding Formula

New teachers' jobs in special education are provided by monies generated through a funding formula in which officials of the LEA and SEA assure representatives of the federal government that children with handicaps are identified, assessed, served, and monitored fairly and consistently. Writers of PL 94–142 stipulated a flow-down formula for monies in which the number of children served is the determining factor of allocated funds provided to each locality. Federal funds are given to the SEA; professionals of the SEA must allot monies to representatives of the LEA. When children are referred as possible candidates for special education, representatives of the LEA are responsible for determining child count figures twice a year. Each area of exceptionality is reviewed for service of students in full-time or part-time programs. SEA representatives report the figures to federal authorities, and monies are allocated based on the needs resulting from the state and local figures.

Members of Congress passed a ceiling level on the number of children to be served for the allocation of EHA funds. The ceiling was initiated to provide an accurate estimation of children requiring services and to restrict SEA or LEA authorities who may count children without handicaps in order to receive more of the allotted funds. Congress intended school officials to receive monies only for students with needs. This stipulation is important for the new teacher who, to some degree, is offered protection from an exaggerated class enrollment or from staggering numbers of students who may not be appropriate candidates for special education and related services.

Referral, Evaluation, and Placement Guidelines

EHA regulations set up priorities for services given to those children who were unserved at the time of the law's passage, and to the most severely involved children within each area of exceptionality receiving inadequate services. EHA also established **Child Find**, a referral system for locating children with special needs. Specific guidelines in the referral, screening, diagnoses, evaluation, placement, and reevaluation of children mandated steps that all teachers are required to follow in order to receive allocated funds. New classroom teachers may be involved in every step of the process—from referral to reevaluation. Each must meet requirements within specific timeframes of the local area and state in order to receive allocated funds and to provide the needed help to students. Figure 2.2 provides a description of the various steps in the process. (Chapter 7 describes the paperwork involved in the referral, evaluation, and placement process.)

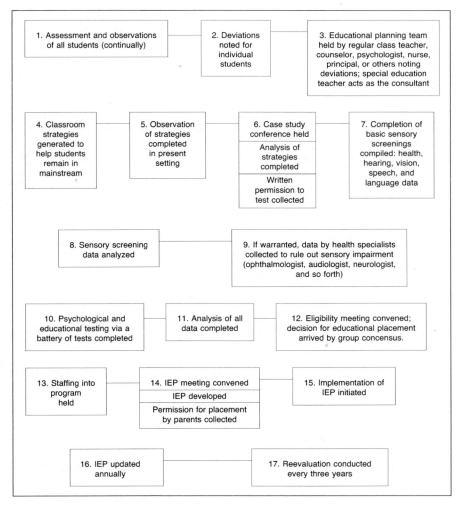

FIGURE 2.2 Steps in the referral process used to determine eligibility for special education and to plan educational programs.

Procedural Safeguards

Every developing and beginning teacher will be involved to some degree in legal proceedings involving students, parents, and professionals. Due process rights, also referred to as **procedural safeguards**, are afforded to participants of the educational process. Parents and classroom teachers are involved directly in the implementation of rights guaranteeing parents' active involvement in their child's educational program. These rights are afforded also to all professional personnel. Procedural safeguards are illustrated in Figure 2.3 including rights in **programming decisions**, **hearings**, and **confidentiality of record keeping**.

PROGRAMMING DECISIONS   EHA requires all educators to follow specific notice, consent, evaluation, and placement procedures for programming to ensure nondiscriminatory evaluation and placement of students.

Notice/Consent Professionals must provide written notice to parents before school officials can initiate or change, or refuse to initiate or change, the identification, evaluation, or placement of students. While implementation of these rights varies according to individual school practices, developing teachers will be involved in the process (e.g., sending the written notices home to parents and holding informal conferences prior to the student's formal testing). All notices must be in the parents' native language or other principal mode of communication. New teachers should work actively to ensure notices are stated clearly to avoid teacher jargon. The notice must include a description of the proposed action, an explanation of the proposal, a summary of all options considered, and information as to why other options were rejected. Parents must be notified of each evaluation procedure, test, record, or report teachers will use as a basis for any educational decision reached.

Parents must grant written permission prior to evaluations and initial placement into any special education program or related service. Beginning teachers should be aware that parents can change their minds at any time to revoke the consent. However, school officials have the right to initiate a hearing in the absence of parental consent. A hearing officer, then, must determine whether the child should be evaluated or placed. In turn, the parent has the right to protest at a hearing any evaluation or programming action by school officials.

Evaluation Evaluation safeguards include the right to an independent assessment by an evaluator of the parents' choosing. The parents have a right to be told where and how the evaluation will be conducted and to be given a list describing any available low-cost or free legal aid in the geographical area in which they reside. Parents have the right to request that the LEA or SEA pay for the independent evaluation if the agency evaluation was done incorrectly or inadequately. All teachers must inform parents that a hearing officer may be asked to order an

---

Evaluation
1. Written permission to evaluate (notice/consent)
2. Comprehensive battery
3. Nondiscriminatory practices
4. Independent educational evaluation
5. Informed results
6. Assessment by a multidisciplinary team

Educational Placement
1. Written permission to place (notice/consent)
2. Participation in educational decisions
3. Approval for proposed changes (notice/consent)
4. Input into creation, maintenance, and monitoring of IEP

Hearings
1. Informal due process hearing
2. Appeal process
3. "Stay put" policy until alternative placement

Records
1. Review
2. Explanations and interpretations
3. Copies
4. Challenge
5. Assurance of confidentiality

FIGURE 2.3 Procedural safeguards involving rights in programming decisions, hearings, and confidentiality of records.

independent evaluation at public expense and of the criteria for the examiner needed to secure payment by the LEA or SEA.

The student must be given a full and individual evaluation using a battery of tests. The testing cannot discriminate on the basis of the student's language or culture. The evaluator must ensure that all testing devices and materials are sensitive to individual needs including differences of sensory, manual, or speaking abilities. All aspects of the student's strengths and abilities should be assessed, especially the areas in which deviations from the norm are recognized by professionals.

Placement Teachers must use more than one criterion when specifying the appropriate educational program based on a student's specific instructional or behavioral needs. EHA mandates that parents be given the opportunity for input into all aspects of the proposed placement. The program must be evaluated and implemented by a multidisciplinary team. Preservice teachers and beginning teachers should note that the student's educational program must be updated annually, and areas of functioning must be reevaluated by a trained evaluator every three years, or more frequently if conditions warrant or if professionals or parents make the request.

Individualized Education Plan (IEP) The student's IEP is the most important document teachers and parents will' determine for the child together. The IEP is formulated from multidisciplinary team input and parents' suggestions. Every student with special needs is provided an IEP that specifies, in writing, goals and objectives proposed for the student during the school year. The plan must be current and in effect at the beginning of every school year. For students identified during the year, teachers must still hold an IEP meeting within 30 calender days from an eligibility meeting specifying the special education and related services to be provided. After parents give written consent for placement, the IEP goes into effect immediately. (Chapter 7 describes the IEP in full detail.)

HEARINGS   Hearings result from court decrees allowing dissenting or aggrieved parties opportunities to question educational decisions. To receive federal monies allocated by EHA, representatives of the SEA and LEA must guarantee federal authorities the adoption of appropriate due process procedures in their locale to present complaints relating to the child's identification, evaluation, or placement, or the right to FAPE. In addition, parties in litigation have the right of review (i.e., they may appeal to a higher court any decision they believe requires further interpretation.)

For example, a new teacher may teach a student in the resource-room class. In the teacher's opinion, the student is placed in an inappropriate special education program and requires a change in placement to a full-time special class. The parents disagree with the need for change and request a due-process hearing. Until a final decision is reached, the student remains in the present educational setting (i.e., resource room) unless an alternative placement is agreed on by all parties involved. The review process may continue until the case is heard before the U. S. Supreme Court. Figure 2.4 describes levels of the review process.

Mediation Each professional, especially teachers in training and those new to the field, should strive for **mediation**, the process of solving disagreements and deciding issues of FAPE, before they escalate into a hearing outside of the educational system. Mediation helps parents and professionals resolve differences prior to involvement of representatives of the legal system. Situations will arise in which there will not always

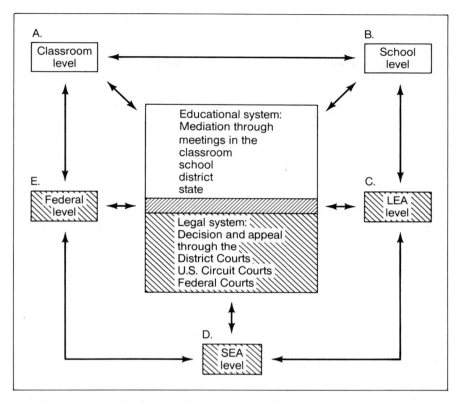

FIGURE 2.4   Levels of the review process used to redress disagreement regarding the education of individual students.

be agreement with others. The following strategies may help professionals new to the field avoid problems in the mediation process or in formal conferences with parents and other professionals:

1. Treat the parents and other professionals with respect in all dealings. Consider both verbal and nonverbal messages of participants during all professional contacts. Record all pertinent messages evolving from mediation attempts.
2. Provide many scheduled conferences to get things out in the open and on the table even prior to initial mention of legal action. Times should be scheduled when students are not present to review academic, behavioral, or social progress, answer questions, or discuss concerns of the administrator, evaluator, teacher, or parent.
3. Inform parents of their due-process rights (i.e., procedural safeguards) in writing during every meeting in which evaluation or

educational decisions are made for their child. This may be done by the teacher, principal, or administrator. Keep a copy of all written material presented during the meeting.

4. Keep on task; confer about student progress in all structured conferences to discuss strengths observed, weaknesses of concern, or proposed changes in behavioral or educational goals and objectives.

5. Have a written agenda to share in all conferences. An agenda will help in the smooth running of the conference and will provide data for the teacher's records if a hearing does follow the mediation process.

6. Always allow all participants a chance to speak at the meeting in order to question, to seek clarification, or to provide feedback on data presented. Demonstrate empathy, listening skills, and approachability.

7. In all mediation efforts scheduled with parents and professionals, come prepared. Meetings will run smoothly and end on time.

8. Provide a copy of all written documentation to every member in attendance.

9. Listen to every concern at meetings and be open to all legitimate solutions to evaluation or programming options prior to a change in placement.

10. Always make officials of the LEA aware of potential problems with parents and other professionals. Report major outcomes of all meetings to those in authority.

11. Never hold a potentially explosive conference alone. Always inform the principal and/or special education supervisor of all conferences when evaluation or placement decisions are to be made or when mediation is in progress.

12. Document meetings. Tell participants in advance the meeting will be transcribed or recorded. Elicit their permission.

13. Encourage all participants to sign, date, and identify their relationship to the student before the meeting gets underway.

14. Devise a written summary of the meeting as soon as possible after meetings conclude. The LEA representative or teacher may complete this. Be sure all data are accurate and dated.

15. Send a copy of the written summary to all participants and administrators in authority who may not have attended.

When many conferences are planned and professionals have the opportunity to discuss evaluation results or placement issues with parents and advocates, the need for involving judicial representatives may be lessened. However, there are times when litigation is unavoidable and legal authorities necessarily are involved in mediation, hearings, and reviews. During this stage, teachers may be asked to provide information they have collected during the year on the student. Mediation, the step prior to initiation of a hearing, often begins by a review of tangible data.

RECORDKEEPING/CONFIDENTIALITY   EHA stipulates that all teachers must ensure students' and parents' rights to fair record-keeping procedures and confidentiality of all records. Records may include informal and formal assessments, anecdotal records, behavioral lists, and checklists. Federal law provides that parents have the right to inspect and review all data about their child. They have the right to copy all information and receive a list of all types and locations of records being collected, maintained, or in any way used by LEA or SEA members. A teacher's data on the student, thus, are very important pieces of information and may be used as evidence in legal proceedings. Parents may ask for an explanation of any information in the records and may ask for changes if they believe the records are incorrect, misleading, or violate privacy rights. They also may initiate a hearing on the issue if school personnel refuse to change the data. Parents can restrict access to the student's records by withholding consent to disclose the data. School officials must inform parents about where and how information is to be used by others and before information in the student's file is to be destroyed.

Major Challenges of PL 94–142 for Developing Teachers

Areas of EHA identified by Abeson and Zettel (1977) pose strong challenges for teachers of special education. These areas summarize the law's major components and bear directly on what the new teacher provides to the student with special needs: (a) fair and nondiscriminatory referral/assessment practices and procedures, (b) ongoing child-find activities, (c) placement of all students in the LRE, (d) development of the IEP for each student requiring special education and related services, (e) confidential data collection and accurate recordkeeping, (f) assurances of equal protection and due process rights, (g) ongoing involvement and input of parents and guardians in all aspects of the educational process.

Federal mandates can make the job of the special education teacher especially difficult. Paperwork, many hours of data collection and conferences, often difficult students or parents, and logistics of operating within a multidisciplinary team can be very frustrating and stressful. However, a new teacher may consider the ramifications of the components of the law as a means of providing structure to the teacher's tasks. Federal and state mandates may help to ensure consistency in the quantity and quality of the services provided. The more experience the teacher has in implementing federal mandates, the easier the teacher's job can be.

How Can Teachers Demonstrate Implementation of the Law?

Preservice and beginning teachers can use and demonstrate a working knowledge of current trends and practices by becoming strong student advocates. They can demonstrate professional standards that lessen the probabilities of legal action initiated by disagreeing parties. Developing teachers can:

1. View education as a process that continually changes in the face of evolving federal and state laws and regulations. In order to survive legal challenges, teachers must be flexible and adaptable within acceptable professional guidelines of their locales.
2. Be articulate consumers of public policy by talking with parents, teachers, community leaders, administrators, and legal representatives. Teachers should be familiar with local philosophies and goals of educational programs. Reading district procedures and other legal policies published by the state or local education office may help new professionals to become familiar with current issues affecting their classrooms.
3. Be familiar with legal and professional guidelines to ensure fairness and appropriateness of their programs and to facilitate program accountability. This includes awareness of prereferral strategies, referral steps, testing procedures, program criteria, and exit criteria for all special education and related services provided.
4. Demonstrate knowledge of the major components of PL 94–142.
5. Seek to upgrade personal knowledge of legal changes that have an impact on them or their students (e.g., legal issues related to teaching practices; research and services bearing directly on public policy) through inservice, recertification and so forth.

An example of the changes new teachers face is the modification of PL 94–142 set forth in 1986. New regulations affecting the provision of services to very young children with special needs have come about through the challenge to public policy on the most effective time to begin special education and related services.

PL 99–457: New Challenges

Parents, teachers, and advocates recognize the need to begin special education and related services as soon as possible to prevent and/or ameliorate handicaps. During the 1980s data were collected by professionals pinpointing the necessity of early intervention for young children with identified handicaps or infants and toddlers at risk for handicaps (Peterson, 1987). In 1986, Congress passed the **Amendment to the Education for All Handicapped Children's Act**, also referred to as **PL 99–457**. This is the most important piece of federal legislation affecting special education and related services since the passage of EHA in 1975. PL 99–457 reauthorized the discretionary programs of EHA and provided incentives to states to serve an estimated additional 70,000 handicapped children ages 3 through 5 who remained unserved. It created a discretionary program to address the needs of handicapped infants and toddlers (birth through age 2) and their families (NASDSE, 1986). The highlights of PL 99–457 identified by Peterson (1987) include: (a) establishment of parent and preservice teacher training centers dealing with preschool needs of at-risk toddlers and infants and young children with identified handicaps, (b) provision of a multidisciplinary assessment of individual child needs and services required to meet such needs, (c) annual individualized program plan developed by a multidisciplinary team, including the parents, describing necessary services, and (d) access to all services described in the state/local early intervention program plan without cost to the parent or guardian.

The intent of PL 99–457 is to reach young infants and toddlers as early as possible in the hope that through early intervention, problems will be eliminated or minimized. Enactment of the law provides special education and related services at public expense to preschool children in need beginning at age 3. By creating funding options to school districts to provide early intervention programs for very young children, services can begin at optimal times. Monies are available to train parents as well as to train and certify teachers in early intervention special education. Individual Family Plans (IFP), developed for parents and each young child identified as requiring help, will contain family goals and objectives in addition to other ways of documenting the young child's progress.

Legal and Professional Responsibilities of New Teachers

Positive educational changes have occurred in recent years for students of all ages from infants to 21-year-old adults with special needs. Transitional needs of students in various life stages are examples of positive educational changes. These changes evolved with the help of dedicated teachers fulfilling their legal and professional responsibilities to students, parents, themselves, and their profession. When past practices were analyzed critically by dedicated professionals, inadequacies were tackled head on and the process of change helped to initiate better practices in meeting the students' needs. Today's preservice and beginning teachers also share responsibilities including: (a) provision of *FAPE* through effective teaching practices and the application of pertinent laws and regulations, (b) efforts exerted within the educational system to promote *communication and teaming*, (c) use of *mediation* and *professional attitudes* during unavoidable litigation, and (d) advocacy for new and better *legislation* to promote educational progress of all students. Figure 2.5 illustrates the major responsibilities of teachers today to guarantee required services to special students in a timely and effective manner.

Providing FAPE

Understanding important regulations and laws and abiding by legal mandates may help to promote progress of all students. New teachers need

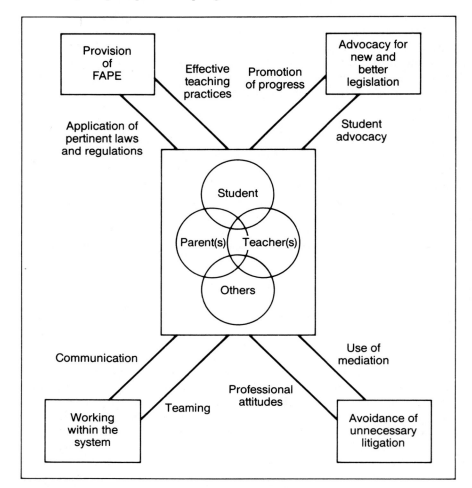

FIGURE 2.5   Major responsibilities of teachers today.

to modify their programs to meet current federal and state laws and regulations, to modify the program according to current teaching practices, and to display professionalism.

EFFECTIVE TEACHING PRACTICES   Changes within individual classrooms may affect the quality and quantity of services provided in the school, the LEA, or the SEA. Teachers can effect changes in their own classrooms in a number of ways.

1. Determine student skills through continual assessment linked to curricula needs.
2. Establish, implement, and evaluate individual and group goals for students.
3. Set realistic criterion levels and evaluation schedules to be followed.
4. Set optimal conditions for learning through control of environmental variables, such as classroom physical arrangement, temperature control, lighting, acoustics, and other stimuli manipulation.
5. Evaluate personal teaching styles and abilities and the effects these behaviors have on students.
6. Plan effective academic and behavioral objectives in which students are on-task for a majority of the instructional time.
7. Provide appropriate instruction based on specific goals and objectives.
8. Use a variety of curricula and materials considering vocational, self-help, cognitive, motor, communication, or social-emotional development of students.
9. Plan and manage transition activities to lessen problems between instructional sessions and learning environments.
10. Manage individual and group behaviors of students by implementing and monitoring a host of management strategies.
11. Observe regularly and keep systematic methods of data collection.
12. Prepare for all events by collecting, maintaining, and analyzing verifiable data.
13. Monitor and make necessary changes as conditions warrant.

AWARENESS OF LEGISLATION AND LITIGATION   All teachers have a legal and professional responsibility to display a working knowledge of legislation and litigation that affects students. Awareness of legislation and litigation can occur through a number of ways. Developing and beginning teachers will be able to maintain knowledge of current practices, laws, and court cases through active participation in conferences, workshops, inservices, or continuing education classes. Subscribing to relevant journals and newsletters may help teachers obtain information on current teaching practices, research, and service activities. Working actively in local, state, or national advocacy groups may widen the contacts teachers have and may aid in political and legal awareness. Becoming an advocate may provide, also, new perspectives to the educational process occurring at the local level so that teachers may work effectively within the educational system.

Working within the Educational System

To facilitate efforts to solve problems within the school, teachers should confer regularly with each other and parents about similarities and differences they perceive of the student or any aspect of the FAPE provided. Energies can be directed toward a team model encouraging parental and professional involvement. The use of effective communication skills during all professional endeavors and the concept of teaming may enhance teachers' abilities to affect positive changes.

COMMUNICATION   Communication is the foundation of all interpersonal relationships and the framework for every meeting with parents or professional contacts with peers. In order for teachers to be effective communicators, real effort is needed. Teachers new to the field can develop and enhance their interpersonal communication skills by setting priorities, demonstrating good rapport-building skills, and being flexible and adaptable. Additionally, new teachers should consider their roles in sending or receiving messages during the communication process. They should speak clearly and correctly with a consideration given to meaning behind discourse. Teachers should listen to what parents and other professionals say and be open to suggestions. They should consider their nonverbal messages, including body language, facial expressions, posture, and stance, and demonstrate empathy, positive regard, and nonjudgmental statements to peers and parents. All of these suggestions may aid in facilitating better communication. To increase positive rapport during meetings or conferences, consideration of the aspects of communication as presented in Box 2.3 may help. The need for legal action may be lessened when individuals closest to the student believe and demonstrate they are working together.

TEAMING   Involving others in the change process often helps if everyone perceives a team effort. Individuals may assume ownership of the functions of the team and often may work harder to lessen inherent difficulties for the benefit of the student. Through the process of multidisciplinary teaming, parents and professionals work together to ensure FAPE to students and lessen legal difficulties. Some general tips to promote teaming can be used within the context of any functional relationship with parents and other professionals.

1. From day one, capitalize on the personal strengths of the student and always demonstrate that the major consideration is the student's best interests.

BOX 2.3

Important Considerations of the Communication Process for Teachers to Use with Peers and Parents

1. *Background and experiences.* All human beings are different and have had life experiences that provide a unique way of perceiving the world and its events. Each person learns, understands, feels, and speaks from his or her own background and experiences. Parents and professionals will bring to the meeting a host of background events and experiences which the teacher should be prepared to acknowledge. A smart teacher can use the variety to his advantage rather than consider variety a hindrance. Being aware of differences in backgrounds and experiences can aid in the communication process and may lessen problems of difficult programming meetings. Teachers should appreciate the competence of other professionals and parents.

2. *Feelings and emotions.* Feelings and emotions are powerful personal forces that vary in duration, frequency, intensity, and expression. People think, act, and speak differently when they feel cool, calm, or affectionate as opposed to when they feel angry, upset, or fearful. Teachers should consider others' feelings and emotions in both informal and formal conferences. The use of empathy and the display of approachability may lessen any negative feelings and emotions brought to educational meetings.

3. *Language meaning.* Words often have more than one meaning, and sometimes they are used inaccurately. Due to varied experiences, words with just one dictionary definition have different shades of meaning for different individuals. In reality, the meanings of words are in people — not in words. It is especially important that teachers consider others' professional language or the family's cultural background when word meaning and usage are used that are different from the teacher's own. Awareness of these differences may be especially important during disagreements of evaluation or placement meetings.

4. *Being self-centered.* Sometimes individuals are so concerned with themselves that they cannot extend interest to others long enough to hear what others have to say. To communicate well, individuals must be conscious of and sensitive to the needs, abilities, and desires of others. When individuals focus on themselves, meanings, intentions, and feelings can be missed and legal action, which might have been avoided, may follow.

(continued)

BOX 2.3 (continued)

It is best to use the process of empathy in which one can place himself into another's shoes. Displaying positive regard for others is important. The ability to listen is very important to help parents and other professionals contribute to educational decisions.

5. *Making snap judgments.* Some people look at outward appearances and become so distracted by the image of the person that they can't hear what he says. This is falling into the dangerous trap of putting people in categories or labels—stereotyping them using unfound biases. This is a type of closed-mindedness that prevents individuals from learning from things or people that are new or different to them. Beginning teachers should be especially aware of this when working with parents and should avoid the use of snap judgments as a means of making false assumptions about parents' intentions, power, or feelings. It is best to use nonjudgmental statements when conferring with peers and parents.

6. *Failing to seek clarification/disregarding feedback.* Anytime teachers are uncertain about someone's meaning or intention, they should ask questions and seek clarification of what others intended. Feedback is made up of the various clues that tell a speaker how messages are being accepted or interpreted (e.g., smiles, frowns, nods, grunts, yawns, questions). To disregard these signals is to risk sending unclear, inadequate, or inappropriate messages to participants attending meetings or conferences. These types of mistakes may lead to unnecessary litigation.

7. *Status of relationship.* The professional in the more dominant role or power position should also avoid the "I'm better than you attitude" and "talking down " attitude to parents that sometimes may crop up at highly emotional referral, placement, or evaluation meetings. Professionals need to take the lead to promote harmony and facilitate the exchange of ideas, feelings, and information among all individuals. This is especially important during educational meetings in which parents may not be able to deal with evaluation results or accept a placement proposed for their child. When individuals perceive themselves as powerless, their emotional expressions may escalate, resulting in undue actions or unnecessary words. Teachers need to acknowledge the emotions of others involved in the relationship and be aware of their attitude towards others.

SOURCE   Based on O'Shea, D.J., & Hendrickson, J.M. (1987). *Tips for using teacher aides effectively.* (Monograph No. 16.) Gainesville: University of Florida Diagnostic and Teaching Clinic.

2. Provide constructive criticism by sharing information and by eliciting from parents and other professionals targeted improvements in the child or ways to initiate improvements. Provide encouragement through a balance of positive statements and corrective feedback statements.
3. Aim criticism with the goal of improved performance. While teachers should never gloss over individual weaknesses that need discussion, always mention some strength of the student at every meeting. It is wise to start and end all meetings with a positive statement. Even one small word of progress may aid in the teaming effort.
4. Strive for consistency in all team meetings by using verifiable data. Don't base information on personal opinion—provide facts. Communicate effectively in speech and in writing the data to parents, colleagues, administrators, and community members.
5. Get continual feedback from parents and other professionals to assess reasonableness of the type and amount of programming requirements and others' role in facilitating the requirements. Ask parents and professionals continually for their suggestions to improve the student's performance.
6. Involve parents and professionals in every step of the educational process. Elicit their suggestions to provide more appropriate programming for the student. Be flexible and adaptive to their suggestions.
7. Always keep others informed of all records, evaluation results, or educational proposals. Keep a written, dated copy of all communication attempts for records. Keep the records where they can be located quickly.

Using Mediation and Professional Attitudes during Litigation

Even with the best efforts during the communication process or teaming, problems may still escalate over which the classroom teacher has little or no control. During this time, mediation efforts require help from other professionals including administrators, peers, or even school attorneys.

There are **mediation steps** classroom teachers can take during in-school mediation to solve disagreements of the student's evaluation or educational placement and plan.

1. Provide many formal conferences to attempt to remediate differences within the student's current placement. Invite all significant individuals to the mediation conference.
2. Designate a leader to chair all mediation attempts. It may be the classroom teacher, principal, supervisor, or legal counsel. Have a written agenda to share in all conferences.

3. Encourage all participants to sign, date, and identify their relationship to the student.
4. Listen to all suggestions in order to ascertain the student's LRE. Strive for a group opinion on new strategies and procedures to try first in the student's immediate classroom environment.
5. Implement all suggested new strategies, procedures, and modifications within 6 weeks of the mediation conference.
6. Be sure to collect baseline data on the student's present levels prior to the introduction of treatments or changes in strategies. Keep data on all progress over time.
7. Document all modifications of the usual classroom techniques and procedures. Observe the student under different conditions within the classroom (e.g., individual assignments, group tasks, peer tutoring) and record all observations. Observe the student in different settings and working or socializing with different individuals.
8. Ask various school professionals and parents to observe the modifications within the class and document their observations on student progress. Compare professional and parent observations to determine interrater reliability.
9. Meet again in a structured conference to compare observation data and the student's progress to date. Strive again for group consensus on the next steps and "iron out" differences. Record the outcomes of all meetings.
10. Devise a written summary as soon as possible when meetings conclude.
11. Send a copy of the written summary to all participants.

These suggestions will help the developing professional to document every attempt to ensure the LRE for the target student. However, parties may still disagree over best practices or specific treatments for individual students. Be assured that with dated, written data new teachers do not have to fear court actions. If litigation still results, preparation and professional attitudes may still provide relief.

INEVITABLE LITIGATION   If repeated mediation attempts fail, the only recourse may be a hearing in which the decision passes from parents and school authorities to an impartial hearing officer who determines the outcome of the case (Schrybman, 1982). It is vital that teachers in training and teachers new to the field not view litigation as an evil process. When seen in the context of past litigation resulting in new and better laws for students, litigation may be considered a healthy and necessary process. When inappropriate management occurs, when procedures need to be redefined or refined, or when public policies require clarification that cannot be agreed on by local participants of the educational process, litigation can and should be looked on as a legitimate step in the process of FAPE for students with handicaps.

Advocacy for New and Better Legislation

Professional attitudes can affect public policy encouraging beneficial changes in the educational system. As demonstrated by past efforts, new legislation can result that will help to guarantee gains in special education and related services. It is beneficial to developing teachers to remember that much litigation evolved during the past because individuals recognized and responded to inadequate services, poor practices, and unfair procedures occurring in schools. Past advocates were willing to work for changes within the system but realized the power of political forces and legal influences were necessary. These individuals acted when data verified warranted changes. Today, new teachers should strive to work within established rules of the school, the district, and the state and strive for mediation first when disagreements arise. They can respond when changes are necessary through simple modifications in school policies or classroom procedures. All teachers need to formulate and follow a professional code of ethics and assume inherent professional roles and responsibilities. However, professionals who care about students and use established methods of intervention can be confident that members of the educational and legal systems will protect appropriate educational programming. An effective role beginning teachers can assume to protect the legal rights of their students is to recognize, implement, and monitor best teaching practices in their classrooms. This role is the foremost assurance that students are afforded legal justice in educational settings.

Summary

This chapter reviewed pertinent laws and court cases that have shaped special education and related services during the past 30 years. Legal themes from the 14th Amendment to the U. S. Constitution were discussed in relationship to laws and litigation prior to and after the passage of EHA in 1975. Major components of EHA were reviewed. Legal and professional responsibilities of new teachers were analyzed in terms of suggestions to increase professional awareness of the best practices in teaching, legal concerns, communication, teaming, mediation, unavoidable litigation, and advocacy for new and better laws. Legal efforts were viewed as healthy components of the changing process of special education.

References

ABESON, A., & ZETTEL, J. (1977). The end of the quiet revolution: The Education for All Handicapped Children's Act of 1975. *Exceptional Children*, 44, 114–128.

AMENDMENT TO THE EDUCATION FOR ALL HANDICAPPED CHILDREN'S ACT (Public Law 99–457). (1986) Washington, D.C.: Office of Special Education and Rehabilitation Services.

BALLARD, J. RAMIREZ, B. A., & WEINTRAUB, F.J. (1982). *Special education in America: Its legal and governmental foundations.* Reston, VA.: Council for Exceptional Children.

EDUCATION FOR THE HANDICAPPED LAW REPORT (1977–1988). Alexandria, VA: CRR Publishing.

MAHEADY, L. (1988). An opportunity for developing instructional diversity. *Special Services Digest, 2,* 4–6.

NATIONAL ASSOCIATION OF STATE DIRECTORS OF SPECIAL EDUCATION (1986). *NASDSE Newsletter.* Washington, D.C.: Author.

PETERSON, K. (1987). *Early intervention for handicapped and at-risk children. An introduction to early childhood special education.* Denver: Love.

REINERT, H.R. & HUANG, A. (1988). *Children in conflict.* (3rd ed.). Columbus, OH: Merrill.

SCHRYBMAN, J. (1982). *Due process in special education.* Rockville, MD: Aspen.

TURNBULL, H., & TURNBULL, A. (1978). *Free appropriate public education, law and implementation.* Denver: Love.

WEINTRAUB, F.J., ABESON, A., BALLARD, J., & LA VOR, M.L. (1977). *Public policy and the education of exceptional children.* Reston, VA: Council for Exceptional Children.

Litigation

Board v. Rowley (1982). Cited in Prasse, D.P. (1986). "Litigation and special education: An introduction." *Exceptional Children, 52,* 311–312.

Brown v. Board of Education, 347 U.S. 483 (1954).

Burlington School Committee v. Department of Education of the Commonwealth of Massachusetts, 105 Super. Ct. 1996 (1985).

Diana v. State Board of Education, C-70 37 RFR (1970).

Doe v. Koger, 480 F. Supp. 225 (N.D. In. 1979).

Frederick L. v. Thomas (1978). Cited in Prasse, D.P. (1986). "Litigation and special education: An introduction." *Exceptional Children, 52,* 311–312.

Hansen v. Hobson, 269, F. Supp. 401 (1967). aff'd sub nom Smuck *v.* Hobson, 408 F. SD 175 (D.C. Cir. 1969).

Honig v. Doe. (United States Court of Appeals for the Ninth District, No. 86–728).

Howard v. Friendswood Independent School District, 454 F. Supp. 634 (S.D. Texas 1978).

Jose P. v. Ambach (1986). Cited in Prasse, D.P. (1986). "Litigation and special education: An introduction." *Exceptional Children, 52,* 311–312.

Larry P. v. Riles (1979). Civil Action No. 71–2270 (N.D. Cal. 1971).

Lora v. NY City Board of Education (1978). Cited in Prasse, D.P. (1986). "Litigation and special education: An introduction." *Exceptional Children, 52,* 311–312.

Luke S. and Hans S. v. Nix (1984). Cited in Prasse, D.P. (1986). "Litigation and special education: An introduction." *Exceptional Children, 52,* 311–312.

Mills v. Board of Education of the District of Columbia, 348. F. Supp. 866 (D.D.C. No. 1939–71, 1972).

PARC, Bowman, et al. v. Commonwealth of Pennsylvania, 334 F. Supp. 279 1257 (E.D. Pa. 1971) and 343 F. Supp. 279 (E.D. Pa. 1972).

S-1 v. Turlington, 635 F. 2d. 342 (5th Cir. 1981).

Stuart v. Nappi, 443 F. Supp. 1235 (D. Conn. 1978).

CHAPTER 3

Setting Up for Instruction

Classrooms for students with mild and moderate handicaps tend to be very busy places. Whether one is student teaching in a self-contained or resource-room setting, a large number and variety of instructional and noninstructional events occur simultaneously. While a student teacher may be conducting a lesson on long division to a small group of students in one corner of the room, it would not be unusual for several other students to be completing seatwork assignments with peer tutors from neighboring classrooms or for still another group to be returning from their mainstreamed music class. If these events were not enough of a management concern, most special education teachers have also been asked to assume a variety of responsibilities that go beyond the boundaries of traditional classroom instruction. In addition to being charged with the usual array of diagnostic and teaching responsibilities, teachers of students with handicaps are frequently called upon to (a) complete full-scale educational evaluations, (b) field-test new and existing learning programs and instructional procedures, (c) monitor students' progress through the curriculum, (d) coordinate mainstreaming activities, (e) initiate and maintain collaborative working relationships with related service personnel, and (f) develop outreach programs with parents and significant others in the community.

Not surprisingly, special education teachers meet these often overwhelming demands with differing levels of success. Variation in degree of success is not, however, a function of magic or luck; those able to deal effectively with the multitude of demands involved in teaching students with mild handicapping conditions succeed because they work hard to produce conditions that promote success. The lesson is short and relatively simple: To successfully manage the daily demands of their busy classroom, special educators must be organized managers of their environments.

All classrooms, regardless of whether they contain special or normally achieving students, contain organizational pressures that influence the teacher/learning process. Table 3.1 describes Doyle's (1980) conceptualization of these complex organizational pressures typical of most classrooms. It is interesting to note that these six factors portray the classroom as a public forum requiring frequent and immediate teacher actions in the face of almost overwhelming and, in many cases, unpredictable environmental variables. The range and intensity of the six pressures can vary according to a teacher's experience level, dedication, level of competence, and even time of year. While many veteran teachers are experienced in managing the busy classroom, preservice and beginning teachers face the challenge of managing the sensory overload of their first days in the classroom. This may be particularly evident in special education classrooms where the unique learning and behavioral characteristics of students require additional external controls.

Fortunately, the early recognition of the organizational pressures of the classroom can allow for the development of strategies to manage these ever-present demands. These strategies are best viewed as preventive — an approach in which the events of a busy classroom are anticipated and planned for by an organized and flexible professional who successfully manages multiple occurring events (Paine et al., 1983). In this

TABLE 3.1   Organizational Pressures of Classrooms

Organizational Pressure	*Definition*
Immediacy	Large numbers of events require immediate attention or action.
Publicness	Teacher is always on stage.
Multidimensionality	Classrooms are crowded and busy places in which limited resources are used to achieve a wide range of goals.
Unpredictability	Events in classrooms change daily and many occurrences are difficult to predict.
History	Events that occur early in the school year set the tone for later happenings.
Simultaneity	Many things happen at the same time in classrooms.

SOURCE   Adapted from Doyle, W. (1980). *Classroom Management*. West Lafayette, IN: Kappa Delta Pi.

chapter, we will examine and provide guidelines for five interrelated preinstructional activities, which will assist student and beginning teachers in preparing for successful teaching: (a) the design of the physical environment, (b) the management of instructional time, (c) the effective scheduling and grouping of classroom activities and students, (d) the formulation of meaningful and relevant classroom rules and procedures, and (e) the coordination of available resources.

Designing the Physical Environment

The first of the many organizational challenges facing beginning, experienced, and, to a certain extent, student teachers is to make effective use of the physical dimensions of the classroom. Chairs, desks, bookcases, tables, room dividers, and countless other pieces of furniture need to be arranged for accessibility and safety. Instructional equipment such as computers, tape recorders, and portable filmstrip projectors need to be arranged for controlled student access and efficient teacher use. Seating patterns for instruction and independent work need to be considered in relation to their effects on discipline and transitions among activities. Finally, those aesthetic features that promote pride in one's classroom, such as displays, plants, and bulletin boards need to be infused appropriately into the existing physical structure of the room.

This monumental task of orchestrating the physical environment of the learning environment is critical because classroom designs are directly related to effective classroom management and student academic performance. This relationship among physical environmental variables and student performance variables is especially pronounced for students with mild and moderate handicaps. These students typically require added structure in all facets of their educational experience. For all students, however, the appropriate arrangement of the physical environment can decrease the rate of student disruptions, improve the quantity and quality of desirable social interactions among students, and increase the amount of time students attend to their assignments (Paine et al., 1983).

Figures 3.1 and 3.2 illustrate several typical classroom configurations for students with mildly handicapping learning and behavior problems. It should be cautioned, however, that the design of the physical classroom environment will vary according to a number of interacting variables including (a) the actual physical layout and location of the classroom, (b) the number, age, and behavioral profiles of students in the class, and (c) the degree or level of service (e.g., self-contained, resource-room, and so forth) being provided. Several generic rules, however, should be considered when arranging the physical layout of a special education classroom.

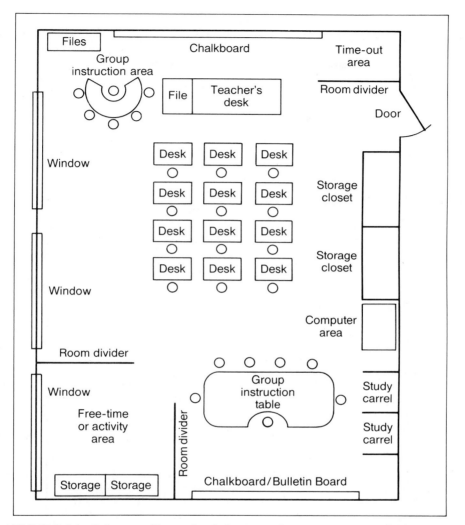

FIGURE 3.1 Primary self-contained classroom for students with mild learning and behavior problems.

Public and Private Space

Regardless of the age or types of problems exhibited by students with mild and moderate handicaps, classroom environments should provide opportunities for work, study, and free time in both public and private areas. Public areas used for group instruction and the majority of independent practice activities should be arranged in such a way that all students can see the teacher's desk or the primary instructional area.

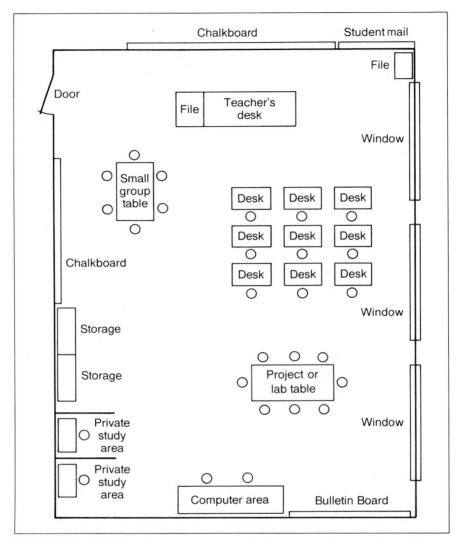

FIGURE 3.2   Middle-school or secondary resource room for students with mild learning and behavior problems.

Because students with mild and moderate handicaps have low rates of time-on-task under the best of conditions, exposure to potential distractors such as windows, free-time areas, and displays should be minimized.

Traditionally arranged student desks, class meeting tables, and large or small group instruction areas should be complemented with private quiet areas where students can work with limited distractions. Such areas can be easily designed through the creative arrangement of bookcases, filing cabinets, and study carrels. Partitions with greater portability and flexibility could be used as room dividers, providing privacy for small instructional groups, peer tutoring activities, or counseling sessions.

Furniture

It is critical that teachers consider patterns of movement typical of busy classrooms and plan furniture and seating arrangements to regulate such movement. Movement around the classroom can be facilitated by keeping high traffic areas free of unnecessary congestion. Students should be able to move to high traffic areas such as the teacher's desk, the pencil sharpener, and the front door without disturbing others. Moreover, these areas should be located in separate areas of the classroom, so that students engaged in other activities are not overwhelmed or distracted by such activities. Open spaces that have no clear purposes should be avoided; such areas often become a breeding ground of problematic behaviors. Furniture should be used to regulate or channel movement in and around the room. Bookcases, room dividers, and filing cabinets can be used to limit movement in those areas that require regulation. For example, furniture can be arranged in such a way that movement around quiet or timeout areas can be easily monitored and regulated.

Easy Lines of Vision

In general, teachers should be able to monitor their students throughout the day. Because many of the instructional goals for students with learning and behavior problems necessitate the direct observation of behavior, it is critical that teachers have an unobstructed view of the entire classroom. The teacher's attention is a powerful reinforcer of appropriate behavior — easily used to manage minor instances of disruptive behaviors. In planning, teachers should also ensure that each student can easily see the key elements of daily lessons: the teacher, the teacher's aide, the chalkboard, and so forth. Each of the key elements should be in full view of students with minimal movement of their heads, desks, or chairs.

Storage of Instructional Materials

As observed by Evertson and associates (1984), easy access to instructional materials and supplies increases the effectiveness of instructional procedures by minimizing the time needed for "getting ready" and "cleaning up" for individual lessons. Materials frequently used by teachers and students should be kept within easy reach at materials stations, activity centers, or other designated areas. Materials used on a more infrequent basis (e.g., overhead projectors, crafts supplies, seasonal decorations, and so forth) should be stored in closets, storage bins, or bookcases.

Aesthetics

Similar to other worksites, classrooms that are pleasing to the senses can communicate a sense of pride to teachers and students. To contribute aesthetically pleasing elements to the classroom, teachers can use any of a number of alternatives including (a) the display of content or seasonally appropriate bulletin boards, (b) the exhibiting of students' work, and, when appropriate, (c) plants and animals.

In summary, the structuring of the physical environment is a critical variable in the design of a successful special education classroom. The levels of structure and intrusiveness required in different settings, however, will vary according to the developmental levels, handicapping conditions, and instructional goals of the students being served. Teachers of young children or students with behavior problems, for example, may find it necessary to assign seats to their students prior to the first day of school and to label desks, chairs, and lockers as belonging to specific students. In such situations, it may also be necessary to use discrete markings on floors and tables to prompt students as to where their chairs, desks, and materials are located during various parts of the day.

Instructional Time

Effective teachers value instructional time and carefully control its allocation. Efficient use of instructional opportunities is critical if teachers are to maximize the effects of special education efforts. Fortunately, teachers of all experience levels — developing, beginning, or master — can become sensitive to and influence time-related factors that rob instructional opportunities. Two interrelated activities can increase the appropriate use of instructional time: (a) an awareness of the different levels of instructional time and how they differentially influence classroom events, and (b) the implementation of generic and lesson-specific strategies designed to increase the effectiveness and efficiency of the time students are in school.

Levels of Instructional Time

As noted in Figure 3.3, instructional time is broadly viewed as a variable that exists in four quantities: allocated time, actual instructional time, engaged time, and academic learning time. **Allocated time** is the amount of time that school systems or individual teachers set aside for the teaching of specific skills, concepts, units, or subject areas. Although school boards typically mandate how much instructional time students should receive in basic curricular areas, the individual teacher decides how much time is allocated to the various skills within the areas. A readily

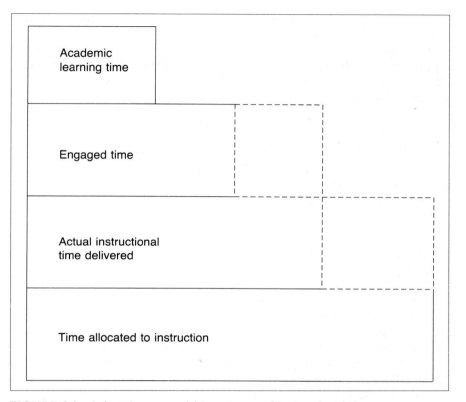

FIGURE 3.3   Subsetting or vanishing nature of instructional time.

available measure of how time is allocated to learning is a teacher's planbook.

Actual instructional time is a measure of how much instructional time is actually delivered to students. Unfortunately, numerous unforeseen events (e.g., fire drills, visiting related service personnel) can reduce the time allocated for instruction. Moreover, noninstructional activities such as secretarial chores, organizing materials, and the management of disruptive behavior can spill over into planned instructional time. Actual instructional time is measured by timing the length of a lesson presented to a group of students regardless of how much time is allocated. In most special education settings, 80% of the time allocated for instruction is actually delivered (Wilson & Wesson, 1986).

Engaged time refers to how much students attend to the actual instructional time. Because engaged time accounts for the possibility that students can only learn material to which they attend, it is generally regarded as a sensitive measure of the effectiveness of how time is used in classroom settings.

However, **academic learning time,** is the most meaningful measure of instructional time. This final level of instructional time is the amount of time students attend to work that is diagnostically and instructionally appropriate. Thus, in evaluating whether academic learning time is occurring, variables such as task difficulty, teacher diagnostic ability, and student success rate must be considered.

Time Management

Strategies that can be used readily by student and beginning teachers to increase the effectiveness and efficiency of instructional time fall into two major domains: generic classroom initiatives and lesson-specific procedures.

GENERIC CLASSROOM INITIATIVES   Three generic strategies can increase the amount of productive time in classrooms for students with mild handicaps. First, teachers should *conspicuously demonstrate that attendance and punctuality are expected and valued behaviors.* Truancy, absenteeism, and tardiness are insidious thieves of instructional time. In addition to highlighting a policy that encourages and prompts school attendance, intermittent rewards for consistent participation and punctuality should be administered. These rewards can fit within the framework of the regular classroom management plan and need not be elaborate or expensive. Moreover, systematic follow-up plans should be made for students who are absent or tardy repeatedly. Telephone calls, letters to students' homes, and other types of parental contacts can reduce instances of tardiness and unexcused absences.

Unfortunately, some children with mild handicaps come from home environments where *parents* need help in getting their children ready to attend school. In such cases, teachers may need to be active resources for parents and recommend strategies that could promote attendance and punctuality. For example, problems with school attendance can be avoided if teachers remind or prompt parents to establish a morning routine. This routine would involve (a) setting out appropriate school clothes that children would wear the next day, (b) using alarm clocks, (c) eating a healthy, relaxed breakfast, and (d) keeping the television *off* in the morning (Bleichman, 1985).

Once students are attending school regularly, consideration should be given to a second concern: *increasing the amount of the school day that is devoted to academic or task-relevant activities.* Research on effective teaching has demonstrated that academic performance thrives in special education settings where teachers maintain an academic focus (e.g., Sindelar et al., 1986). In such settings, effective teachers conduct a greater number of instructional activities and make more frequent use of directed questioning than do less effective teachers. However, clear danger signs of an environment at risk for a low academic or task-relevant focus include:

1. Excessive amounts of time in open-ended, undirected discussions about personal opinions and beliefs.
2. Too much time allocated for noncontingent recess or free activity periods.
3. Large amounts of time spent on the management and discussion of discipline problems and disruptions.
4. Exceedingly long periods of time spent on attendance and other housekeeping or organizational chores.
5. Unscheduled but regular discussions of sporting events, movies, and television programs during academic work periods.
6. More than 25% of the day devoted to nonacademic activities, such as arts, crafts, and music.
7. High numbers of seemingly harmless, social interruptions from teachers' colleagues during academic periods.

Planning and *regularly scheduled monitoring of how time is used* can ensure that appropriate amounts of time are delivered to academic or task-relevant activities. In terms of planning, it is important to be prepared for the teaching of lessons; instructional procedures should be mastered, and materials necessary for the entire lesson should be accessible. Teachers should regularly analyze how time is used in their own classroom settings. These continuous analyses can range from informal self-monitoring exercises to more systematic and precise observational regimens that require the help of peer observers. Regardless of the method chosen, it is critical that teachers determine how they use class time and, when necessary, consider alternative teaching methods that emphasize academics or task-relevant activities. A straightforward method for gathering data about instructional time during a typical school day is provided in the form found in Box 3.1.

The final generic classroom initiative to maximize the effectiveness of instructional time is to *facilitate fluid transitions among activities*. The great majority of classrooms for students with mild handicaps have many activity shifts, which typically require movement from one area of the classroom to another, or, in settings where there is resource-room programming or extensive mainstreaming, from one part of a school building to another. Transitions are unavoidable by-products of comprehensive educational programs; the greater the variety provided to students, the more they will need to switch locations and behavior. Because students are not working during transitions, valuable instructional time is lost. Transitions also tend to be disruptive and create circumstances that often require the use of planned instructional time for classroom management activities rather than teaching.

BOX 3.1

Monitoring of Instructional Time

Directions: For each classroom activity, record the amount of instructional time allocated and actually delivered. Also, indicate if the major use of the delivered time involved teacher-directed instruction (TDI), seatwork (SW), or a nonacademic activity (NA). Use the formulas to calculate how instructional time is used. An illustration is provided on the first line of the form.

Activity	Allocated Time	Time Started	Time Ended	Actual Minutes	TDI/SW/ NA	Comments
Check H.W.	15	8:33	8:43	10	TDI	Discipline Problems

Total TDI
minutes _____

Percentage of instruction delivered $= \left(\dfrac{\text{Actual minutes}}{\text{Allocated time}} \right) =$ _____

Total SW
minutes _____

Percentage of delivered instruction that is TDI $= \left(\dfrac{\text{TDI}}{\text{TDI + SW}} \times 100 \right) =$ _____

Total TDI/SW
minutes _____

Total NA
minutes _____

BOX 3.2

Transition Cues

1. Teacher gives verbal cues to group.
2. An appointed child gives verbal cues to group.
3. Teacher gives verbal cues to individuals.
4. An appointed child gives verbal cues to individuals.
5. Teacher touches children to dismiss.
6. An appointed child touches children to dismiss.
7. Lights blink, a bell rings, a piano sounds, a buzzer buzzes, and so forth, to signal dismissal.
8. Teacher begins a song that routinely tells children to move.
9. Teacher makes a routine gesture or stands in a routine place to signal dismissal.
10. Teacher or an appointed child hands out individual necklaces or bracelets with a color, number, word, or symbol keyed to the children's intended destinations.
11. Teacher or an appointed child distributes cards with symbols for the destinations printed on them.
12. Teacher calls for all children wearing a certain color, type, or pattern of clothing.
13. Teacher gives each child an object that will be needed in the next activity.
14. Teacher holds up something (e.g., coat, library book) for its owner to recognize and take to the destination.
15. Teacher tells children to go and find their names at the destination.
16. Teacher dismisses children by physical characteristics (e.g., brown eyes, red hair).
17. Teacher dismisses children by gender.
18. Teacher dismisses children by letters in name.
19. Teacher shows a letter, number, or word and asks for volunteers to identify it. Correct answers earn dismissal.
20. Teacher dismisses children by tables at which they sit.
21. Teacher calls on all children who received stickers or "smiley faces" on this day to leave first.
22. Teacher calls first on those students who completed a valued task (e.g., remembered to clean out your cubbie yesterday, took a nap, said your telephone number).
23. Children look at a picture list on the chalkboard or cue card to learn where to go next after finishing an assigned activity.
24. Teacher dismisses using an if/then sentence (e.g., "if you have teeth in your mouth, then go . . . ," "if you could be a father when you grow up, then go . . . ").

SOURCE   Rosenkoetter, S.E., & Fowler, S.A. (1986). Teaching mainstreamed children to manage daily transitions. *Teaching Exceptional Children, 19*(1), 20–23. Copyright 1986 by The Council for Exceptional Children. Reprinted with permission.

To facilitate efficient transitions, teachers need to arrange the physical environment appropriately, establish and enforce rules that encourage smooth transitions, and use signals to indicate clearly that activity shifts are to occur. To teach effective transitioning skills, teachers should (a) analyze tasks and model appropriate methods of shifting between activities or locations, (b) provide directed practice in activity and location changes, (c) use a variety of group and individual cues to signal transitions, and (d) frequently evaluate the effectiveness of the types of transition signals used. Twenty four different transition cues are listed in Box 3–2.

LESSON SPECIFIC PROCEDURES   The most productive method for maximizing the use of time during lessons is to ensure that students attend to diagnostically and instructionally relevant instruction. A number of monitoring systems and corresponding instrumentation exist for the observation of on-task behavior. Each of the available alternatives can be adapted to the unique features of any classroom. Box 3.3 contains a generic form for the measurement and recording of on-task behavior, which can be adapted for use under varying instructional conditions. Specific strategies for increasing on-task rates during both teacher-directed instruction and practice sessions are summarized in Box 3.4.

Scheduling Activities and Grouping Students

The complicated, interrelated tasks of scheduling activities and grouping students are typically completed when preservice teachers enter a student teaching situation. Consequently, those preparing to be teachers rarely have supervised experiences in these frustrating activities. The following is provided as an advance organizer for developing teachers who will be faced with scheduling and grouping responsibilities, and as a set of guidelines for beginning teachers who are faced with the task of organizing their first classrooms.

Scheduling

Effective classrooms for students with mild handicaps are places where (a) schedules of daily tasks are relatively fixed and (b) routines consistently facilitate the completion of assigned tasks. When planning activities, two tools can facilitate the development and implementation of effective schedules: a **master schedule** and **individual schedule cards**.

THE MASTER SCHEDULE   The most difficult and logistically complex step in developing consistency and predictability in the learning environment is the development of overall class schedule. This overall or **master**

BOX 3.3

Recording Rates of On-Task Behavior

Directions: At 10-second intervals, record a plus sign (+) if the target student is on-task and a minus sign (−) if off-task. Operationally defined, on-task means that the student is looking at the appropriate individual or instructional stimulus. Alternate among the targeted students at the prearranged 10-second intervals. Use a tape-recording of a low audible sound to signal an observation.

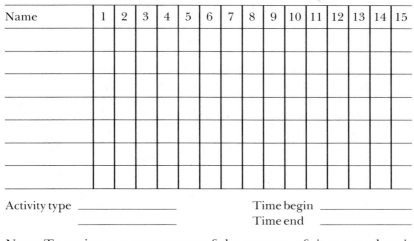

Name	1	2	3	4	5	6	7	8	9	10	11	12	13	14	15

Activity type _____   Time begin _____
              _____   Time end   _____

Note: To arrive at a percentage of the amount of time a student is on-task, use the following formula:

$$\frac{\text{number of plus signs } (+s)}{\text{number of plus signs } + \text{ number of minus signs } (+s + -s)}$$

schedule is directly related to the allocation of instructional time; teachers need to determine how much of the school day is to be devoted to specific skill instruction and other relevant activities. Obviously, much of this information is gathered from students' records, recent IEP data, and current diagnostic test information. The master schedule is, however, a direct reflection of the relative emphases that will be given to content-area instruction for each student in the class. The schedule also reflects the level of each student's participation in regular education or mainstreamed activities as well as the amount of related service activities received each week.

Master schedules need to contain (a) the precise times the scheduled periods are to begin and end, (b) a general label representing the subject

BOX 3.4

Strategies for Increasing On-Task Behavior during Teacher-Directed Instruction and Independent Practice

TEACHER-DIRECTED INSTRUCTION

1. *Teach more and test less.* Rather than replicating diagnostic testing and repeatedly asking students to tell what they already know about the instructional subject matter, devote time to instructing students in what they need to know.
2. *Question students frequently.* Frequent questioning increases opportunities for students to respond. Pose randomly sequenced questions on a frequent basis. Whenever poss ible, have students respond both in unison and individually.
3. *Ensure that all students participate.* Structure instructional tasks so all students can be actively involved in responding to learning opportunities.
4. *Use signals and prompts to indicate transitions and other attentional shifts within the lesson.* Signals can ensure smooth movement between the various components of lessons.
5. *Be enthusiastic.* Students participate more when teachers are excited about what they are teaching. Ways to show enthusiasm involve a touch of the "ham" in all of us and can include humor, animation, and gimmicks.

PRACTICE SESSIONS

1. *Reward correct student responses frequently.* Because students with learning and behavior problems tend to have high rates of off-task behavior when assigned independent practice, teachers need to devise methods to provide frequent reinforcement of appropriate behavior. Methods that can be used include (a) directed content-related praise, (b) tangible reinforcers such as pencils, books, food, and so forth, (c) generalized reinforcers such as tokens, points, or checkmarks, or (d) activity reinforcers such as computer time, library time, or free time.
2. *Develop clear and concise rules, procedures, and instructions for practice activities.* How and what students should do both during and upon completion of practice activities should be highlighted as a classroom rule. Procedures for the correct method of obtaining assistance should also be clearly defined.
3. *Use interesting and motivating practice activities.* In addition to using traditional "ditto" pencil and paper seatwork activities, intersperse assignments that require the use of microcomput-

BOX 3.4 (continued)

ers, learning centers, language masters, and portable filmstrip projectors.

4. *Have private study spaces available.* Highly distractible students may find a "private office" helpful in maintaining the sustained attention necessary for the completion of practice assignments.

5. *Use peer-mediated or cooperative-learning strategies.* Tutoring systems and cooperative-learning strategies have been reported to be effective in increasing the number of opportunities students have to respond, as well as improving the academic achievement of students with mild handicaps.

SOURCES Adapted from Rosenberg, M.S., & Baker, K. (1985). Instructional time and the teacher educator: Training preservice and beginning teachers to use time effectively. *The Teacher Educator, 20,* 195–207, and Wilson R., & Wesson, C. (1986). Making every minute count: Academic time in LD classrooms. *Learning Disabilities Focus, 2,* 13–19.

area or general activity to be covered, (c) the adult (i.e., teacher, paraprofessional, parent volunteer) responsible for leading or supervising the period, and (d) the location where the assigned task should be completed. These components are illustrated in Figure 3.4 for several students with mild handicaps attending a self-contained setting. This type of scheduling format can be adapted for resource placements as well. Any type of sturdy chart paper can be used for the construction of the master schedule, although large sheets of paper having preprinted rows and columns will result in a product that is neat and easy for students to read.

The master schedule should be posted in an area that is accessible in the classroom; smaller copies of the chart should be placed in the teacher's and instructional aide's planbooks. The master schedule should serve as a resource for (a) students who may have forgotten or misplaced their own personal schedule, (b) substitute teachers who need to ensure that quality programming continues when regular personnel are absent, (c) building administrators who may need to know where a student should be during a particular instructional period, and (d) parents and other interested visitors needing a guide to classroom activities.

THE STUDENT SCHEDULE CARD To personalize the master schedule, each student should receive a personal schedule card. The card should be small enough to fit into students' pockets, purses, and wallets, or, when necessary, be attached to the students' desks. Activities related to the construction of student schedule cards should be started on the first day of a new school year.

Opening exercises 8:45–9:00

Name	Period 1 9:00 9:35	Period 2 9:40 10:15	Period 3 10:20 10:55	Recess 11:00–11:20	Period 4 11:25 12:00	Period 5 12:05 12:40	Period 6 12:45 1:15	Period 7 1:20 1:55	Period 8 2:00 2:30
Jane A.	Reading decoding group A Bk. group table w/ Mrs. Fisk	M Art w/class 3-303 MTWTh Music—F Rm. 202	Math group A Fr. group table w/ Mr. Ross	Recess	Lunch	Spelling w/ peer tutor MWF TTh—PE	Reading compreh. group A Fr. table group w/ Mr. Ross	Written expression Group A w/ Mr. Ross	Social studies MW: Science; TTh: Free time; F: all
Hector B.	Speech R Rm 302 MWF w/ Mr. Brooks TTh—PE	Reading group C Fr. group table w/ Mr. Ross	Math group A Fr. group table w/ Mr. Ross	Recess	Lunch	Spelling w/ peer tutor TTh MWF—Art Rm. 202	Reading compreh. group B Bk. table group w/ Mrs. Fisk	Written expression Group A w/ Mr. Ross	Social studies MW: Science; TTh: Free time; F: all
Dale C.	Reading decoding group A Bk. group table w/ Mrs. Fisk	Math group B Bk. group table w/ Mrs. Fisk	Spelling w/ peer tutor MWF TTh—PE	Recess	Lunch	M Art w/ class Rm 3-301 MWF Music—F Rm. 202	Reading compreh. group A Fr. table group w/ Mr. Ross	Written expression Group A w/ Mr. Ross	Social studies MW: Science; TTh: Free time; F: all
Louise Z.	Reading decoding group B Fr. group table w/ Mr. Ross	Math group B Bk. group table w/ Mrs. Fisk	Spelling w/ peer tutor MWF TTh—PE	Recess	Lunch	M Art w/ class 3-301 MTWTH Music—F Rm. 202	Reading compreh. group B Bk. table group w/ Mrs. Fisk	Written expression Group B w/ Mrs. Fisk	Social studies MW: Science; TTh: Free time; F: all

Dismissal at 2:35

Teacher: Mr. Ross

Aide: Mrs. Fisk

Key:

[M] ▶ Indicates a "mainstream" activity

[R] ▶ Indicates a "related service" activity

FIGURE 3.4 Master schedule for a self-contained setting.

Grouping Students

Grouping students for effective instruction is not an easy task; the process tests teachers' diagnostic, organizational, management, and decision-making skills. In special education, the process of grouping is tied directly to individualization of instruction. Individualization is based on the assumption that the adaptation of instruction to the individual characteristics or needs of students results in desired rates of learning. Individualization, however, must not be mistaken with one-to-one instruction; instruction appropriate to a learner's individual needs can be and often is presented in small and large groups.

Although compelling arguments can be made for most grouping alternatives (e.g., within class ability grouping, learning-style approaches, specific-skill grouping), two preconditions must exist prior to the consideration of any such alternative in special education settings. First, the alternative must result in success and achievement for **all** members of the group. Second, there must be no stigma or negative feelings associated with group membership. To meet both of these preconditions, student and beginning teachers should keep in mind the following:

1. *Make grouping decisions based on the principle that each student possesses specific strengths and weaknesses.* It is possible that a student will be placed in an advanced group for writing instruction while requiring a slower pace for math, story problems, and measurement.
2. *Assignment to groups should not be considered permanent.* As students progress through their programs, factors influencing group success may require changing a group's composition. Reassessment of student characteristics and, when necessary, reorganization of groups highlight that the ever-changing individual characteristics of students are regularly monitored and addressed.
3. *Consider the necessity of grouping.* Content areas, such as science and social studies, that do not have the "building block" character of math or reading may be best presented in large group settings (Slavin, 1986).
4. *Program for the size of groups based on the ability levels of students.* For average or high performing students, groups of 6 to 10 students may be appropriate. Low performing students may require a group size of 3 to 5 and very low achieving students may need tutorial groups consisting of no more than 3 students (Paine, 1982).

When grouping for instruction, students should be divided into groups on the basis of (a) criterion-referenced placement tests, (b) standardized test scores, (c) previous performance observations, (d) typical rate of acquisition, and (e) learning-style preferences. Attention should be paid to students' actual knowledge and skills rather than on the basis of inappropriate behavior. Once students are grouped, instruction should be tailored to meet the needs of each group. This tailoring typically involves adjustments to the content level assigned, the pace of the lesson, and the dominant mode of presentation. For example, one group in a self-contained class of students with mild handicaps may require 3 lessons to master the math content that another group of students can acquire in just 1 lesson. Moreover, the group requiring the additional instructional time may require substantially more visual cues for content mastery. Appropriately implemented grouping allows for these important adaptations.

Developing Meaningful and Relevant Rules and Procedures

Organization and management, two factors critical to the successful functioning of classrooms, produce large amounts of apprehension between students and beginning teachers. These concerns are well-founded; a teacher's ability to organize and manage classrooms is related to a student's academic performance and social-emotional behavior and both teachers' and students' attitudes toward school. Teachers demonstrate or present their organizational and management expectations through two general delivery systems: **rules** and **procedures**. Rules identify, define, and operationalize a teacher's specific principles of acceptable behavior. Procedures specify a protocol of behaviors necessary for the appropriate completion of an activity, task, or classroom operation.

The need for clear, unambiguous, and concise rules and procedures for students with mild handicaps cannot be overstated. As a result of their unique learning and behavioral difficulties, these students tend to have difficulties in learning and/or complying with many of the more obvious standards of conduct typical of schools and classrooms. Rules and procedures, however, can also serve as discriminative stimuli, or antecedents, of appropriate situation-specific behavior. When used correctly, rules and procedures become the overt guides, models, and prompts for desired student behavior. They remind and motivate students to meet the standards of a specific learning environment. Finally, classroom rules and procedures, when used in a positive context, can serve as specific behavioral targets to which teachers can direct reinforcers such as attention, praise, or tokens. The success of rules and procedures depends on (a) how they are introduced and presented to students and (b) how teachers plan for maintaining the integrity of their stated expectations.

Introducing Rules and Procedures

Classroom rules and procedures should not be designed in a quick or frivolous manner. Considerable forethought and trouble-shooting is necessary to ensure that stated procedures match a particular school's and teacher's expectations of student behavior. The following guidelines, adapted from a number of sources (Evertson et al., 1984; Paine et al., 1983; Rosenberg, 1986; and Strain & Sainato, 1987), can assist developing and beginning teachers in planning and introducing rules and procedures.

1. *Be aware of school district policies.* Have a working knowledge of the expectations for all students within the LEA. Design classroom rules and procedures to be congruent with the prevailing expectations.
2. *Identify the specific behaviors and procedures expected of students.* Reconstruct these expectations into overt, behavioral, and measurable pinpoints. Ensure that agreement as to the occurrence or nonoccurrence of such expectations can be attained between *teachers* and *students*.
3. *The first order of business on the first day of school should be to discuss and teach classroom rules and procedures.* Because rules and procedures govern how daily classroom activities and events should occur for the entire school year, it is important they be in place and reinforced as soon as possible.
4. *Present a solid rationale as to why classrooms need well-defined rules and procedures.* Because a teacher's approach to the presentation of the need for structure can influence student compliance, discussions about rules and procedures should be conducted in a patient, businesslike, and sincere fashion.
5. *Involve students in the development of the rules and procedures.* Solicit opinions as to what the consequences should be for *both* compliance and noncompliance. By promoting a sense of ownership in the classroom system, students will feel a greater sense of allegiance to the rules and procedures identified.
6. *Keep the number of rules and procedures that students need to follow small.* For each of the rules generated, ensure that the wording is kept simple and to the point. Students often view stated rules and procedures literally, and extraneous verbiage should be avoided. When specifying procedures, such as what a student should do upon completing a seatwork assignment, an easy to follow step-by-step sequence of behaviors is most effective.
7. *Phrase rules and procedures positively rather than negatively.* Instead of accentuating what students should not do (e.g., "Do not call out during lessons"), highlight appropriate behaviors that students should engage in regularly (e.g., "Raise your hand if you wish to get the teacher's attention").

Maintaining the Integrity of Rules and Procedures

Unfortunately, the potency of classroom rules and procedures seems to diminish as the school year progresses. A number of factors account for this loss of effectiveness ranging from lapses in students' memories to lack of consistency in providing consequences for rule and procedure compliance and noncompliance. The following guidelines, adapted from a number of sources (Evertson et al., 1983; Paine et al., 1983; and Rosenberg, 1986), will assist in promoting long-term compliance to the stated behavior expectations of classrooms.

1. *Keep rules posted in an area visible to all students.* Prominently displayed rules and procedures can be powerful cues for appropriate student behavior and can serve to prompt busy teachers to provide consequences for student compliance and noncompliance on a regular basis.
2. *Ensure that there are different rules for various situations.* One set of rules will not hold for the range and variety of activities typical of most special education classrooms. For example, during highly structured instructional activities such as directed reading and math lessons, rules and procedures should reflect the need for quiet, order, and a high degree of engagement to the task. In contrast, less ordered activities, such as art and discussions or debates of citizenship issues, would require a different, more relaxed set of rules.
3. *Teach and provide practice for all rules.* Both overall classroom rules and activity-specific rules need to be taught and reviewed just like any other material teachers wish students to acquire. Lessons scheduled early in the school year can ensure rapid acquisition of the various rules and procedures of the classroom; brief reviews of rules prior to lessons can serve to remind students of the expectations for that specific lesson. The potency of brief reviews of rules should not be underestimated. Rosenberg (1986) found that brief reviews (1–2 minutes) of lesson-specific rules just prior to instruction increased rates of time-on-task and the number of opportunities to respond over levels found when no such reviews were provided.
4. *Model classroom procedures.* Most classroom procedures, whether involved with the correct way to behave during a fire drill or to line up for lunch, involve a complex series of behaviors. To ensure that students learn the correct way to comply to standard classroom procedures, it is recommended that teachers (a) model or demonstrate how specific procedures are to be performed, (b) provide opportunities for guided practice in the initial performance of the procedures, (c) reinforce correct performance of the procedures, and (d)

provide corrective feedback immediately if procedures are not followed correctly.

5. *Self-monitor performance with the documented rules and procedures.* A major reason for the lack of maintenance in classroom organization and management systems are teachers' failures to be consistent in the following of class procedures and the lack of regular enforcement of the rules. To promote high levels of consistency in the administration of classroom management systems built on a foundation of stated rules and procedures, teachers should (a) regularly sample, through peer observation or self-recording, their performance in providing consequences for rule and procedure compliance and noncompliance and (b) develop a personalized system to prompt regular and consistent enforcement of the class rules.

Coordinating Resources

The final category of guidelines related to the successful organization of special education classrooms involves the coordination of the resources and personnel available to teachers. By creating or coordinating several key instructional resources and using the strengths of other school personnel, developing and beginning teachers will find that much of the time typically spent searching for or organizing materials and information could be replaced with the more relevant activities of teaching or lesson planning. Three specific types of coordinating activities are considered: using the IEP as a living and working document, the organization of files and materials, and the preparation of substitute teaching packets. Using the strengths of other personnel in the school environment is discussed in Chapters 8 and 9.

Using the IEP as a Living and Working Document

In most programs that prepare individuals to teach students with handicaps, considerable time is devoted to Individual Educational Programs (IEPs). As noted in Chapter 7, developing teachers require considerable practice in structuring the IEP document to ensure that it meets local, state, and federal standards. Sometimes overlooked in the activities related to technical and legal compliance is the notion that students' IEPs should be treated as **working documents** related directly to the ongoing instructional activities of the classroom.

Treating the IEP as a living and working document begins at the time of its preparation. When writing the document, the annual goals and short-term objectives should be treated as the foundation for the lessons that will be presented to students. When initially completed, IEPs should be placed in an accessible area close to the teacher's desk. The IEP should be monitored frequently regarding (a) the status of the goals and objectives listed, and (b) the specific activities or instructional modifications necessary for successful attainment of the listed goals and objectives. When communicating with parents or professionals involved in the education of a student, the IEP should be used as the definitive record by which educational progress is measured and recorded.

Keeping Files Organized and Accessible

The time devoted to the organization and accessibility of files and resource material can pay rich dividends throughout a school year and, in many cases, a teacher's full career. Quick and easy access to student records, instructional materials, and test protocols is an example of how a systematic filing system can save time and stress. Student records should be close to the teacher's desk; in case of emergencies, it is essential to have the parent's or guardian's address, places of employment, and telephone numbers. Curricular materials can be filed according to subject areas, specific skills, or instructional objectives. McCoy and Prehm (1987) recommend that teachers file their material by sequenced instructional objectives within broad content categories. Material related to each objective is coded according to a task-analytic hierarchy related to skill acquisition and the specific-learning adaptations that each activity provides. Time devoted to the ordering of new instructional materials also can be saved if catalogs for instructional materials are filed according to this same system.

Preparing a Substitute Teacher's Packet

Under the best of conditions, the job of substitute teacher is difficult. Even the best of students behave as if there is a lessening of standards when the regular teacher is absent. In special education settings serving students with mild handicaps, reports of disarray and confusion from substitute teachers are not uncommon. Consequently, many school districts have found it difficult to arrange for substitute teachers to fill in for ailing special education teachers.

All student and beginning teachers should plan ahead for the occasional need of a substitute teacher. Because there is no way to know for certain when sickness or emergencies will strike, a generic substitute teacher packet should be prepared at the beginning of the school year. The packet should contain all the information needed to teach and manage the students left in the substitute teacher's charge. Platt (1987) has recommended that information be provided in six broad areas: policy information, schedules, specific student information, classroom procedural information, daily plans, and alternative activities. These six areas are further defined in Table 3.2.

TABLE 3.2   Components of a Substitute Teacher's Packet

Major Areas	Specific Information to Be Included
Policy information	Floor plan or map of school. Names of individuals to contact in case of emergencies, problems, or questions. Entry, lunch recess, and dismissal policies and procedures. Emergency and fire drill procedures.
Schedules	Master schedule of student activities. Teacher's duty schedule (e.g., lunch, recess, and so forth). Schedules of parent volunteers, aides, peer tutors, and related service personnel.
Specific student information	Seating chart and description of students. Medication needs of students. Names, addresses, and phone numbers of students' parents or guardians.
Classroom procedural information	Attendance, charting, and record-keeping procedures. Brief description of classroom management program. Location of instructional materials and equipment. Free-time activities.
Daily plans	Location of students' IEPs. Location and guide to teacher plan book or daily lesson plans.
Alternative activities	Bag of tricks containing fun and motivating student activities. Structured recess plans.

SOURCE   Adapted from Platt, J.M. (1987). Substitute teachers can do more than just keep the lid on. *Teaching Exceptional Children, 19*(2), 28–31

Summary

We conclude this chapter with the same message with which we started: to manage busy classrooms successfully, special educators must be organized. In this chapter we have provided a number of practical suggestions for improving the organization of classrooms serving students with learning and behavior problems. A theme that emerged throughout the chapter is that organization required for successful teaching can be acquired, practiced, and mastered.

The first topic discussed was the challenging task of arranging the physical environment. Five basic rules of classroom design were outlined, and specific illustrations related to the physical layout of special education environments were provided. Second, the management of instructional time was considered. The different levels of instructional time were operationally defined, and both generic and lesson-specific strategies were presented for using instructional time effectively and efficiently. Third, the logistically complex tasks of scheduling classroom activities and grouping of students were discussed. Strategies for organizing the school day into manageable segments were reviewed, and guidelines for the grouping of students were examined. The fourth topic covered the development and maintenance of meaningful and relevant classroom rules and procedures.

The chapter concluded with ideas related to the coordination of resources. Included were suggestions regarding IEP utilization, the organization of files and materials, and the preparation of substitute teaching packets.

References

BLEICHMAN, E. A. (1985). *Solving child behavior problems at home and at school.* Champaign, IL: Research Press.

DOYLE, W. (1980). *Classroom management.* West Lafayette, IN: Kappa Delta Pi.

EVERTSON, C. M., EMMER, E. T., CLEMENTS, B. S., SANFORD, J. P., WORSHAM, M. E. (1984). *Classroom management for elementary teachers.* Englewood Cliffs, NJ: Prentice Hall.

MCCOY, K. M., & PREHM, H. J. (1987). *Teaching mainstreamed students: Methods and techniques.* Denver: Love.

PAINE, S. C. (1982). Setting up for instruction. *Association for Direct Instruction News, 2,* 8–9.

PAINE, S. C., RADICCI, J., ROSELLINI, L. C., DEUTCHMAN, L., & DARCH, C. R. (1983). *Structuring your classroom for academic success.* Champaign, IL: Research Press.

PLATT, J. M. (1987). Substitute teachers can do more than just keep the lid on. *Teaching Exceptional Children, 19*(2), 28–31.

ROSENBERG, M. S. (1986). Maximizing the effectiveness of structured management programs: Implementing rule-review procedures with disruptive and distractible students. *Behavioral Disorders, 11,* 239–248.

SINDELAR, P. T., SMITH, M., HARRIMAN, N. E., HALE, R. L., & WILSON, R. J. (1986). Teacher effectiveness in special education programs. *Journal of Special Education, 20,* 195–207.

SLAVIN, R. E. (1986). *Education psychology: Theory into practice.* Englewood Cliffs, NJ: Prentice Hall.

STRAIN, P. S., & SAINATO, D. M. (1987). Preventive discipline in early childhood. *Teaching Exceptional Children, 19*(4), 26–30.

WILSON, R., & WESSON, C. (1986). Making every minute count: Academic time in LD classrooms. *Learning Disabilities Focus, 2,* 13–19.

CHAPTER 4

Planning for Instruction

In any systematic approach to a task, planning is central. Consequently, effective teachers spend significant amounts of time planning for instruction in a variety of ways. The purpose of this chapter is to provide developing teachers with a rationale for planning, to show how planning relates to diagnostic teaching, to specify the components of well-designed plans, and to provide suggestions for writing unit and daily lesson plans. This will help developing teachers approach teaching in a systematic, premeditated manner.

Why Plan Lessons?

Many teachers are skeptical about the need for written lesson plans. Some argue that the time spent writing plans could be better used developing or adapting materials, thinking through lessons, or consulting with other teachers. All of these activities are important elements of instruction and certainly there never seems to be enough hours in the day to complete all of the planning and teaching functions expected of teachers. However, written plans that specify objectives of a lesson and detail the instructional activities that will be used to attain the objectives have been shown to be attributes of effective teaching. The reasons why written plans are valuable teaching tools are described below.

Planning Increases the Probability of Effective Teaching

As the old axiom applies to travel—if you don't know where and how you are going, you won't be able to get there—it applies to instructional planning as well. Specific goal statements provide a destination for teachers and students and the basis for evaluating the effectiveness of the instructional activities and materials in aiding students to arrive at some prescribed skill level. Detailing the means by which students are to attain objectives, through activity descriptions, is necessary as well. Researchers have shown that teachers who set specific objectives and write more detailed lesson plans are more effective than those teachers who write broadly stated goals and superficial lesson plans (Cooper, 1986).

An important distinction needs to be made between written and mental planning. Many hours of mental planning precede the act of writing plans. Thoroughly thinking through instructional objectives and activities is often a necessary, but insufficient, means of planning. Mental planning alone still leaves a high probability that objectives and activities will be vague and loosely structured. Preparing a written document increases the chances that objectives will be clearly stated and that activities will be thoroughly organized.

Planning Increases Confidence, Security, and Direction

Plans remind teachers what they are to do during a lesson. Considering the range of variables that teachers deal with during instruction, having a plan they can refer to tends to increase teachers' confidence and sense of security. Effective teachers know that if worse comes to worse they can have a quick glance at their notes and continue with their lesson (Clark & Yinger, 1979; McCutcheon, 1980).

Planning Helps to Establish Good Habits

Being consistent in writing lesson plans helps developing teachers establish a systematic approach to instruction. Using a particular format for sketching out what and how to teach forces teachers to examine each element of a lesson, to sequence activities more carefully, and to organize materials more thoroughly. Once this routine is established and followed, it should be maintained and used when planning to teach any new content.

Developmental Aspect of Lesson Planning

Novice teachers will have more extensive written plans than more experienced teachers. This is a function of beginning teachers' unfamiliarity with students, materials, and content.

Written lesson plans provide the first steps for developing teachers to learn to manage and carry out daily instructional activities. Although a time-consuming and often tedious activity, writing out plans helps developing teachers to structure their thinking about teaching which results in a more systematic course of action. Eventually, beginning teachers gain sufficient experience so that the need to write down detailed daily lesson plans diminishes (i.e., there is point when teachers can taper off the amount of written planning they do). Based on interviews with experienced teachers, researchers have found that ultimately teachers covertly think through rather than write down their daily plans (Clark & Yinger, 1979; McCutcheon, 1980). To get to this point, however, it is necessary to practice writing out detailed plans in an efficient manner. Over time, developing teachers will spend more time mentally planning lessons and attending to broader long-term planning needs rather than focusing on writing out details of individual lessons.

Relationship of Planning to the Diagnostic Teaching Model

The **Diagnostic Teaching Model** (DTM) is a framework for conceptualizing teaching as a hypothesis-testing process. Teachers systematically examine the variables (e.g., students' present skill levels, available teaching materials, strategies for presenting content, practice activities, and so forth) associated with learning and how they apply to their students. They then construct a hypothesis in the form of an instructional plan. The plan is implemented, and student performance is monitored. If the plan to manipulate learning variables in certain ways changes the performance of students, then the hypothesis is supported. If the plan does not manifest the intended effects, then teachers are able to analyze their plan to determine where changes are needed. Consequently, instruction is approached in a systematic way that acknowledges teaching as an inexact science and teachers' limited ability to determine the cause-and-effect relationship of the multitude of variables that exist in any learning environment (Cartwright, Cartwright, & Ward, 1981).

The Diagnostic Teaching Model contains five core steps that teachers follow in planning for instruction: (a) identifying attributes, (b) specifying objectives, (c) selecting strategies, (d) selecting materials, and (e) testing strategies and materials.

Step 1 involves the collection of information about the classroom setting, the behavior and learning attributes of students, and any other relevant variables. Teachers collect baseline data prior to intervention, allowing them to form a picture of what is occurring in the classroom under existing conditions. Next, they must determine what skills or behaviors they want to decrease, maintain, or increase by specifying clear

and behaviorally stated objectives that reflect how the target students
are to respond (e.g., see-say, hear-write, see-write, and so forth) and
what criterion level they are to attain (e.g., 90% accuracy, 60 movements
per minute, and so forth) (step 2). Teachers then select alternative strategies (e.g., self-monitoring, semantic webbing, concept induction, and
so forth) and any accompanying materials (e.g., tangible reinforcers,
reading books, concrete examples, and so forth) for accomplishing the
stated objectives (steps 3 and 4). Once implemented by the teacher, the
strategies and materials are tested through subsequent observations and
data collection (step 5).

Based on the information gathered, teachers analyze students' performance on daily or weekly measures and determine whether the objectives
have been reached. Accordingly, the sequence is repeated in one of two
ways (see Fig. 4.1). If objectives have been reached, the teacher moves
the student on to the next objective in the curriculum hierarchy (step
2) and continues through the other steps as described. On the other
hand, if objectives are not reached, they reexamine the accuracy and
appropriateness of the baseline data, stated objectives, strategies, and
materials. If modifications in any of these areas are necessary, they make
the changes and the sequence is continued. When all steps seem to be
accurate and appropriate, teachers implement the strategies and materials again and retest. (See Box 4.1)

One other point requires consideration. Often teacher-training programs prepare their preservice teacher trainees to follow the steps in
the sequence provided above. However, researchers who have surveyed
actual planning patterns followed by teachers in the field suggest that
teachers typically plan in a different sequence. Often the first steps
involved in planning focus on activities, content, materials or resources
(Peterson, Marx, & Clark, 1978) instead of on specifying goals and objectives. In other cases, planning may not be a sequential process. Instead,
teachers go back and forth among these steps, simultaneously working
on each of the steps. Regardless, the steps within the DTM are considered
critical despite variations in the sequence with which they are carried out.

Strategic and Tactical Planning

There are two basic levels of planning: strategic and tactical planning.
Strategic planning refers to the broad, overall rationale for providing
instruction to a particular student. It includes justification for the content, activities, materials, and objectives that are included in the day-to-
day operations of a classroom. Typically at the strategic level, teachers
reflect on their philosophy of instruction and the ultimate outcomes that
should result from sound instructional programs. An example may be
that teachers consider what the needs of students will be once they leave
school and enter some vocation, how those needs can be most effectively

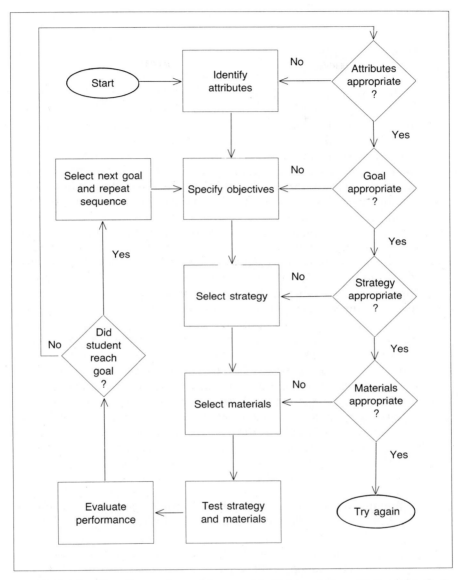

FIGURE 4.1 The diagnostic teaching model. (Adapted from Cartwright, G. P. & Cartwright, C. A. (1972). Gilding the lily. *Exceptional Children, 39*, 231–234.)

met, and how the curriculum can be structured to provide the highest probability that those needs will be met.

Based on strategic considerations, teachers then consider how, on a day-to-day, week-to-week basis, they can provide instruction that builds on the bits and pieces of previous learning to attain the long-range goals of a program. These daily operational considerations, which take the

BOX 4.1

Case Study

Bob, a sixth grade student, has just been referred to Ms. Stoddard, a resource-room teacher in an elementary school. Bob has been having difficulties in responding to comprehension questions. Ms. Stoddard decided she wanted to confirm his reported reading level by administering an informal reading inventory based on words, passages, and questions from the reading materials in the resource room. In addition, she has collected interview data from Bob's classroom teacher and parents regarding the reading environment in the regular classroom and at home. She also asked Bob what he does while he reads. Based on the information gathered, Ms. Stoddard concludes that Bob can recognize words using phonic and semantic cues and can fluently read material written on a fourth grade level, but is able to answer comprehension questions with only 60% accuracy. He is provided opportunities to read in the regular class, and his parents appear to provide a good reading environment at home (i.e., both parents read magazines and newspapers daily and encourage Bob to read as well). When asked what he thinks about during reading and how he reads, Bob reports that he reads the words and sometimes he thinks about other things. He apparently does not correctly review what he has read, ask himself questions, or try to predict what will happen in the passages he reads.

Based on the attributes derived from her assessments (step 1 of DTM), Ms. Stoddard specified the following objectives (step 2 of DTM):

- When given a passage at the fourth grade reading level, Bob will paraphrase the content after each paragraph read with 100% accuracy.
- When given a passage at the fourth grade reading level, Bob will see-write answers correctly for 7 out of 8 comprehension questions.

To improve Bob's writing answers to comprehension questions, Ms. Stoddard decides to train Bob to paraphrase the content of each paragraph read during daily 15-minute sessions of small group instruction (step 3 of DTM). She selects a set of passages and accompanying comprehension questions written at the fourth grade level to use for practice and as evaluation probes (step 4 of

BOX 4.1 *(continued)*

DTM). Ms. Stoddard then implements her teaching strategy and records Bob's performance in using the paraphrasing strategy and writing answers to comprehension questions (step 5 of DTM). If Bob's performance increases at an acceptable rate (i.e., he increasingly uses the paraphrasing strategy and answers more questions correctly), then Ms. Stoddard will continue with her intervention program. If not, she will have to reevaluate each of the steps of the DTM process and make necessary modifications.

form of daily lesson plans or unit plans, are the essence of **tactical planning**. Tactical planning includes determining prerequisite skills acquired by students, setting short-term objectives (e.g., what they will be teaching the next day), describing specific teaching activities and related materials to present particular concepts or skills, and designing daily evaluation procedures.

An example of strategic and tactical planning is reflected in the preparation for the implementation of a learning strategies program. A group of content-area secondary teachers and the special education resource and consulting teachers meet to discuss how they can better facilitate the needs of students with learning problems (strategic planning). Through discussion of observational data, they conclude that these students appear to have little or no skills in monitoring and regulating their own learning. The teachers decide to set up a learning-strategies course to be offered by the resource teachers. In addition, the content-area teachers will modify their demands for content mastery, particularly during the first term of the school year, and provide opportunities for students to practice the use of the strategies they have learned. The expectation is that with improved learning processes, students will be able to master more content.

With the overall plan sketched out, the teachers identify specific objectives to be mastered and learning strategies they believe need to be taught. In addition, they identify the Strategies Intervention Model (Deshler & Schumaker, 1986) as the set of procedures to be used. They then begin work on unit plans for the courses on learning strategies and plans for content-area teachers to facilitate the use of strategies in their classrooms (tactical planning).

In sum, planning takes place at a variety of levels moving from more global to more specific considerations. It is important for new teachers to realize that the process of strategic and tactical planning is not necessarily sequential whereby teachers make strategic plans then move onto tactical planning. Teachers often move back and forth between global and specific considerations until both levels of planning are complete.

Components of Successfully Planned Lessons

Effective planning is characterized by definable components that contain information on where and how students are going to reach some specified goal. These components include: prerequisite skills, instructional objectives, instructional activities and materials to be used, methods to evaluate lessons, anticipated problems, and self-evaluation of lesson plans.

Prerequisite Skills

To provide effective instruction, teachers must determine the present educational levels of their students. That is, they must determine what individual students can and cannot do vis-à-vis the curriculum hierarchy. If one envisions a skill hierarchy for a given content area (e.g., reading, math, language, and so forth) organized in some rational sequence, then determining students' present educational levels entails teachers pinpointing which skills students have mastered and which skills they must learn or continue to practice. In some cases, published skill hierarchies may not be available, making it necessary for teachers to determine the subskills for a given task.

Determining the present educational levels of students entails collecting some baseline data. Depending on the target skills, baseline data may be derived from probe sheets, teacher observation, formal assessment devices, and so forth. In any case, these assessments enable teachers to specify the target skills that will form the basis for instructional objectives.

Instructional Objectives

Effective teachers know where they want to take their students. They have explicit goals and make students aware of them. Differences in how they guide students to reach those goals may not be as important as the need to specify where students are going. By setting clear and specific goals, developing and new teachers can more easily determine what types of activities will better facilitate students achieving their goals. Without specific goals, teachers and students may flounder around completing one activity after another, yet not make any progress toward the mastery of some predetermined skill or concept.

CHARACTERISTICS   Behaviorally stated instructional objectives contain phrases identifying the target students, the behavior they will demonstrate, the conditions under which they will demonstrate the behavior, and the criterion for mastery. They are written in a clear and concise language that makes it easy for others to understand the focus of instruction. The behavior is stated in observable, measurable terms indicative of the response mode the student will use (e.g., see-write, hear-say). Behavioral objectives are student focused (i.e., they reflect what students will do or accomplish, not what the teacher will do). For example, the following statement contains all the attributes of a behavioral objective:

> When given a probe sheet with words beginning with bl, cl, and fl consonant blends, Johnny will see-say the words at a rate of 60 words per minute with two or less errors.

Often teachers run into problems when they make unclear statements such as, "The teacher will work on decoding." It is unclear because "work on" connotes numerous possible activities. The same statement is flawed because it does not indicate a desired outcome, instead it refers to the process of "working on." There is no mention of students in the statement either. The most common error is the lack of an observable, measurable behavior that indicates specifically how the student will respond to a stimulus.

Behaviorally stated objectives are focused on some desired outcome of instruction. This does not limit the utility of objectives to the end-product of an academic task. Processes (e.g., metacognitive strategies, verbal rehearsal, self-instruction) used in attaining some end-product (e.g., reading faster, comprehending more, or writing better essays) can also be the targeted behavior(s). For instance, a student with writing difficulties may be asked to employ a learning strategy such as TOWER (i.e., think, order, write, error monitor, and revise) in generating an essay (Mercer & Mercer, 1985). The objective could be stated in terms of the strategy, not the end-product (i.e., the characteristics of the essay). The objective below is an example:

> When asked to write an essay, the student will show evidence of using each step of the TOWER strategy with 100% accuracy for 3 consecutive days.

A second objective could also be written to reflect the intended effect of using the TOWER strategy (i.e., to be able to write a more coherent essay). Such an objective may read:

> When asked to write an essay, the student will think-write topics and supporting material that are coherently ordered as judged by the teacher in three consecutive essays.

FUNCTIONS   *Lesson Planning* Once teachers determine where students are functioning in a skill hierarchy, they determine how far up the hierarchy a student should go over some period of time. With the objectives of instruction identified, teachers can begin to select activities and materials that will help students attain the objectives. Like a Sunday driver, a teacher without specific objectives may take a windy path in some unknown direction and never reach the appropriate destination (i.e., instructional objective).

Selection of Activities and Materials Activities and materials act as vehicles for reaching some objective. They are generated from a sense of purpose; they must help students to acquire an understanding of a concept or to remember the steps of an academic rule and provide sufficient practice to develop mastery. For instance, if the objective of instruction is for students to discriminate between squares and rectangles, then the instructional activities and materials should focus on students identifying the attributes that make one shape different from the other. These activities would involve the teacher stating or having the students discover the attributes of each figure, listing them on the board, and having students methodically examine examples and check to see that all the attributes are present. If, on the other hand, students can already discriminate between a square and a rectangle, but the discrimination responses are slow, then the activities and materials should focus not on what the attributes are, but to a quick and accurate response to examples and nonexamples of each. These activities and materials may involve students quickly naming shapes using flash cards. Consequently, the activities and materials change as the objectives change.

Assist Teachers, Administrators, Parents, and Students to Track Their Progress Clearly stated objectives indicate what students should be learning. All those with an interest in the students' progress can draw conclusions about the effectiveness of instruction based on whether or not students are reaching their objectives. Consequently, objectives form the basis for evaluation of instruction and accountability.

Task Analysis and Enroute and Terminal Objectives Objectives are generated from analyzing the components of a superordinate task or skill. Once a task or skill is selected for instruction, teachers or curriculum specialists often break down the task into steps. Instruction is then focused on students mastering individual steps and sets of steps leading to mastery of the entire task or skill.

Depending on the complexity of the target task or skill and the existing skills of the students, the number of steps (i.e., enroute objectives) leading to mastery of the task (i.e., terminal objective) will vary. Another factor in determining the number of steps or enroute objectives used to master a terminal objective depends on who makes the distinction between a task being the terminal objective or being an enroute objective leading toward the mastery of some greater objective. One person may call mastery of consonant blends a terminal objective, while another may identify it as an enroute objective leading to the mastery of phonics. Both persons may be right. The point is that teachers make the determination as to what they want to call enroute or terminal. In any case, the skill needs to be mastered. A rule of thumb for developing and new teachers is to break down tasks or skills to the largest unit appropriate for the instructional situation. Some students can master multiple steps at once while others will have to focus on each step individually. Using the example of consonant blends, some students can master a set of blends containing the /L/ sound while others may have to work on bl, fl, and cl, separately.

Task analysis of many basic academic tasks has already been done by curriculum specialists and publishers of instructional materials. These skill hierarchies are lists of sequentially ordered subskills that lead to some terminal objective. Consequently, new teachers do not have to spend as much time analyzing the components of a task or skill. However, hierarchies or curricula may not be available for a particular content area. In those cases, teachers need to complete their own task analysis. Even when skill hierarchies or curricula are available, some task analysis may be needed to fit them to the learners' needs.

The benefit of following skill hierarchies is that planning is guided in a logical or sequential fashion. Teachers know where students are and where they need to go—they can see both the trees and the forest. This allows them to anticipate where instruction is going, make adaptations, and better assist students in reaching some terminal objective.

Instructional Activities and Materials to Be Used

Instructional activities are designed to assist students in the realization of targeted objectives. Designing instructional activities requires that teachers consider the stage of learning to which the activity is directed. A simple four-stage model (i.e., acquisition, fluency building, maintenance, and generalization) illustrated in Figure 4.2 can be used to show how learning proceeds. The first stage of learning, **acquisition**, is characterized by high rates of inaccurate responses. Students have little or no skill at this stage. However, with careful teacher-directed instruction, the rate of accurate responses rises and the rate of inaccurate responses declines.

When the responses reach 90% accuracy, students are moving into stage two, **fluency building.** At this stage, instructional time involves students practicing their newly acquired skill to increase the speed of

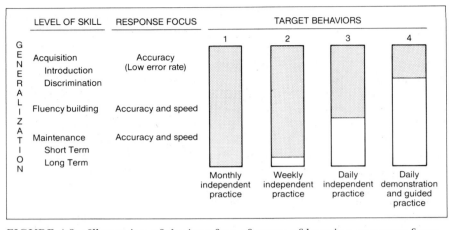

FIGURE 4.2   Illustration of the interface of stages of learning, response focus, and instructional activities.

responding accurately. For instance, instead of solving computational math problems at a rate of 40 digits per minute with 5 or less errors, students practice building their speed to a rate of solving 60 digits per minute with zero errors.

Once students respond fluently, instructional time for the target skill can be gradually reduced, but students must be provided practice at the **maintenance** stage of learning. During the maintenance stage, students are largely engaged in periodic independent practice to ensure that they can still perform previously taught skills at an acceptable rate of speed and accuracy.

The fourth stage, **generalization**, involves preparing students for using newly developed skills in different settings and at different times than those used during acquisition and fluency building. This is accomplished by reducing the level of prompting and reinforcement used by the teacher so that the student can demonstrate the behavior independently.

Instructional activities will be different at each of the four stages. Activities at the acquisition stage require intense teacher-student interaction where the teacher models a response and students imitate. The teacher explains the steps to a skill or the definition and characteristics of a concept. Numerous cues are used to assist students to respond accurately. Fast responding is not the focus of instruction; the numbers of correct responses and errors are the dependent measure. During fluency building, teacher–student interaction continues, but the interactions are largely a function of providing corrective feedback as students work on daily independent practice activities. These activities require less teacher supervision than at the acquisition level. The supervision entails periodic checks of student work and reminders to students of the need to respond quickly and accurately. Maintenance stage activities are much the same type of independent practice activity used at the fluency-building stage, except that a little more review may be required beforehand and the practice is distributed over intervals of a week or month. Generalization stage activities are imbedded into activities at all the previous stages and therefore do not occur necessarily as discrete independent activities. Further description of these stages and the types of strategies and learning activities used are provided in Chapter 5.

Regardless of the stage of learning, lessons contain a beginning, middle, and end. This not-so-novel concept is surprisingly absent from the conceptualization of many developing teachers. The beginning of a lesson for effective teachers usually entails telling students what they will be doing during the lesson and linking previous lessons with the content of the current lesson. This often takes the form of a lesson-initiating review. Next, teachers provide some demonstration of a concept or academic skill and appropriate practice activities for students. Finally, the lesson should end with some form of closure that indicates to students the transition from one session to another. A lesson-ending review often fills this need. The following sections detail the various sections of a lesson.

LESSON INITIATION   It is necessary to prepare students for a lesson by telling students what activities they are going to do and how it fits in with previous and future lessons. Consequently, the first step in lesson description should be to note the activities of the lesson. For example, an advanced organizer may be used, "Today we are going to discuss nouns and verbs. Then we are going to look at some magazine ads to find nouns and verbs. Finally, I have a worksheet for you to complete." To link this lesson with the last lesson, a teacher may make the statement, "Yesterday we talked about nouns. We defined them and came up with some examples. Today we are going to do the same, but we are going to discuss verbs also." What may follow is a review of the definition and examples of nouns either by the teacher simply stating this information or preferably by having the students respond to teacher questioning. The later strategy provides students with an additional practice activity as well as a link to the previous lesson.

DEMONSTRATION   Once an initial review is conducted, instruction on new content begins. Instruction initially involves a demonstration of target concepts, facts, skills, principles, or value judgments. The demonstration entails the teacher either **providing a model** or **inducing the model** from the students. For instance, in teaching the concept of a square, the modeling strategy would begin with the teacher presenting a diagram of a square and telling students what it is. Next, the teacher would write the definition of a square on the board, "A square is a quadrilateral with 4 congruent sides and 4 congruent angles." Using a diagram of a square, the teacher would then show how the example has 4 congruent sides and 4 congruent angles. On the other hand, in using an induction strategy, the teacher would present a diagram of a square without naming its shape and proceed to ask the students leading questions about the number of sides and angles and other attributes that distinguish a square. Using that information, the teacher may have the students write a definition and give a name to the diagram. In either of these two cases, the target content is explicitly provided to students in a systematic fashion.

Another dimension to the demonstration phase of a lesson is the type of subject matter students are learning. When teaching **academic rules**, the students must be exposed to a stated rule (e.g., *bl* makes the */bl/* sound). Then the students must apply the rule (e.g., sounding */bl/* in the word *blue*). When teaching **concepts**, teachers need to expose students to the definition or attributes, to give examples and nonexamples (e.g., a square is a quadrilateral with 4 congruent sides and 4 congruent angles). In cases where the concept is too abstract to define for students, the teacher may simply use examples and nonexamples to teach the concept (e.g., in teaching the concept of a square to children functioning at the preschool level). Special types of concepts are called **laws** and **lawlike principles**. Laws and lawlike principles refer to cause-and-effect relationships usually found in the sciences. They are taught by explicating the causal agent and the effect and by linking the two together. For example, the cause-and-effect relationship between temperature and moisture and the formation of rain is illustrated in Figure 4.3.

Teachers need to specify whether they are going to provide a teacher model or use an inductive strategy and indicate what type of subject matter will be taught. Clear statements of the facts, academic rules, concepts, and principles, along with examples and nonexamples should be written in the plan.

GUIDED PRACTICE   Once the target subject matter has been demonstrated, the teacher engages students in guided practice activities. Guided practice is characterized by teacher–student interactions involving high amounts of teacher cues and prompts in a closely supervised activity. Examples of guided practice are asking students to state in unison the definition of a checking account, questioning students about the attributes of a checking account, and asking students to evaluate examples and nonexamples of checking accounts. During guided practice, teachers model responses, lead students in practicing responses, and test students' skills in making responses with decreasing amounts of cues and prompts.

Often the shift from demonstration to guided practice is indistinguishable, especially when teachers use an inductive teaching approach. Being

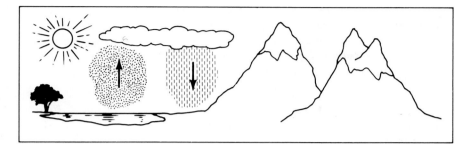

FIGURE 4.3   Teaching steps for explicating the cause-and-effect relationship between rising moist air and cold air in atmosphere in the formation of rain.

1. The teacher demonstrates the effect of rising moist air by reviewing a previously taught concept of evaporation (i.e., the sun's heating effect on bodies of water and atmosphere).

2. The teacher uses the diagram above to illustrate.

3. The teacher explains to students that the air high in the atmosphere is much colder, as illustrated in the diagram.

4. The teacher explains that, as the heated, moist air rises up into the cold air, the little droplets of water begin to join and make bigger and bigger drops of water. When they are big and heavy enough they begin to fall through the air down to the ground in the form of rain.

5. The teacher shows students the following and explains:

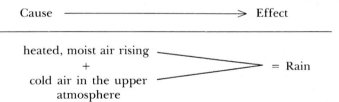

6. The teacher next demonstrates the cause-and-effect relationship by heating a pot of water on a hot plate and holding an aluminum tray filled with ice above the pot of water. Soon steam (hot, moist air) begins to rise and, as they reach the tray, drops form on the bottom of the tray. As the drops get larger or condense they begin to "rain" down.

Variation: Instead of teacher "explaining" each step, the teacher may ask a series of probing questions to *induce* the steps in the cause-and-effect relationship.

able to make the distinction as to exactly when a lesson moves from demonstration to guided practice is not of primary concern. What is important is that the subject matter be clearly and explicitly presented and students be given numerous opportunities to respond with high rates of accuracy (Greenwood, Delquadri, & Hall, 1984).

INDEPENDENT PRACTICE   When students respond accurately during guided practice, they are ready to work for fluency through independent practice activities. Independent practice refers to activities in which students engage in repeated responding and require little teacher supervision. Fluency refers to fast as well as accurate responding. Therefore, the focus of independent practice activities is on attaining a high rate of correct responding. Students are ready to work independently on a target skill when they have attained 90% accuracy. If students are unable to respond accurately and teachers ask students to practice independently, students will either make numerous errors or constantly ask for assistance while the teacher attempts to work with others.

Demonstration and guided practice are used to prepare students for independent practice. It may take one or several lessons involving only demonstration and guided practice on a target skill before students are able to work independently. Consequently, for a particular group of students, an instructional period may include either demonstration and guided practice; demonstration and guided and independent practice; or demonstration and guided practice plus independent practice on another previously acquired skill.

When designing independent practice activities, two points need to be considered for students with special needs. First, practice sessions need to be massed (i.e., daily practice) at the early stages of fluency building and then distributed on weekly or monthly intervals to facilitate short- and long-term maintenance. Second, practice activities should be considered in terms of the number of opportunities to respond provided for the learner. Some gamelike activities are highly motivating, but students only get a few chances to respond after waiting for other students to take their turns. Other activities, such as worksheets, require students to make a high number of responses in a relatively short period of time. Consequently, teachers in special education need to balance their practice activities so they are exciting and motivational and provide the opportunity to students to make a sufficient number of responses.

SUMMARY REVIEW   The final step of a lesson should be a summary review of the content being taught or practiced (Good, Grouws, & Ebermeier, 1983). A review allows teachers to highlight the major points of their lesson, which helps students to organize material. A review becomes practice when teachers ask students to respond to questions about the major points of the lesson. Review provides a sense of closure to the lesson, gives students a sense that the lesson has an explicit ending, and helps prepare them for the transition into the next lesson.

Methods to Evaluate Lessons

Effective teachers monitor and evaluate their instruction. Teachers must identify a behavior or academic task, set goals, collect data to establish a baseline, introduce an intervention, and record the results over time until the goal has been reached or until no further progress has been demonstrated. A technique frequently used is the direct measurement and recording of student performance using data charts or graphs (Fuchs & Fuchs, 1986).

GRAPHING PERFORMANCE   Graphs allow data organization and visual analysis of the effects of an intervention on behavior or academic achievement. In addition, the use of pictorial rather than a narrative form saves time and space (Deno & Mirkin, 1977). Two basic types of graphs may be used by developing teachers to record data on a daily, weekly, or monthly basis: performance graphs and progress graphs.

Performance Graphs Performance graphs depict a regular, frequent measure of the student's performance and behavior changes on a specific task over time (Fig. 4.4). An example is the number of times a pupil interrupts during a 30-minute interval. Plotted on the abscissa is the time interval during which the observations are recorded, and on

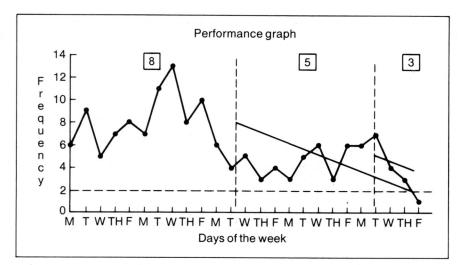

FIGURE 4.4   A decrease in the frequency of targeted behavior.

the ordinate, the level of performance on that particular task. Periods of time or phases when specific instructional strategies are implemented are indicated by vertical lines. The baseline phase is first and shows that no instruction occurred or current instructional procedures remained the same. Data from this phase are used to identify the students' current level of functioning and to set instructional objectives. Next, a goal line is plotted (i.e., dotted line). Based on the median performance of a target student (represented by teardrop shapes on the graph), the estimated time of intervention available, and the goal, a decision line is plotted (i.e., the diagonal line beginning at the end of baseline and running until the estimated ending date for intervention).

After the baseline phase, intervention phases are implemented as needed. Each of these phases represents implementation of a different strategy or mix of multiple instructional strategies. Student performance is monitored and continuously compared with the pattern of performance displayed during baseline. Data points are plotted until the goal is reached, or until no further progress is made.

As the data points are plotted, teachers make decisions to continue or modify an intervention. Specific decision-making rules are used to make these determinations:

1. If for 3 consecutive sessions the data points fall above the decision-making line (when attempting to decrease a behavior) or fall below the decision-making line (when attempting to increase a behavior), then the treatment phase is terminated and a new or modified treatment is initiated.
2. After 3 weeks (15 sessions) of the same treatment, modify or change the treatment (to maintain interest and performance levels).

When necessary, additional intervention phases are introduced, with goal lines and decision-making lines reformulated. Teachers evaluate the effectiveness of their instruction based on changes in the level of student performance (i.e., how much higher or lower is the student's current performance level to the baseline performance) and the rate of change in student performance (i.e., how quickly the student's performance is improving).

In the example, the first intervention was the teacher talking to the target student about his behavior. Talking appeared to be effective, as indicated by the data points falling below the decision line. This decrease in the frequency of the behavior changed, however, as indicated by the last 3 data points of this phase, which fell above the line. This prompted the termination of the first intervention and the implementation of a second intervention of planned ignoring. A new decision line was constructed using the median performance level as the endpoint and drawing a line parallel to the first decision-making line. Ultimately, the target student did reach his goal during the second intervention phase. In fact, all four data points during this phase fell below the adjusted goal line for phase two.

Progress Graphs A progress graph (or chart) is intended to measure the time it takes a pupil to master a set of instructional objectives. The abscissa indicates the time, and the ordinate expresses the series of objectives. Data points are plotted sequentially on the relevant intersection of the vertical (objective) and horizontal (time) lines and connected with a straight line, thereby illustrating graphically the pupil's progress in achieving the desired objectives. Unlike the performance graph, a progress graph is cumulative. That is, the data points never descend, they either remain at the same level or ascend. Regardless, the same decision rules are used in both performance and progress graphs.

The progress graph example provided in Figure 4.5 is based on a district-wide primary-level mathematics curriculum goal of mastering 3 objectives per week. Donna, a first grade student, mastered only one objective after 6 weeks of instruction. The teacher referred Donna to the resource teacher, and, in consultation, it was decided that a goal of 3 objectives per week was appropriate, even though Donna would be functioning slightly below grade level at the end of the school year. Initially, a trained fifth grade student tutored Donna on her arithmetic skills for 15 minutes daily. This extra practice proved insufficient, and individual work with the resource teacher for 15 minutes daily was added to the intervention. In the third phase, Donna was given 25 minutes of daily practice with the resource teacher.

Graphs are an effective means of monitoring student performance on

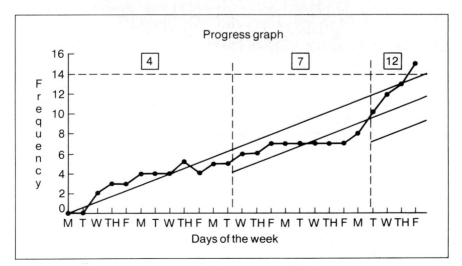

FIGURE 4.5   Cumulative mastery of curriculum objectives.

specific instructional tasks and progress through sets of curricular objectives. The choice of a performance graph or a progress graph depends on the type of data to be charted. If the rate of mastering a set of instructional tasks is of greater importance, the use of a progress graph is recommended. If changes in the level of performance on a specific task is to be highlighted, then the preferred medium is the performance graph. In both cases, graphs provide a means for succinctly displaying the achievements of students and consequently the effectiveness of instruction. This can motivate the students, teachers, parents, and other individuals interested in the student's attainment of educational goals. It should also be remembered that graphs also provide a vehicle for clear communication among teachers, administrators, and parents.

Anticipated Problems

The final step before implementing a lesson plan is to anticipate potential instructional and behavioral problems that might arise during the lesson. Regardless of how well teachers prepare materials and activities, they may still have to deal spontaneously with glitches in the subject presentation or disruptive behavior by individual students. Such problems frequently can be addressed on the spur of the moment. However, planning ahead can help either avoid these problems before they occur or deal with them with a minimal loss in instructional time. For example, developing teachers often have difficulties determining how long activities will take to complete and do not prepare back-up activities when students complete the primary activity sooner than expected. By preparing a contingency plan, they can quickly move students into another activity and avoid the potential behavior problems associated with students not being engaged in constructive activities. (See Box 4.2.)

Lesson Plan Follow-Up: Self-Evaluation

To benefit fully from the experience of carrying out each instructional plan, teachers must spend time after the lesson analyzing and evaluating what occurred during the lesson. This process affords teachers the opportunity to determine the strengths and weaknesses of the lesson. The foci of the post-lesson evaluation are teacher and student performance. In evaluating their own performance, teachers may analyze their organization and lesson development, presentation of concepts or skills, and their management of classroom behaviors. For example, they may determine whether or not a sufficient number of examples were used to illustrate a target concept. In addition to their own performance, teachers need to analyze the performance of students in terms of their participation in instructional activities and attainment of specified objectives. Consideration might be given to the degree to which students were motivated by an instructional activity. On the other hand, teachers need to consider

BOX 4.2

Case Study

Mr. Gollery, the teacher of an elementary resource room, uses a theme approach to teach units of concepts and skills. During one term, the theme was pirates. Students attending the resource room for reading and language arts read about pirates, listened to stories about sailing, and wrote compositions about pirates and the sea. During math instruction, word problems and computation skill development were set in the context of pirates calculating distances and navigating the seas. With anywhere from 5 to 15 students working at different skill levels and on different types of activities at the same time, Mr. Gollery designed activities to fill in any "dead time" between activities. He used learning centers that involved activities students could complete with little or no assistance from Mr. Gollery or his aide. (When activities required instruction, Mr. Gollery appropriated a specific time to teach the necessary skills.) So when students finished an instructional activity, they could spend time completing the paper-mâché pirate ship or sit at the listening post with a story book and read along with a tape-recorded story. Importantly, the activities had five characteristics:

1. "Dead time" was reduced.
2. Independence was promoted.
3. The learning of theme concepts and skills were enriched.
4. The teacher was able to work with other students.
5. The activities served as a reward for completing previous activities (Premack principle).

the students' mastery of the content. If students did not attain criterion performance levels, then teachers may need to recycle students through the DTM. If mastery has been reached, consideration needs to be given to the next objective in the skill hierarchy. In any case, self-evaluation of the teacher's ability to conduct an instructional activity and to direct students' behaviors is critical if effective teaching behaviors are going to be maintained and ineffective ones reduced or eliminated.

Lesson-Plan Formats

Teachers plan at a variety of levels: they make year-long plans, semester or term plans, unit plans, and daily plans. The focus of this chapter is on unit and lesson plans. Selection of the unit plan or a daily lesson-plan format must be based on classroom variables and individual needs at any given time.

Daily Lesson Plans

The most commonly used format for writing lesson plans is the traditional group instructional plan. Such a plan lists objectives and provides a relatively detailed description of the materials, activities, and evaluation procedures for multiple small-group or single large-group instruction. Teachers using this format write when and how they are going to provide instruction. An alternative format is the daily activity schedule, a succinct list designating when instruction will take place with little reference to how instruction will be carried out. Often this format is used in conjunction with a unit-plan format or in resource rooms where students work predominantly on their own with their assignments for each day listed in a work folder.

TRADITIONAL GROUP INSTRUCTIONAL PLAN   Traditionally, preservice teacher trainees have been taught to construct daily lesson plans with the assumption that at any given time they would be working with a single large group or two to four small groups simultaneously. The generic format of lesson plans includes a statement of the lesson objective and a description of the materials, activities, and evaluation procedures to be used. This format continues to be used extensively because of its ease of use and applicability. In many classrooms for mildly handicapped students, large and simultaneous small group instruction and practice is provided. However, in those classrooms where students are individually placed at different points in the curriculum, the traditional lesson-plan format is not feasible.

In fact, the section entitled *"Components of Successfully Planned Lessons"* contains the categories used in the traditional daily lesson plan. Box 4.3 illustrates how the categories are laid out in the traditional lesson plan. Sections 1 through 6 are the contents of the actual plan while the remaining sections are used to self-evaluate the lesson after the plan has been implemented. The following steps are needed to complete the lesson plan:

1. Provide the teacher's name, date, and the student's or group's name in the header.
2. Write behaviorally stated objectives that indicate how students will respond to demonstrate mastery.
3. In the activities description section, write step-by-step procedures for each activity. Content information, such as definitions of concepts, academic rules, and so forth, should be included as well.
4. List all materials to be used in the lesson.
5. List evaluation tools/measures and indicate whether the measures will

BOX 4.3

Traditional Lesson-Plan Format

LESSON PREPARATION AND ANALYSIS FORM

Name: Ms. Baldwell   *Date:* 5/12/89
   Student(s) or Group: Cary, Carlos, Bill, Su-Lee, and Tyrone

1. *Behavioral objectives of activity*
   When given a passage to read, students will be able to under-
   line two important words or phrases for each paragraph with
   90% accuracy.
      When given a passage to read, students will be able to see-
   write answers to 7 out of 8 comprehension questions for three
   consecutive passages.

2. *Description of activity*
   Demonstration
      Explain purpose of underlining strategy (i.e., to help student
      identify and recall important information). Tell students that
      the teacher is going to show them how to use the underlining
      strategy. Model the strategy by reading the first paragraph of
      the passage aloud. Verbalize the steps to the strategy:
         "I need to underline two important words or phrases."
         "Important words or phrases tell me about the main idea or
            details."
         "Underline."
         "Ask myself, why is this important?"
         "Go on to the next paragraph."
   Guided practice
      Have students read the second paragraph.
      Lead the students through verbalizing the steps above.
      Repeat guided practice with paragraphs 3 and 4.
      Lead students in summarizing the content of each paragraph
         using the underlined key phrases.
      After finishing the passage, lead students in using underlined
         phrases to read-write answers to comprehension questions.
   Independent practice
      None.

3. *Measurement*
   Note each student's use of self-instruction statements.
   Note each student's underlining of two words or phrases per
      paragraph.
   Tally number of comprehension questions answered correctly.

(continued)

BOX 4.3 (continued)

4. ***Materials***
   Story "Animals with Pouches."
   Highlite pens.
5. ***Adaptations***
   Engage students in choral practice on self-verbalizations.
6. ***Problems that might be encountered***
   Students may not be able to discriminate important from unimportant words or phrases. If so, ask students to justify the importance of the words and phrases they underlined. Provide feedback on selections and justifications.
7. ***Problems that actually arose***
   Students had difficulty with identifying important words and phrases. Feedback was provided, and student selections were shaped into more appropriate responses.
8. ***Behavioral techniques used during activity***
   Strategy modeling and specific academic praise for accurate self-verbalizations and underlining.
9. ***What you learned from this activity***
   Students respond well to modeling strategy steps. The model and lead steps provide sufficient support to students so that they can make accurate responses and enjoy their success.

be taken at daily, weekly, or monthly intervals. The evaluation tools selected should be designed to assess the mastery of the objectives, not the activity.
6. List any special adaptations needed for individual students.
7. Anticipated instructional or behavior problems should be described along with strategies to deal with any problems if they arise.
8. After the lesson has been implemented, note any problems that occurred and the strategies used to resolve them. Provide information that will be helpful in dealing with problems in the future. Note any other information that would be helpful in preparing for the same lesson.

ACTIVITY SCHEDULE   The activity schedule replaces the traditional daily lesson plan with a daily timeline depicting when instruction will take place. Teachers list the sequence of activities. In addition, teachers document who will supervise each activity (i.e., teacher, aide, or student). The activities listed on the activity schedule are derived either from (1) a unit plan, which contains a list of instructional objectives, materials to be used, a description of the activities, and evaluation procedures that monitor progress toward attaining the objectives; or 2) a set of materials from an individual student's work folder. The activity schedule provides planned activities without the details for each day of instruction.

Completion of a daily activity schedule is designed to:

1. Provide consistent, accurate, and meaningful planning for each student.
2. Provide a written record of previous activities to facilitate future planning, monitoring, and recordkeeping.
3. Provide a plan of action for the implementation of the unit plan.

Alternative forms: Option A
Instructions for completing activity schedule option A (see Figure 4.6):

1. Enter your name and date.
2. According to the time blocks you determine, enter each student in the appropriate column:

   • *Activity with teacher* — Teacher-directed activities are typically used to introduce, continue development, or review acquisition and/or provide guided practice.
   • *Activity with aide* — These can be teacher-directed activities used by the teacher aide as above to introduce, continue development, or review acquisition skills.
   • *Independent activity* — These are practice activities to help the student maintain or develop fluency on previously acquired skills. They are characterized by the student's ability to complete the activity with little or no teacher assistance once the directions for the activity have been overviewed.

3. Beside the student's name, list each activity. Be specific as to page number, cassette, filmstrip, disk, and so forth. Also indicate whether the activity entails demonstration, guided, or independent practice.

Helpful hints

1. If your schedule remains the same on a daily/weekly basis, fill in students' names, time periods, and so forth. Then make a master copy of the activity schedule. As a result, you will only have to complete the activity columns from day to day or week to week.
2. A student can be a group, if consistent and clearly labeled initially.
3. A code may be developed to correspond to your unit plan. For example: In the unit plan, reading activities can be numbered such as R-1, R-2, and so forth; math activities as M-1, M-2, and so forth. Then, when entering activities on the activity schedule, R-1 or M-2 could be used to refer to specific items on your unit plan.

ACTIVITY SCHEDULE

Teacher: **Ms. Ley**   *Date:* Wednesday, April 19

Groups:
G1: Willie, Brett, Jose, Errol & Juanita   G5: Mike, Maria & Bo
G2: Barb, Sam, Myron, Amal & Robert   G6: Greg, Jack, Carol & Paul
G3: Lindsay, Kelly & Chris
G4: Conor, Patrick, Kevin & Shannon

Time	Activity with teacher	Activity with aide	Independent practice
8:30–9:30	**G1** Flash card drill (sums to 10)	**G2** Language master: fluency building on phrases to 100 wpm	**Kevin & Conor** computer (Spell Blaster)
9:30–10:30	**G2** Reading comprehension, pp. 42–48: underlining strategy training with explicit text questions	**G1** Handwriting: copy and edit last week's language experience sentences	**G5 & 6** Peer tutoring, 2 digit × 2 digit multiplication w/ regrouping
10:30–11:30	**G3** Oral repeated reading, pp. 31–36: fluency building to 120 wpm	**G4** Mastery test: fractions **G6** Probe: 2 × 2 multiplication	**G1** Listening post: spelling quiz **G2 & 5** Sustained silent reading
12:15–1:15	**G4** Reading comprehension, pp. 98–107: paraphrase strategy training with explicit text questions	**G5** Handwriting: copy and edit last week's language experience stories	Lindsay: Implicit text questions from passage Chris: Listening post: Main idea from "Over the Fence"
1:15–2:00	**G3, 4, & 5** Written expression topic: fossils (based on field trip)		

FIGURE 4.6   Completed activity schedule for option A.

Alternative forms: Option B
Instructions for completing activity schedule option B (An advantage to this format is each student and teacher can readily see daily routines and expectations. See Figure 4.7.):

1. Use one sheet for each day of the week.
2. Fill in students' names across the top. Arrange by classes/grade levels to facilitate groupings. If pencil is used and space on the schedule is a priority, new students can replace those who leave your program.
3. Enter time (standard time) notations down the left-hand side (8:00, 8:30, 9:00, 9:30, and so forth).
4. Enter each student's daily schedule (including lunch, recess, regular classroom activities, other specialists, and so forth). If desired, use consistent color coding for each different activity.
5. Block out periods in your classroom setting.
6. Record specific daily activities (reading, math, language, spelling, and so forth) directly on sheet. If plastic or separate sheet is used, master schedule can be reused each week/day.

UNIT PLAN   Individualized programming is not exclusive to special education settings, but it is a more predominant practice than in regular education. In addition, the heterogeneity of many special education settings is more extreme than in many regular class programs. As a result, many special education teachers provide instruction to students who are functioning within a broad range of skills. Often this means that separate instructional activities have to be prepared for each student. Because of these factors, preparing daily lesson plans can be an enormous task. To ask developing teachers to write traditional lesson plans for each student or small sets of students at each skill level each day is unrealistic. The unit-plan format is a viable option to accommodate the need to write effective lesson plans within the context of many resource rooms.

The unit plan is the vehicle whereby the specific objectives are translated into and correlated with specific activities, materials, and evaluation methods. A unit plan is designed to:

1. Provide a comprehensive plan for curriculum implementation.
2. Provide a foundation and rationale for all instruction.
3. Develop creative planning from determination to implementation and evaluation of instructional objectives.

Alternative forms: Option A
Instructions for completing unit plan option A (see Figure 4.8):

1. Enter the student's or group's name, subject, major goal, dates of initiation and completion, and charting method (i.e., progress or performance graphs).
2. Enter specific objectives that correspond to a major objective.
3. List all materials that might be used.

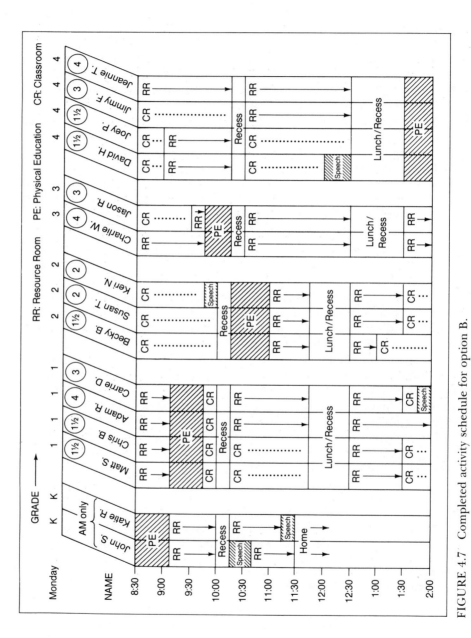

FIGURE 4.7   Completed activity schedule for option B.

Reading Unit Plan

Students: Groups 1 & 2

Date of Initiation: September 18

Annual Goal: Students will improve reading comprehension

Date of Completion:

Objectives

1. When given passage at their instructional level, SWBAT see-write correct answers to seven out of eight comprehension questions related to text explicit and implicit information for three consecutive sessions.

Materials

Stories from basal and supplemental reading series.

Activities

Semantic Webs (SW)

1. Set purpose for reading (e.g., predicting events, main ideas, related facts, and so forth).
2. Discuss theme of story and relate to students' background experiences.
3. Have students read first and second paragraphs.
4. Assign third paragraph. Have students predict what will happen next in the story.
5. Formulate a core question and write on the board.
6. Elicit possible answers to core question and write in list separate from web.
7. Ask students to accept, reject, or modify answers.
8. Draw web.
9. Build support for web strands. Ask students to examine them and accept, reject, or modify. (Students may reread prior to doing this.)
10. Guide students to relating strands (two to three relationships maximum).

Evaluation

Probe containing eight comprehension questions will be completed at the end of each passage.

FIGURE 4.8   Unit plan format for option A.

4. List activities that will help students reach the stated objectives. Under each activity, describe the specific step-by-step procedures. Content information, such as definitions of concepts, academic rules, and so forth, should be included as well. The activity description will only have to be entered at the initial entry point in the unit plan. If you wish to use the same activity to reach another objective, the teacher only needs to list the activity title in the activity column next to subsequent objectives.
5. List evaluation tools/measures and indicate whether they are daily, weekly, or monthly. The evaluation tools selected should be designed to assess the mastery of the objectives, not the activities.

Helpful hints:

1. Be as broad-based as possible. Build and adapt objectives, activities, and materials across groups and skill levels.
2. Be creative and flexible. Design a mixture of creative high-interest activities along with less elaborate drill activities.

Alternative forms: Option B
Instructions for completing unit plans option B (see Figure 4.9):

1. Develop a card file of successful activities. Code activities according to skill area.
2. Activity cards might include: name of activity, identifying code, materials needed, objective, appropriate instructional level, and so forth.
3. Copy several cards onto one sheet of paper to be included with your unit plan.

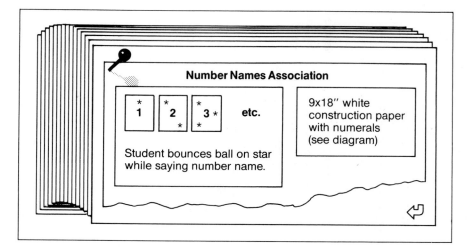

FIGURE 4.9   Activity card for unit plan format, option B.

4. This technique permits using the same activity with several skill levels without recopying the same information. In addition, the cardfile will be an invaluable resource.

Summary

The bottom line for effective teaching is that teachers need to invest a substantial amount of time in preparing to teach. Although many developing and beginning teachers would like to think there must be a short cut, there is none. To be effective, teachers have to work hard to develop their lessons and revise and polish them continuously.

This chapter provides beginning teachers with an overview of the rationale and principles of planning that set the foundation for effective teaching. Plans help teachers to identify clearly what they hope to accomplish and specify the means for accomplishing their goals. They help to foster confidence and security. Plans provide the basis for an organized educational plan that ensures the success of students in developing academic and functional skills. In order to derive these benefits, plans must contain objectives, sound instructional and practice activities, and a method for evaluating attainment of the objectives (Garland,1982).

Several suggested formats have been presented that provide a starting point in developing a system of planning. Teachers need to examine the generic principles of effective planning and examine some possible formats for writing out their plans. Then they can devise a system that fits their own needs.

References

CARTWRIGHT, G.P., CARTWRIGHT, C.A., & WARD, M. (1981). Educating special learners. Belmont, CA: Wadsworth.

CLARK, C.M., & YINGER, R.J. (1979). Three studies of teacher planning. East Lansing: Michigan State University, Institute for Research on Teaching, Research Series No. 55.

COOPER, J.M. (1986). Classroom teaching skills (3rd ed.). Lexington, MA: D.C. Heath.

DENO, S., & MIRKIN, P. (1977). Data-based program modification: A manual. Reston,VA: Council for Exceptional Children.

DESHLER, D.D., & SCHUMAKER, J.B. (1986). Learning strategies: An instructional alternative for low-achieving adolescents. *Exceptional Children, 52*, 583–590.

FUCHS, L.S., & FUCHS, D. (1986). Effects of systematic formative evaluation: A meta-analysis. *Exceptional Children, 53*, 199–208.

GARLAND, C. (1982). Guiding clinical experiences in teacher education. New York: Longman.

GOOD, T., GROUWS, D., & EBERMEIER, H. (1983). Active mathematics teaching. New York: Longman.

GREENWOOD, C.R., DELQUADRI, J.C., & HALL, R.V. (1984). Opportunity to respond and student academic performance. In W.L. Heward, T.E. Heron, D.S. Hill, & J. Trap-Porter (Eds.), *Focus on behavior analysis in education* (pp. 58–88). Columbus, OH: Merrill.

MCCUTCHEON, G. (1980). How do elementary school teachers plan their courses? *Elementary School Journal, 81,* 4–23.

MERCER, C.D., & MERCER, A.R. (1985). *Teaching students with learning problems.* Columbus, OH: Merrill.

PETERSON, P.L., MARX, R.W., & CLARK, C.M. (1978). Teacher planning, teacher behavior, and students' achievement. *American Educational Research Journal, 15,* 417–432.

CHAPTER 5

Delivering Instruction

The central function of teachers is to deliver instruction to their students in the most efficient and effective manner possible. Developing teachers need to take into account the various elements of instruction and weave them into a form that will clearly communicate to students what target responses are expected. The purpose of this chapter is to describe for developing teachers a set of instructional elements that are related to effective instruction. These instructional elements are derived from two instructional models prominent in classrooms today: Direct instruction (DI) and guided discovery learning (GDL). These models form the conceptual and procedural basis for a variety of other instructional approaches. For example, DI steps are found in the strategies intervention (Deshler & Schumaker, 1986) and class-wide peer tutoring models (Greenwood, Delquadri, & Hall, 1984). The GDL steps form the basis of the reciprocal teaching model (Palincsar & Brown, 1984). These and other instructional models are important and effective, certainly worthy of further study. However, the limits of this chapter prohibit discussion here. Table 5.1 lists other models incorporating elements of DI and GDL that may be of interest to the reader.

In addition to the generic procedures of DI and GDL, the second section of the chapter contains specific procedures for presenting concept and academic-rule subject material. Both are found to varying degrees in all school curricula content areas.

The third section of the chapter is used to describe the stages of learning that students must pass through in order to master the subject matter being presented. The lesson development section contains a description of instructional elements associated with initiating instruction, engaging students, and ending a lesson.

The final section of the chapter is a synthesis of the above material

TABLE 5.1   Teaching and Learning Models That Incorporate Elements of DI
or GDL

Model	Source	Description
Strategies intervention model	Deshler & Schumaker (1986)	The generic model used to teach acquisition and generalization of learning strategies.
Informed strategies learning	Paris, Cross, & Lipson (1984)	Program for teaching students about the existence and use of various metacognitive strategies
Reciprocal teaching	Palincsar & Brown (1984)	A system of dialogue between student and teacher involving the modeling and imitation of metacomprehension strategies.
Peer tutoring	Greenwood, Delquadri, & Hall (1984)	A program of peer-mediated instruction that focuses on increasing students' opportunities to respond.
Self-instruction	Wollery, Bailey, & Sugai (1988)	A system for using self-statements to guide students in the completion of academic and behavioral tasks.
Precision teaching	Precision Teaching Project	A system for mastery learning that entails direct, daily monitoring of student responding rates using timed probes.
Academic strategy training	Lloyd & de Bettencourt (1982)	A method for teaching students routines for completing various academic tasks.

and is designed to present the chapter content in an integrated form. Also, a discussion of when particular elements of instruction should be used is provided.

Throughout the chapter a variety of examples from different content areas are provided to show how the suggested strategies can be applied in different contexts.

Direct Instruction and Guided Discovery Learning: Principles for Effective Instruction

The two most broadly applicable models of instruction, which are often considered to be diametrically opposed, are DI and GDL. The proponents of DI have focused on the need of students to master specific curriculum content; the proponents of GDL have focused on the importance of students learning procedures for problem solving and learning how to learn. In the former case, the outcome of instruction is viewed as the demonstration of specific skills and knowledge about reading, math, social science, science, and so forth (e.g., being able to sound out words and knowing facts about state capitals). In the latter case, the outcome of instruction is viewed as the demonstration of skills and knowledge about the process of learning (e.g., how to implement steps for solving problems or how to use study skills). DI procedures can be found underlying a variety of instructional programs such as DISTAR. GDL rationale can be found in currently popular instructional models such as metacognitive strategy training.

Although the philosophical underpinnings may be accurately described as in opposition, the application of the procedures derived from these models can be viewed by developing and beginning teachers as complementary. Each model has its strengths and weaknesses, and the weaknesses of one are compensated by the strengths of the other. Therefore, to counter any shortcomings of DI, teachers can use GDL techniques in appropriate situations and vice versa.

The section below contains a description of both models and the key components of each. Examples of how lessons are taught using each are also provided. It is important to realize that the instructional procedures attributed to either DI or GDL are not so precise that variation in their implementation will lead to significant reductions in their effectiveness. Developing teachers, instead, should be encouraged to use the procedures outlined below as guidelines from which they can vary to meet their needs based on the content being presented and the educational state of the learners.

Direct Instruction

In the areas of special and remedial education, the methodology of DI has grown in popularity like no other instructional approach over the past decade. Its roots date back to the mid-seventies when Rosenshine (1976) coined the term in reference to effective teaching behaviors. By extensive classroom observation, Rosenshine (1971) and others (Anderson, Evertson, & Brophy, 1979; Fisher et al., 1980) identified critical teacher behaviors that correlated positively with student academic gains. Englemann and associates (Becker, Englemann, & Thomas, 1971; Carnine & Silbert, 1979; Englemann & Carnine, 1982) expanded the term *direct instruction* to include not only specific teaching procedures, but also to include the use of highly structured curriculum materials. These materials are designed to help teachers systematically direct students in making accurate responses. Scripted lesson plans are designed to ensure that precise communication occurs between teacher and student. During instruction, teachers **model** target responses, **lead** students in making the response, and periodically **test** students' skills to respond without teacher cues.

DIRECT INSTRUCTION DEFINED DI refers to teacher-guided instruction directed toward the mastery of specific skills and includes students working in small groups with high rates of engagement. Success is facilitated through the use of structured lessons that are fast-paced, structured curricula, corrective feedback procedures, and performance monitoring. The critical aspect of the DI model is that teachers control instruction. They determine what and how subject matter content will be presented (i.e., they demonstrate target responses and lead students in making responses). As teacher cues are gradually faded, students are increasingly able to respond independently. Extensive practice is provided so that students have sufficient opportunities to make responses and thus master the target skills. Practice activities are fast paced so that there is a high density of responses during instructional periods. During initial learning, teachers work with students in small groups to monitor the accuracy of their responses and ensure that they are engaged in academic tasks. When students err, teachers respond to provide corrective feedback that entails taking students through the model, lead, and test sequence.

PRINCIPAL COMPONENTS OF DIRECT INSTRUCTION The three principal components of DI include the **demonstration, guided practice,** and **independent practice stages** of lesson development. During each of these stages, teachers execute instructional behaviors in a standard, systematic manner. If teachers use predictable steps in lesson development, students are able to participate in activities and perform responses in a more consistent manner.

Demonstration The demonstration stage of lesson development entails teachers **modeling** target responses for students. The responses relate to the performance of an academic rule (i.e., sets of procedures for performing academic tasks such as solving computations with re-grouping) or the formation of concepts (i.e., well-defined categories of information used for classification, such as types of plants). For instance, if the target response for students is to see-say a set of words containing the medial short vowel sound /a/, then the teacher would point to each target word and sound out the letter sounds contained in the words (e.g., c-a-t, m-a-t, r-a-t). If the target response being taught to the student were to state a concept name and say the definition, the teacher would model the response by stating the target word and its definition (e.g., a square is a quadrilateral that contains 4 congruent sides and 4 right angles).

Guided Practice The second stage of lesson development is super-vised practice that entails teachers using cues and prompts to emit target responses. Teachers **lead** groups of students in making the desired re-sponse (i.e., the teacher and students perform the response simultane-ously). As the students demonstrate accurate responses, the teacher gradually fades his degree of leading. Instead of making the response with the students, the teacher presents the stimulus and has the group of students respond. **Unison responding**, groups of students making responses simultaneously, allows students more opportunities for re-sponding during a period of time. Teachers must monitor the response of individual students in the group during unison responding to deter-mine whether all students are responding accurately. In addition, teachers **test** students by calling on individual students to make responses on their own.

As students become more accurate in their responding, teachers shift the performance criterion to fast and accurate responding. Teachers concentrate on asking for as many responses as possible during a guided-practice session. This increases the opportunities to respond and helps to ensure skill mastery.

If teachers were continuing the lesson on see-say words with medial short vowel sounds, after the sounding out demonstration, teachers would have the students sound out the words with them simultaneously. Similarly, in teaching the hear-say response for the concept of a square, teachers would demonstrate the response and then lead students in stating the definition with them.

During the interactive process of instruction, these two stages of lesson development often overlap with little discernible differentiation where one stage ends and the next begins. Making such a differentiation when implementing these procedures is much less important than the teacher ensuring that responses are demonstrated and that students have numer-ous opportunities to practice the responses while the teacher leads.

Independent Practice Once students have performed responses accurately without cues or prompts, the third stage of lesson development is initiated to provide students the opportunity to practice response accuracy and speed. Independent practice, therefore, is minimally supervised practice in which students respond with a 90% or better response accuracy.

Two important and closely related features of independent practice assist in skill development and efficient management of classroom activities. First, teachers can work with other groups of students while one group practices independently. Second, students must be making accurate responses so they can *truly work independently of the teacher* (i.e., without a constant parade of students moving over to the teacher to ask questions about their seatwork).

When students engage in independent-practice activities, the teacher should prepare them and monitor their progress in completing the assignment. The following sequence is typical: (a) give directions to complete the activity tasks, (b) lead students in completing example tasks, (c) indicate deadline for completing activity, (d) circulate and assist students as needed, and (e) review student responses to activity tasks.

OTHER COMPONENTS Other components of DI have been developed for use during the different stages of lesson development. They are used by teachers to ensure that instruction is systematic and that students are engaged in academic tasks to the maximum extent possible and evaluated continuously for their progress toward skill mastery (Carnine & Silbert, 1979).

Small-Group Instruction In an ideal world, there would be one teacher for every student. However, such an instructional arrangement is hardly practical. On the other hand, a ratio of one teacher for 100 students would provide excellent economic efficiency but is not an effective instructional strategy. The practical compromise is to have 10 to 15 students in a special classroom or 20 to 30 students in a regular classroom. Under these conditions, the most efficient and effective arrangement is to work with students in small groups when engaging in demonstration and guided practice. For a special classroom, 3 to 5 students would be considered a small instructional group; in a regular classroom, 5 to 8 students would be a small group.

Small-group instruction allows teachers to fulfill the criteria for effective instruction listed below. They can keep students engaged more easily, have students respond in unison, monitor group and individual performance, and provide corrective feedback. The close proximity of the teacher to students in small-group situations is a controlling force. Students are more likely to engage in desired tasks and to be responsive to teacher cues and prompts.

Engaged Time Engaged time is the amount of time students spend actively performing the academic tasks presented to them. The concept of engaged time is simple — the greater the proportion of engaged time to allocated instructional time, the greater the academic performance of students. When students are off-task, overtly or covertly performing nonacademic tasks, they are not working toward mastery of target responses. Teachers maximize engaged time by efficiently using instructional time, monitoring the rates of engagement in their classrooms, and avoiding dead time. Dead time occurs when teachers delay the start of instructional periods or do not have materials ready and close at hand, when students take unnecessary time to make transitions from one activity to another, and when discussions go off on tangents unrelated to the responses being taught. These can all be minimized by developing teachers being aware of the importance of engaged time and monitoring the rates of engagement in their classrooms.

Unison Responding During small-group instruction, teachers seek to maximize the number of opportunities students have to perform target responses. Unison responding, a technique used to maximize the efficiency of practice time, is the simultaneous performance of a response by a group of students. A synonymous term is choral practice. Each student is provided more practice under unison responding than if individual students were asked to make a response one after the other. The result is more efficient use of instructional time. This increases the likelihood of them mastering the response in the shortest amount of time (Greenwood et al., 1984).

Signaling Signaling is used during unison responding. Teachers visually or auditorially prompt students to make the desired response to ensure that the responding is truly unison. Without signaling, some students will lag behind and wait for another student to begin the response before they join in. For example, if a teacher has the word *mate* written on the board and does not train students to react to a signal, some students will wait for others to begin sounding out the /ma/ sounds before starting their response. It is difficult for teachers to determine who is capable of making the response independently without cues.

When teachers begin to use unison responding, they must teach students to respond to their signal. Without explicit training in responding to signals, some students will persist in delaying responses.

Pacing DI lessons are also characterized by fast-paced practice sessions. Not only does a fast rate of stimulus presentation facilitate the efficient use of instructional time, it helps to maintain interest and decrease off-task behavior.

Monitoring To ensure appropriate instructional decisions, developing teachers need to know how well students are progressing toward skill mastery. Direct and continuous monitoring of students' rate and accuracy of responding allows developing teachers to determine the daily instructional needs of each student. Daily monitoring better ensures that students will not proceed through an extended series of lessons with high-error rates before instruction is modified to improve response accuracy. Monitoring can take the form of simply tallying the number of correct and error responses students make during an oral practice session or on a paper and pencil seatwork assignment. These frequencies can be kept in a daily log or a bulletin board chart, or can be plotted on a graph. Chapter 4 contains a discussion on charting techniques for monitoring student performance and progress.

Corrective Feedback The teaching precision under the DI model is designed to increase the probability that students will make accurate responses. Accordingly, ideal instruction occurs when instructional procedures are so carefully designed that students make no errors; however, students invariably err regardless of the teaching precision. In such cases, the following set of corrective feedback procedures is to be used with the DI model in small groups: (a) praise students making correct responses, (b) model correct response, (c) lead students in correct response, (d) test students by asking them to respond on their own, (e) alternate between erred example and other examples, and (f) give delayed test later in the lesson.

For high-level responses, restate or ask students to restate the rule or strategy used to arrive at the correct response. For instance, in teaching the spelling rule i before e except after c, students can state this rule and then spell the word.

Box 5.1 contains excerpts from a DI lesson that includes the primary components—demonstration, guided practice, and independent practice.

Guided Discovery Learning

From a philosophical perspective, the antithesis of DI is the pure form of discovery learning of which guided discovery is a derivation. Barlow (1985) defines discovery learning as a process of presenting students with problem situations and encouraging them to identify solutions through group interactions or individually. Assumptions are made regarding the learners' psychological state (i.e., learners are viewed as processors of information and problem solvers who are curious and motivated to learn, and who want to make sense of a situation).

Discovery learning methods emanate from a child-centered view of learning in which students make decisions about what they learn and how learning proceeds. There is little structure provided for students by teachers. The tight control that teachers maintain under a DI model is largely absent with GDL. There are few specific teaching behaviors to be followed, and the content and materials are not prearranged or tightly structured.

Jerome Bruner is the leading proponent of the discovery model. Based on his conceptualization of **"cognitive structure,"** Bruner (1966) emphasizes the importance of students learning the structures and re-

BOX 5.1

Example DI Lesson

The target skill being taught is two digit plus two digit addition with regrouping. This lesson has been preceded by instruction on prerequisite concepts (e.g., place value, regrouping, and so forth) and skills (e.g., basic math facts, procedures for regrouping, and so forth).

DEMONSTRATION

Ms. van Noord **models** the procedures for example problems by writing the computations and vocalizing the steps as she completes them:

"We begin with the ones column and add the two digits, 7 ones + 6 ones = 13 ones."

$$\begin{array}{r} 2\ 7 \\ +4\ 6 \\ \hline 13 \end{array}$$

"13 ones can be regrouped into 1 ten and 3 ones."

"So we can replace the 1 ten in the tens column and leave the 3 ones in the ones column."

$$\begin{array}{r} ^127 \\ +46 \\ \hline 3 \end{array}$$

"Next we add the digits in the tens column including the 1 ten we regrouped. 1 ten + 2 tens = 3 tens; 3 tens + 4 tens = 7 tens."

$$\begin{array}{r} ^127 \\ +46 \\ \hline 73 \end{array}$$

"Our complete sum is 7 tens and 3 ones or 73."

Ms. van Noord then introduces a second example problem, and, depending on the attentiveness of her small group of students, she may begin to include them in verbalizing parts of the computation or steps for completing the computations.

"Let's look at another example of two digit plus two digit addition with regrouping."

"We begin with the ones column and add the two digits. Let's say the addition together." (**Unison responding**.)

$$\begin{array}{r} 53 \\ +29 \end{array}$$

Ms. van Noord **signals** the students to respond together by pointing to the 3 and says "Begin." The teacher and group respond:

"3 ones + 9 ones = 12 ones."

$$\begin{array}{r} 5\ 3 \\ +2\ 9 \\ \hline 12 \end{array}$$

(continued)

BOX 5.1 *(continued)*

Ms. van Noord continues with the demonstration.

"Twelve ones can be regrouped into 1 ten and 2 ones."

$$\begin{array}{r}^{1}53\\+29\\\hline 2\end{array}$$

"So we replace the 1 ten in the tens column and leave the
2 ones in the ones column."

"Next we add the digits in the tens column including the
1 ten we regrouped. Let's say the addition together."

Ms. van Noord signals by pointing to the regrouped 1 ten and
says, "Begin." The teacher and group respond:

"1 ten + 5 tens = 6 tens; 6 tens + 2 tens = 8 tens."

$$\begin{array}{r}^{1}53\\+29\\\hline 82\end{array}$$

Ms. van Noord continues:

"Our complete sum is 8 tens and 2 ones or 82."

GUIDED PRACTICE

During guided practice, Ms. van Noord **leads** students in completing the computations and vocalizing the steps as **they** complete
them. The students write the computations on their worksheet
and together with the teacher they vocalize the steps. As more
examples are completed, the teacher fades her vocalizations until
students "talk through" the computations and steps by themselves.
Together the teacher and group of students complete the computations in the right column and vocalize the steps in the left column:

"Start with the ones column and add the two digits;
8 ones + 7 ones = 15 ones."

$$\begin{array}{r}2\ 8\\+3\ 7\\\hline 15\end{array}$$

"15 ones can be regrouped into 1 ten and 5 ones."

$$\begin{array}{r}^{1}28\\+37\\\hline 5\end{array}$$

"Replace the 1 ten in the tens column and leave 5 ones."

"Add the digits in the tens column. 1 ten + 2 tens = 3 tens;
3 tens + 3 tens = 6 tens."
"The sum is 6 tens and 5 ones or 65."

$$\begin{array}{r}^{1}28\\+37\\\hline 65\end{array}$$

These procedures are continued with other examples in **unison**.
Ms. van Noord intermittently has the members of the group com-

BOX 5.1 *(continued)*

plete an example individually (**tests**). When an individual student (John) errs, then Ms. van Noord initiates the **corrective feedback procedure**.

"Everyone is adding the ones column correctly and stating the steps."	Step 1 — Praise students making correct responses.
"Let's make sure that we replace the tens in the tens column."	Step 2 — Model correct response.

Ms. van Noord **models** the steps to example emphasizing the replacement steps. She continues with the corrective feedback procedures:

"Let's complete the same example problem together. Add the ones column. . ."	Step 3 — Lead students in correct response.
"John, say the steps that you followed to complete this example."	Step 4 — Test students individually.
"Do the next example problem by yourselves. As you write the additions, say the steps quietly to yourselves."	Step 5 — Alternate between erred example and other examples.

Ms. van Noord **monitors** students as they complete the examples.

"John, write the additions and say the steps for the last problem we did. . ."	Step 6 — Give delayed test later in the lesson.

INDEPENDENT PRACTICE

Once students have demonstrated 90% accuracy in responding during guided practice, then the teacher can have the group practice example problems on their own in the form of seatwork. Independent practice on the target skill 2 digit plus 2 digit addition with regrouping may not occur during the first few lessons. Instead, independent practice on the target skill is delayed until students are firm on the procedure. The first lessons usually involve demonstration and guided practice only.

lationships of structures of a field of study. By teaching generic problem-solving and information-processing techniques, students can learn how to learn independently. This "heuristic economy" is purported by Bruner as a means for accommodating the vast amounts of information that individuals must manipulate. School curricula should contain courses that transcend subject matter content and teach critical thinking skills.

From a discovery learning perspective, the purpose of instruction is to teach students to be independent problem solvers, to learn the generic steps to scientific inquiry and logical thinking. By learning the generic process of problem solving, it is believed that information from other content areas can be readily learned. Instruction is directed toward transferring the use of problem-solving strategies to new material and situations. Specific content information is learned incidentally through the introduction of novel problems requiring similar problem-solving strategies and involving new but similar information. The bottom line is that the process of problem solving supersedes any learning of content material (Ausubel, Novak, & Hanesian, 1978; Beihler & Snowman, 1982).

Proponents of discovery techniques argue that DI techniques are too simplistic and authoritarian. It is believed that DI methods are effective for low-level cognitive tasks, but discovery techniques using induction better facilitate the use of high-level cognitive skills. Also, the tight control that DI teachers exercise over content and instructional activities is criticized on the basis that students are taught to be passive and overly dependent on teachers and extrinsic rewards. With discovery techniques, students learn to be more independent learners, able to determine their own instructional needs.

GUIDED DISCOVERY LEARNING DEFINED   A variation of the pure form of discovery learning has been developed by Gagne (1970). Under Gagne's GDL model, curricular content and structure are integrated with a bottom-up, inductive approach to learning. Gagne asserts that learning is most effective when content is presented starting with the specific and moving to the general (i.e., bottom-up). Concepts or rules are learned by assembling the examples, making comparisons, identifying patterns, and then identifying the concept or rule that links the examples. A teacher's cues or hints and structured curricula are used to assist students to induce the concept or rule identification. Curricula are to be analyzed and the hierarchy developed from the top-down, but instruction begins at the bottom and moves to the top (Belkin & Gray, 1977).

Guided discovery methodology focuses on gaining specific content as well as on teaching generic problem-solving skills. Instead of solely focusing on teaching students to be independent problem solvers as is the case with the general format of discovery learning, GDL focuses on teachers guiding students through a logical series of problem-solving steps to better facilitate learning specific content.

PRINCIPAL COMPONENTS OF GUIDED DISCOVERY LEARNING

There are several components of GDL that are the foundation of its effectiveness. However, proponents of the guided discovery model do not delineate these components as clearly as the proponents of DI delineate its components. From what can be discerned, a set of identifiable components that characterize GDL is provided below (Ausubel et al., 1978).

Contrasts Contrasts are emphasized throughout this process by identifying and comparing the distinctive features of like concepts. These distinctive features determine the relationship among concepts and help students to discriminate concepts, such as a square from a rectangle. For instance, teachers guide students to identify the features of squares, such as the length of the sides, comparative length of different sides, the inside angles formed by each set of perpendicular sides, and its two-dimensionality. Other nonrelevant features also may be examined, such as the size and color. The distinctive features are then compared to other figures with the characteristics of squares used as the basis for the comparison.

Example Selection Example selection is critical for contrasts to be made. Examples are carefully selected and grouped by distinctive features so when they are presented to students void of a classification scheme, students will be able to identify the relationships themselves. By presenting numerous examples applicable to the target skill or concept, the teacher adds further cues as to the relationship shared by the concepts. For instance, in teaching the concept of a chair, a kitchen chair would be a good first example. It contains the standard features of a chair, and it is a form of chair that students would see frequently and in a number of different settings. Providing other examples of chairs with some variations from a kitchen chair, such as a living room chair (different shape and material) or a secretary's chair (different shape with wheel bases), would help students to form a concept set that accommodates varieties of form and enables students to identify distinctive features (e.g., the seat) and irrelevant features (e.g., wood and material). Gradually, less typical forms, such as a bean bag chair, can be introduced to further elaborate the concept set.

Informed Guessing Students are encouraged to make informed guesses by using information they have identified as the basis for asking questions that lead to further information about the concepts. In reading a story, for instance, a student may be using a self-questioning strategy that entails writing and answering questions about the content of each paragraph read based on information gained from previous paragraphs. The questions are used to aid in identifying and analyzing the concepts presented in the passage. Consequently, students are being taught to reflect on their state of understanding at any given time and to use questions to guide their acquisition of new information.

Awareness of the Underlying Problem-Solving Process If students are asked to focus on the process steps they use to solve problems, they can form their own self-regulating strategies for problem solving. An obvious example is solving math word problems. Students are given problems to solve and asked to state the steps used to determine the operation and identify the variables and constants.

Active Participation   Participation is encouraged by arranging students to work in various capacities as part of a group. In a group assignment, for example, students may be assigned or volunteer to record answers to questions or research other sources of information. The purpose of active participation is to ensure that students are actively involved in the process of solving problems, classifying information, or establishing rules.

The **concept teaching model** (Gregory, 1985) provides an example lesson format that incorporates the components of guided discovery.

1. Three to five well-chosen examples of the concept are presented one at a time. As they are presented, the teacher states, "This is an example of [concept name]."
2. Three to five well-chosen nonexamples are presented one at a time. The teacher states, "This is not an example of [concept name]."
3. Other stimuli representing the target concept or other concepts from the same form class are presented to the students. Students are asked to answer yes or no when asked, "Is this an example of [concept name]?"
4. The teacher, using leading questions, asks students to list the attributes of the examples and the nonexamples.
5. The teacher has the students construct a definition of the concept based on a list of attributes.
6. The teacher provides practice by pointing to examples and nonexamples of the concept and having students answer the question, "What is this an example of?"

Box 5.2 contains excerpts from a GDL lesson that include the steps from the concept-teaching model.

Presentation of Subject Matter

In addition to concerns about how to teach, developing and beginning teachers often worry about what to teach. Although the scope of this chapter does not include specific curricular content, a description of the type of subject matter taught by most teachers is presented. In most classrooms, two basic forms of subject matter, **concepts** and **academic rules**, are the focus of teaching and learning during any given day. These types of subject matter necessitate the use of specific steps that can be included within the more *general* procedures involved in using

BOX 5.2

Example GDL Lesson

The target concept being taught is story setting, a story grammar that describes the context in which a story takes place.

EXAMPLE AND NONEXAMPLE PRESENTATION

Mr. Elkins presents 3 examples listed on the chalkboard excerpted from narrative prose that illustrate story settings. Students are asked to read each silently.

"This is an example of a story setting from the story, 'Back of Burke.'"

The small western town was at the base of a range of steep mountains. Most people in Burke owned cattle ranches that surrounded the town.

"This is an example of a story setting from the story, 'Letter to the Editor.'"

Before he got dressed for school, Alan sat in his room with dirty clothes every-where. Posters of his favorite sports players hung on all four walls. Alan typed quickly on his new computer.

"This is an example of a story setting from the story, 'The Guilty Witness.'"

The sirens grew louder in the hot summer night's heat as the ambulance approached. Pat stood dazed by the sight of the bloody victim. Her mind raced back through the visions of what had just happened.

Mr. Elkins points to an adjacent chalkboard and has students silently read three nonexamples of story settings.

"This is *not* an example of a story setting."

It was all over. Adrian's cattle were back and the town was a safe place to live.

"This is *not* an example of a story setting."

Alan wasn't going to let that stop him. He was deter-mined to interview his hero.

(continued)

BOX 5.2 (continued)

"This is *not* an example of a story setting."	The jury returned their verdict to the judge. Pat knew what they had found from the expressions on their faces.

Mr. Elkins proceeds to have students open their textbooks to specific pages and read brief excerpts from several stories. After reading each, he asks, "Is this an example of a story setting?" The students respond either yes or no (**informed guessing and active participation**).

DEFINITION OR RULE INDUCTION

Next, Mr. Elkins asks a series of questions about the attributes of the examples and nonexamples in order to explicate **contrasts**, and the students respond.

"Let's look at our examples and nonexamples of story settings. What did you learn about the story in the first example?"	"The story is in a little town." "The name of the town is Burke." "People raise cows and stuff."

Mr. Elkins lists the students' responses on the chalkboard and continues to ask more leading questions.

"By learning these kinds of things, what does the story setting do for the reader?"	"Tells us things about the story."
"Yes, it does, but what kind of things does the story setting tell us?"	"Where the people live." "If it's day or night."
"Yes, good thinking. The story setting tells us information about where and when the story takes place."	

To confirm this conclusion, Mr. Elkins directs the students to look at the nonexamples to confirm that the statement, "story

BOX 5.2 (continued)

setting tells us information about where and when the story takes place," adequately distinguishes the examples from nonexamples (**contrast, informed guessing, and active participation**).

"Let's look at the nonexamples and see if they tell us where and when the story takes place. Read the first nonexample. Does this statement allow us to answer the questions where or when the story takes place?"

"Sort of, it says the town."

"But that could mean any town."

"Well, I guess it really doesn't tell exactly where."

"What about telling us when the story takes place?"

"No."

After reviewing a few more nonexamples, Mr. Elkins induces students to **construct a definition** of story setting.

"How can we complete the following sentence beginning—Story settings tell us. . . ."

"Where the story happens."
"When it takes place."

"Good, you've figured out the purpose of story settings. When in the story do we usually find the story setting?"

"In the first couple of pages."

"Yes, story settings tell us where and when a story takes place and is usually found at the beginning of the story."

Mr. Elkins posts this definition of a story setting on a bulletin board and uses it in subsequent lessons when asking students to identify story settings in their reading passages.

either DI or GDL. For instance, in using a DI format, what the teacher models, leads, and tests will be somewhat different when teaching concepts as opposed to teaching academic rules. Nonetheless, the same *general* DI procedures are used regardless of subject matter. This is equally true when using a GDL approach. Therefore, the relationship between the DI and GDL models and the presentation of concepts and academic rules is that the latter dictates more specific steps within the general framework of the former. Below is a description of how these two types of subject matter are presented effectively.

Presentation of Conceptual Knowledge

Concepts are the basis for categorizing and organizing our understanding about the world. They provide a hierarchical structure for superordinate and related subordinate categories of ideas or information. By categorizing information, we are better able to understand similarities and differences among various ideas or events and use information in more efficient ways. To describe conceptual structure, the analogy of a file cabinet is often used. Superordinate categories are the file drawers and within each drawer there are file folders, the subordinate categories, and within the file folders are sets of papers, the second tier of subordinate categories.

Before entering school, young children develop an extensive array of superordinate and subordinate concepts that help them to understand the relationships among people, places, and ideas. For instance, a 1-year-old child looks out the window and grunts with excitement at seeing a dog in the yard. Responsive parents point to the dog and say "dog." After repeated incidents, the child looks out the window, points and says "dog" much to the delight of his proud parents. A few days later, a cat strolls through the yard and the child points and says, "dog." The deflated parents say, "no, cat." Thus, the child begins to build a cognitive structure for classifying information about animals. In time, he will be able to classify and discriminate dogs from cats and that both are animals and not plants.

In school settings, a similar process takes place except that instruction is more formal and structured. Additionally, the concepts taught in schools are often more complex and abstract. Consequently, teachers structure the curriculum and activities to teach concepts in addition to responding to spontaneous incidents, or "teachable moments." Concept instruction, when done systematically, can maximize teaching efficiency and effectiveness.

Conceptual knowledge is the basis for all content areas. Language arts involve a seemingly infinite set of concepts about the human experience and the world in which we live. These concepts deal with the struggle among people, nature, and even supernatural powers. The foundation of mathematics comprises a set of fundamental concepts about numbers and their manipulation. The natural and social sciences also deal with a host of concepts used to categorize plants and animals and people and places. There is even a special category of concepts in the sciences called **laws and principles**. Both involve cause–effect relationships that explain natural and social phenomena. In the physical sciences, for instance, Newton's third law of motion is an explanation of the equilibrium of forces acting on each other. In the social sciences, principles are used to explain causal relationships such as the economics of supply and demand. Laws differ from principles in that they carry a greater deal of certainty about their ability to account for what happens in nature. Natural laws are absolute, but principles are only guidelines that have exceptions. Although concepts differ from subject to subject and there are special categories of concepts such as laws and principles, the teaching of conceptual knowledge can be presented using a common set of principles to guide instruction.

HOW TO TEACH CONCEPTS   Presentation of conceptual knowledge is centered around definitions of the concepts being taught. In order to teach students the category of information subsumed by the concept name, developing teachers must set the limits for what fits and what does not fit. This can be thought of as a conceptual basket. A determination must be made as to what will fit in one basket and not another, just as though the concept of sorting as applied to clothes washing was being taught in a secondary daily living skills class for Educably Mentally Handicapped students. First, the hierarchical structure of the categories must be determined (Fig. 5.1). With reference to the selector dial on the washing machine, Mr. Gunn, the teacher, might plan to start with three categories: permanent press, heavy duty, and regular. Next, remembering his bachelor training, the teacher separates whites from colors. So now Mr. Gunn has planned a two-tier system of sorting clothes requiring six baskets. In order to set limits, the teacher has to state the characteristics of the clothes that go into each basket, so he lists the essential attributes of the clothes for each basket. For example, to define white permanent press clothes, the teacher might say that it is those clothes that are 90% or more white (when clean) and made of a permanent press material. He now has a definition of white permanent press clothes that can be used to classify the heaps of filth piled up in the laundry room.

The definition has three components: **concept name** (e.g., white permanent press); **class term** (e.g., clothes); **essential attributes** (e.g., 90% or more white when clean and made of a permanent press material). The concept name simply serves as a label for the concept. The class term links the target concept to a broader conceptual category to which it belongs. The essential attributes define the parameters of the target

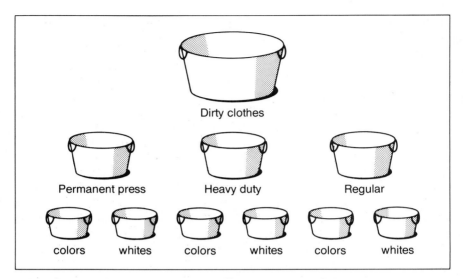

Dirty clothes

Permanent press   Heavy duty   Regular

colors   whites   colors   whites   colors   whites

FIGURE 5.1   Hierarchical structure of the categories of clothing used as analogs for the hierarchical structure of superordinate and subordinate concepts.

concept and help distinguish it from other related concepts (e.g., dark permanent press clothes or white heavy-duty clothes).

Definitions alone are insufficient for presenting conceptual knowledge. They are abstractions that need to be translated into more concrete examples. To do so, the class term and the essential attributes are used to identify those items that fit into the conceptual basket and those that do not. In examining the clothes pile, the students are taught to place each item of clothing in its appropriate basket by examining the item and first asking themselves whether or not it is a piece of clothing (the broad class of items) or some other item found in the dirty clothes pile. If it is a piece of clothing, then the students examine it more closely to determine the match between the essential attributes of conceptual baskets and the characteristics of the piece of clothing. If the piece of clothing is a white shirt (i.e., 90% or more white when clean) and made of a permanent press material, then it would be a good example of clothes that go into the white permanent press basket.

To complete the process of conceptualizing, the teacher needs to determine what does not fit in the baskets (i.e., nonexamples). The critical item for selecting nonexamples is the class term because it serves as a screening device for two types of nonexamples. Those items that are not members of the broader class are **between-class nonexamples**. They do not possess the essential attributes to even be a member of the broad class let alone a member of one of the subclasses. A wallet found in the middle of the clothes pile would be a gross nonexample of clothing. On the other hand, a pair of blue jeans would fit the class of clothing but

BOX 5.3

Procedural Options for Teaching Concepts

Define (give concept name, class term, and essential attributes), give examples and nonexamples

or

Give examples and nonexamples.

would not share either of the essential attributes for the white permanent press basket. Consequently, it would be a **within-class nonexample**. Within-class nonexamples have varying relations to the target concept (i.e., the more essential attributes an item of clothing shares with the target concept the more alike it is and the finer the discrimination needed to sort it). For example, in the white permanent press category, there are only two essential attributes that clothing must have in order to fit. So the degrees of fineness are limited to two, those pieces of clothing that have none of the essential attributes and those that share one essential attribute, but not the other.

These distinctions are important because the use of examples and varying degrees of nonexamples are critical in teaching students to discriminate among related concepts. By using clear examples that possess the essential attributes of the concept, students can more efficiently construct a stimulus set. After students have worked with a group of good examples and are firm on what fits in the conceptual basket, then the use of effective nonexamples can be used to decide what fits and what does not. This confirmation process is aided by moving from between-class to within-class nonexamples. It enables students to shape and fine tune their understanding of the target concept.

The presentation of conceptual knowledge is operationalized in one of two ways. First, teachers may use a **definition, examples, and nonexamples** to teach a concept (Box 5.3). They may model the concept by defining it and then show students a set of examples and nonexamples to form a more concrete understanding. This sequence is congruent with the DI teaching method. On the other hand, a teacher may introduce a set of examples and nonexamples and induce students to formulate a concept definition based on common characteristics. This approach is more typical of a GDL approach commonly used at the upper elementary grades and above when complex related concepts are taught in science, math, and literature.

Second, a teacher may choose to give (DI) or to induce (GDL) **examples and nonexamples** without stating a formal definition. This strategy is applicable to situations where a formal definition may be too complicated to be of value to the learner (e.g., teaching the concept of redness and blueness to preschoolers) or at the early stage of a spiral curriculum where a concept is developed at progressively higher levels throughout students' educational careers (e.g., the concept of a square when taught to preschoolers as a visual discrimination of shape versus teaching the concept to an elementary school child as a geometrical plane with essential characteristics involving sides, angles, and closedness (See Fig. 5.2).

Presentation of Academic Rules

A second type of subject matter that is taught on a large scale is an academic rule. Academic rules are procedures taht are followed to complete an academic task. Academic rules contain two elements: (a) a **situation or condition**, which denotes when or where a procedure is to be used, and (b) a **command**, which pinpoints what is to be done (Box 5.4). For example, students are taught when writing a paragraph to indent the first line. The situation or condition is "when writing a paragraph"

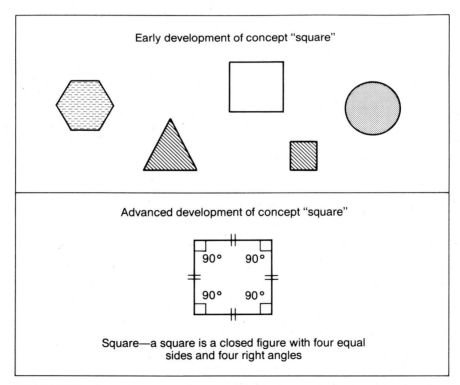

FIGURE 5.2   At early stages of concept development during preschool and primary grades, students learn to discriminate using examples and nonexamples; later in a spiral curriculum, concepts are further developed through formal definitions, examples, and nonexamples.

BOX 5.4

Steps for Teaching Academic Rules

1. State the academic rule.
   - Condition or situation.
   - Procedural step(s).
2. Apply the rule to examples.

---

and the command is "indent the first line." More complex academic rules contain a situation or condition and a series of commands that represent the steps needed to complete a task. For instance, students being taught to use Multipass (Alley & Deshler, 1979), a study-skill strategy, are instructed that when you set out to read a passage, first do a survey pass, then a size-up pass, and finally a sort-out pass.

Academic rules also operationalize the application of conceptual knowledge. A prime example is mathematics. There are numerous procedures for doing computations and problem solving that entail the use of conceptual knowledge. An example is the concept of place value, the idea that in a base 10 system the placement of a number in a left to right progression will determine the factor of the units it represents. For students to understand what it means to "carry" or "regroup" a number from one column to another, they must learn the concept of place value. Then, the academic rule for "carrying" or "regrouping" makes sense to students (i.e., they recognize that the digit they are regrouping represents sets of 10, 100, and so forth).

How to Teach Academic Rules   The principles for teaching academic rules are relatively simple. A teacher needs to state (DI) or induce students to formulate (GDL) the rule including the condition or situation and the command(s). Next, the rule must be applied to examples, and, ultimately, students need to be able to distinguish when and where the rule is used appropriately. For instance, when the academic rule for decoding CVCe words is being taught, the rule must be stated or discovered and applied to words that fit the pattern. Students then practice decoding the sounds of example words. Using a DI procedure, the teacher points to the chalkboard and states the academic rule as written:

- "When a consonant, vowel, consonant is followed by a final e (CVCe), the vowel is long and the final e is silent" (**model**).
- "All right. When I signal, say the rule with me. When a consonant. . . ." (**lead**).
- "What is the rule, Sandra?" (**test**).

After several opportunities to practice, the teacher demonstrates the application of the rule and provides guided practice.

1. "Let's look at the words on the board and see how the rule works."

| came |
| sale |
| tide |

2. "I'll write the pattern above the word and sound the word" (**model**).

came	CVCe
	came

sale	CVCe
	sale

tide	CVCe
	tide

3. "Let's try the next two together. When I signal, say whether the letter I am pointing to is a consonant, a vowel, or the final e" (**lead**).

| CVCe |
| mine |

| CVCe |
| pole |

4. Let's sound out each word when I signal" (**lead**).

mine

| CVCe |
| mine |

pole

| CVCe |
| pole |

5. "Write the pattern above the next word and sound it out. . . ." (**test**).

| cake |

After students have accurately stated and applied the rule using examples, then nonexamples would be introduced in this or a subsequent lesson so that students learn when the rule is appropriate (examples) and not appropriate (nonexamples).

Learning Stages

Another consideration in using either a DI or GDL approach is the progression of students through the stages of skill development. As students' conceptual knowledge and academic skills improve, the DI and GDL procedures are modified to accommodate mastery. When initially learning a new concept or skill, the student characteristically makes numerous mistakes, requires cues and prompts, and needs corrective feedback. But, with instruction and practice, students gradually become able to conceptualize information or execute the skill. This is clearly evident when they are learning to decode and recognize words in print. At first, they read each individual word slowly, often saying the wrong sound or leaving a sound out. Teachers have to model letter-sound correspondences and sounding-out procedures. Gradually, young readers decode or recognize words with greater speed and accuracy as a result of instruction and practice. Ultimately, they are able to read fluently many varied types of reading material at school and home. Learning to read exemplifies the stages of learning through which students pass when learning a new concept or skill. These stages include concept or skill **acquisition, fluency building, maintenance,** and **generalization** (Fig. 5.3).

Acquisition (Introduction and Discrimination)

The acquisition stage of learning is characterized by naïve learners and the precision of developing teachers. Students at this stage typically make frequent errors when attempting to use a target concept or skill, but gradually respond more and more accurately. Teachers provide effective **instructional antecedents**, which are characterized in this stage of learning by extensive direction or guidance, prompts, and cues that assist students in responding accurately. Through careful selection of examples and clear definitions of concepts or clear rule statements, teachers structure learning in ways that decrease the complexity of the learning environment and increase the probability that students will respond in a desired fashion.

The key principle associated with instructional antecedents at the acquisition stage is clear communication (Englemann & Carnine, 1982). This is accomplished by the teacher either providing directly or guiding students to develop clear concept definitions or academic rules. Definitions contain distinctive attributes that set the target concept apart from other similar concepts. Academic rules effectively describe the situation in which rules are appropriate and provide clear steps to execute the skills. Additionally, clarity of communication is provided through the selection of effective examples. During the acquisition stage, examples should contain the prototypical dimensions of the concept or provide

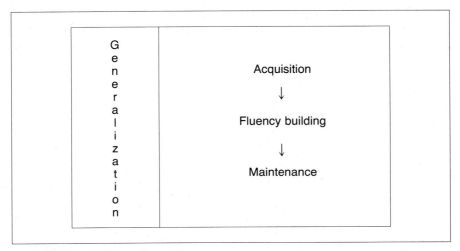

FIGURE 5.3 Stages of learning.

an easy stimulus for executing an academic rule. The reference earlier to using a kitchen chair as a prototypical example is applicable here. Similarly, using the word *mat* would be a good example for introducing the CVC sounding-out rule, whereas the multisyllable word *material* would not.

The acquisition stage can be divided into two levels: introduction and discrimination. The differences between these two levels are minimal but significant. The **introduction level** entails the use of examples only, and the **discrimination level** entails the use of examples and nonexamples. During the introduction level, the examples-only format helps to establish a pattern of accurate responding. When students respond accurately, those responses are reinforced by the students' sense of success and by teacher praise. During the discrimination level, learning is solidified by having students distinguish between examples and nonexamples (i.e., they are able to determine whether or not the stimulus fits the concept category or fits the situation for using an academic rule).

The two levels occur sequentially when using DI procedures but are presented in a more simultaneous fashion when using GDL procedures. Students move from the introduction to the discrimination level when they respond accurately to examples of the target concept or rule. The time spent at the introduction level varies with the complexity of the response being taught. The presentation of 3 or 4 examples during 5 minutes of instruction may be sufficient. On the other hand, instruction at the introduction level may require numerous examples being presented over 3 or 4 days before nonexamples are introduced. Similarly, several lessons may be needed at the discrimination level before mastery is attained.

Teaching the reading strategy of skimming can be used to exemplify instruction of an academic rule at the acquisition stage of learning. Using a DI approach, the teacher lists the steps for the procedure on posterboard and uses it as the focus of a bulletin board in the front of the room (permanent model). Before reading a passage, the teacher first **demonstrates** the steps. Later, the teacher **leads** the students in reading the steps and applying them to their daily reading passage. The skimming procedure, to this point, is applied to appropriate passages for which skimming is suited (i.e., introduction level using examples only). As students respond by accurately following the steps, the teacher gives them passages that are very short, for which skimming is not necessary (i.e., discrimination level using examples and nonexamples).

If a teacher uses a GDL approach to teach skimming, he would demonstrate using appropriate example passages and say, "This is an example of skimming." Then the teacher would fully read the short passages (i.e., nonexamples) and say, "This is *not* an example of skimming." The next step would be to ask a series of guiding questions to induce students to identify the steps for skimming and to determine when it is appropriately used. Under the GDL approach, the presentation of examples and nonexamples is done in more of a simultaneous rather than sequential manner.

Fluency Building

The second stage of learning, fluency building, is characterized by students maintaining high rates of accuracy and increasing the speed with which they make a response. Once students have demonstrated consistent accurate responding, the focus of instruction changes to speed and accuracy. Instructional activities at the fluency-building stage involve the student in fast-paced drill. The use of 1-minute timings to measure the student's rate of performance, as done in precision teaching, is an example of a fluency-building activity. Guided and independent practice sessions are scheduled on a daily basis to provide massed or concentrated amounts of practice. Once a prescribed level of fast and accurate responding is attained, the skill is considered mastered.

During the fluency-building stage and continuing through the maintenance stage, the basic strategy is to wean students from their dependence on the teacher and the structures that have been built into the learning environment, such as demonstrations of the skill, instructions to perform the skill, and prompts to perform the skill (Wollery, Bailey, & Sugai, 1988). **Fading out** means that developing teachers monitor student progress and, as appropriate, they decrease the intensity and frequency of instructional antecedents. In the skimming example, for instance, the teacher moves students through the introduction and discrimination levels with elaborate and frequent demonstrations, prompts, and praise for accurate responding. As students are able to discriminate when and when not to use skimming, the teacher begins focusing on fast and accurate responding in the fluency-building stage. At this time, the teacher reminds students intermittently of the steps and instructs them to use the bulletin board as a reference.

The same fading procedure is necessary for those events that follow the use of a target skill (i.e., consequences). Teachers diminish the intensity of positive reinforcement. By moving from a continuous schedule to an intermittent schedule, the frequency of positive reinforcement is reduced. Initially, students are praised every time they successfully implement the skimming steps. As they become more accurate, the teacher praises them every 2 instances, then every 5.

Maintenance

Maintenance is the third stage of learning during which previously acquired concepts or skills are practiced for retention. The weaning process is continued by further fading of antecedent procedures and consequences.

For example, once students demonstrate fluent skimming, the teacher begins implementing maintenance strategies. First, the posterboard containing the skimming steps is replaced with a poster containing a simple prompt — "skim before you read." The poster is moved from a prominent position in front of the room to the side of the room. Second, the teacher intermittently reminds students to skim when they appear not to be using the strategy.

These steps are taken to help students adapt to using skimming in a more natural environment. The teacher transforms the antecedents from contrived instructional techniques (i.e., demonstration and leading) to more naturally occurring events (i.e., the poster prompt and intermittent verbal reminders to skim). Importantly, it is necessary to recognize that the beginning steps for maintaining skills are initiated from the first stages of instruction (Wollery, Bailey & Sugai, 1988).

As in the fluency-building stage, speed and accuracy are emphasized in maintenance activities. However, the practice sessions are spaced apart in intervals ranging from 1 week to 1 month. They may take the form of an **end-of-the-week** or **end-of-the-month review**. As with the instructional antecedents and consequences for skimming, the regularity of explicit practice and review of the procedures are gradually faded. Maintenance is based on the axiom, "What you don't use, you lose."

Generalization

The ultimate educational outcome that underlies every instructional activity is to have the students function better in the world outside the school, either during or after their school years. This is achieved by fostering generalization of what is learned to other situations and times. Exhibiting learned responses in places other than where they were taught is referred to as **setting generalization**. For responses learned in a resource room, setting generalization occurs when the responses are performed in the regular classroom or at home. When responses are made after training conditions have been faded completely, then a second form of generalization, **time generalization**, has occurred. For example, a month after a unit of instruction on skimming, a student uses the strategy when reading a magazine during free reading time.

In facilitating both forms of generalization, three sets of variables need to be considered: antecedent, response, and consequence (Wollery et al., 1988). As mentioned above, instructional antecedents take the form of teachers demonstrating, leading, and prompting students in making a conceptual or academic rule response. To facilitate maintenance, the intensity and frequency of antecedents need to be faded out gradually with the aim of using naturally occurring antecedents to trigger a response. The objective is to maintain the response, but an additional objective is to facilitate setting generalization. **Naturally occurring antecedents** are operationally defined as those antecedents that occur in the setting to which the child needs to generalize the response. If resource room teachers want to prepare students to generalize a concept or rule to the regular classroom, they need to observe how the regular classroom teacher triggers responses. Using the skimming example, if the regular classroom teacher uses a verbal prompt (e.g., "remember to skim your passage before reading"), then the resource-room teacher should use the same prompt so the student can make a setting generalization. Often, though, simply matching the antecedents will not suffice. The resource-room teacher may need to tell students to use the procedure in the regular classroom and vice versa. Ultimately, both teachers should fade out their prompts completely.

Behavior variables are attributes of the responses that students are taught. Generalization is more likely to occur if the behaviors selected for instruction have a high degree of utility in the target setting or over time. Students must be able to recognize that exhibiting the target academic behavior will be beneficial in some way. The benefits may be in the form of gaining reinforcement or the independence derived from learning new skills. These benefits should be conveyed explicitly to the students so they are made aware of why they are learning a concept or academic rule.

Careful structuring of **consequence variables** can aid generalization significantly. The first strategy for manipulating the consequences of behavior to promote generalization is to develop the use of social reinforcers. Social reinforcers are important because they are naturally occurring and are used most frequently in classrooms as the primary means of reinforcement. Social reinforcers come in a variety of forms including smiles, verbal praise, pats on the shoulder, eye contact, and teacher attention. The second strategy is to prepare students for the usually thin schedule of reinforcement that occurs in most classrooms. In remedial and special classrooms, students are often systematically or arbitrarily put on a very dense schedule of reinforcement. Without thinning to levels equivalent to those in the regular classroom, the behavior may not generalize at all or will extinguish after a short period of time. The third strategy is to increase systematically the gap between the occurrence of the target response and the introduction of reinforcement. Such delays are designed to acclimate students to classrooms with larger numbers of children and fewer adults. In such environments, teachers and paraprofessionals or volunteers are unable to get to every child as often as in a remedial or special classroom where the adult to student ratio is lower. The fourth strategy also helps students to adjust to thin reinforcement schedules or delays in reinforcement by others. Teach students to self-reinforce for appropriate use of conceptual knowledge and academic rules. Self-verbalizations such as, "you did it, big guy," a discrete little dance around the desk, or "low-fiving" themselves are effective ways in which students can self-reinforce.

Lesson Development

The discussion to this point has been focused on the principal elements of effective instruction for the sake of identification and analysis. Of course, developing and beginning teachers should realize instruction is never a neat little prescriptive package with totally distinct and separate parts. It is an integrated mass of interactive elements that vary in their form and sequence. The section below presents this integrated whole in the context of a sequence of lesson development. It is a description of three very general sequential elements of a lesson: initiating a lesson, engaging students during instruction, and closing a lesson. The section on lesson formats that follows is more detailed, providing the specific sequence for lessons that incorporate **direct instruction** or **guided discovery techniques** for teaching **concepts** and **academic rules** at different **stages of learning.**

Introducing a Lesson

The beginning of a lesson should accomplish three basic objectives: gain students' attention, orient students to the lesson content and format, and link old content to new. (See Box 5.5.)

GAINING ATTENTION   Learning is characterized by active participation in the manipulation of concepts and rules either covertly through mental activity or overtly through responses like talking or writing. Regrettably to those who are looking for an easy way to learn, unconscious, inattentive activities like listening to foreign language audio tapes while sleeping does not result in learning. The first step in lesson development is to gain the students' attention before engaging them in conscious efforts to manipulate concepts or rules.

There are some very simple and easy ways this can be done.

1. Effective developing teachers start lessons on time, so that students come to expect that a schedule is in place and will be followed.
2. They cue students that the lesson is to begin either by sounding a bell or buzzer, making a statement like "let's get started," or switching the lights on and off.
3. Teachers can become more creative in their lesson initiation by using more elaborate techniques that spur student interest and curiosity. For example, a pet rattlesnake placed in a conspicuous location in

BOX 5.5

Example of Lesson Introduction

Mr. Ketcher is in the middle of a unit plan on home budgets. During the past couple of weeks, he has been covering concepts and academic rules related to using a checking account. Mr. Ketcher has already introduced concepts such as current balance, check charges, debits, and credits. Also, he has introduced the academic rules for filling out checks and maintaining a running record of transactions. Today, he is going to introduce the concept of an Automatic Teller Machine (ATM) and the procedures for its use. Mr. Ketcher uses the following discourse to introduce the lesson, including **gaining attention, orienting,** and a **lesson initiating review**:

"OK, class, park it and eyes on the front of the class—that includes you, James." **(gaining attention)**

"Remember, that we have been discussing home budgets for the past couple of weeks; the last few days we have focused on checking accounts. Today, we are going to discuss Automatic Teller Machines and the procedures for using them. We are going to practice using an ATM using our computer, and next week we are going to apply for ATM cards." **(orientation)**

"Let's review first what we have covered so far relating to checking accounts. First, we discussed the concept of current balance and said that it is the amount of money that remains in your account to date." **(teacher stating review material)**

(continued)

BOX 5.5 *(continued)*

"We also talked about the concept of a running record. How did we define the term running record?"

"Yes, Clyde, the running record is the section in the check book where we enter the amount of withdrawals, deposits, and current balance."

"Hey, I have used some of those fancy banking terms like withdrawal and deposit. What is the difference between withdrawals and deposits?" (**teacher asking review**)

"Good man, Henry, withdrawals are the amounts of money we take out of the account and deposits are the amounts we put into the account."

"It is the part of the check book where we write down how much checks were and any money we put in."

"We take out money. That is a withdrawal. When we put in money, that's a deposit."

Mr. Ketcher continues the review of major points by asking students further questions about how to keep the running record, and so forth, and then moves into the new material on ATMs. Students should now be aware of the important concepts and rules they have already covered and be ready to use that content in conjunction with the discussion of ATMs.

the classroom is sure to get students to focus their attention on the upcoming lesson.

4. Soliciting students to participate in an exciting lesson-initiating activity, such as playing word bingo, is effective.
5. Wearing an article of clothing that is unusual and related to the lesson topic can also stir interest.

ORIENTATION Orienting students by providing a brief overview of the lesson sequence will make them aware of content to be covered and the activities they will engage in during the lesson. For instance, in orienting students to a reading lesson, a teacher may say, "Today we are going to read a story about a pirate ship manned by a crew of ghosts. First, we are going to talk about pirates and ghosts, then we are going to review the self-questioning procedures we have been using during silent reading. Then we will read and discuss the story." In addition to telling the students about the lesson to follow, the teacher has established a bridge among what has been taught in previous lessons, the self-questioning strategy, and what is to take place during the present lesson. This helps students to recognize the link among successive lessons by cueing them to the fact that concepts and rules taught earlier will be used in subsequent lessons.

LESSON-INITIATING REVIEW   To establish further the links among a set of lessons, teachers often engage students in a lesson-initiating review. During a block of time, usually between 2 and 10 minutes, teachers highlight pertinent information in one of two ways. They may simply state for the students the relevant information for the upcoming lesson, emphasizing critical information. A second form may have the teacher ask a series of questions in order to have students rehearse information about concepts and academic rules. This form of review has the added benefit of providing an overlapping practice session: information is not only reviewed, but students practice verbalizing or applying the content.

ENGAGING STUDENTS DURING INSTRUCTION   Teaching at any stage of learning is going to entail a varying degree of interaction between the student and the teacher. Two critical features of teacher–student interactions are the teacher's questioning skills and treatment of students' responses.

Questioning Students The teacher's questioning skills are important because the questions frame the responses received from students. They determine the complexity of students' responses in terms of the level of cognitive processing required and the degree of elaboration. For instance, teachers may ask students questions that require knowledge, comprehension, application, analysis, synthesis, or evaluation of information (see Box 5.6). It is important that teachers know the type of cognitive processing and response desired and are able to form questions that emit the desired response (Martin, 1979). In teaching a lesson on the concept of helping, for example, a teacher may want students to recall some basic facts from a story about a mouse, an elephant, and a lion, and therefore asks, "What two animals helped each other?" This requires a relatively low level of cognitive processing and a brief response. In contrast, the teacher asks the class, "Why is it so odd that a mouse saved the elephant?" Here students are asked to analyze the relationship between the animals, which requires a more complex level of cognitive processing and a more elaborate verbal response.

A related strategy for questioning is **mixing the types of questions** so that a variety of responses are required (Dunkin & Biddle, 1974;

BOX 5.6

Hierarchy of Questions Ranging from Low-Level to High-Level Cognitive Processing Related to Social Studies

Knowledge:	Who is the president of the United States?
Comprehension:	Why are there two Houses in the U.S. Congress?
Application:	What is an example of a legislative "pork barrel"?
Analysis:	What is the relationship between the spread of communism and the president's defense policies?
Synthesis:	How do interest rates, inflation, and trade deficits affect monetary policy?
Evaluation:	Has the president done an effective job in stimulating the economy?

Low-Level Thinking ⟶

High-Level Thinking ⟵

Rosenshine, 1971). Often developing teachers fixate on lower-level recognition and recall questions. These are certainly the easiest type of question to ask, but the content of academic instruction should require students to do more than recognize and recall. Once basic factual information is presented or developed, teachers need to require students to make responses that involve comprehension, application, analysis, synthesis, evaluation, and judgment. The above questioning example involving the helping relationship between the elephant and the mouse illustrates how teachers can take basic factual information (i.e., recall of who the animals were) and build on that base to the level of analyzing this relationship to determine why animals, and for that matter people, help each other.

In addition to knowing what types of questions to ask, developing teachers need to know how to ask questions. Two strategies need to be applied. First, it is important that the teacher **pose a question first**, then call on a student to respond, rather than calling a specific student's name and then asking the question. For instance, the more effective strategy would be to ask, "Why did the mouse help the elephant?" . . . (pause) . . . "Yes, Miguel," rather than, "Miguel, why did the mouse help the elephant?" The first strategy enables the teacher to get more "bang for their buck" (i.e., all students must covertly process a response because they do not know who will be called on to make the overt response). Consequently, a teacher can emit an overt response and several covert responses with a single question. A second benefit is that students are less likely to engage in off-task behaviors because they are less able to predict who will be called. When the student's name is called before the question is posed, other students are inclined to believe they are off the hook and do not need to attend to the question that follows.

The second strategy is called **wait time** (Rowe, 1974). One form of wait time, **wait-time I**, refers to the gap in time between the presentation of a question and when a student is called on to respond. By waiting 3 to 5 seconds after posing the question, the teacher provides students with time to formulate a response. The use of wait time I results in a greater frequency of accurate responses. Wait time I is used at the early stages of skill acquisition and when desired responses entail higher levels of cognitive processing. However, during fluency-building drills and practice activities, when speed and accuracy are being developed, wait time is not desirable.

A second form of wait time, **wait time II**, refers to the gap in time between the completion of the student's response and the subsequent teacher's response. Using the above story of the helpful mouse, wait time II would occur following Miguel's response to the teacher's question, "Why did the mouse help the elephant? . . . (wait time I) . . . "Yes, Miguel." Miguel replies, "Because the elephant had helped the mouse." . . . (wait-time II) . . . Miguel continues, "When the lion was going to eat the mouse, the elephant scared him away and the mouse was saved." Wait time II provides students with time to contemplate their response and subsequently elaborate or modify it. This results in increased accuracy and more elaborate responses. Wait time II is used more often when teachers ask questions that require responses generated from higher levels of cognitive processing.

Providing Feedback Once questions have been asked and responses made, teachers evaluate the students' responses and provide feedback. For accurate responses, teachers usually praise students, but often they do not inform students as to what was praiseworthy about their response. Statements that praise students and provide information that indicates how they can receive praise in the future is referred to as **specific academic praise**. Such statements refer to the cognitive processes, strategies, or behaviors used to formulate the response. For example, the statement, "Excellent answer, Lindsay. You made the connection between the two important events in the story," contains a praise component and indicates to the student that "making the connection" is what was praiseworthy. In contrast, by simply saying, "Excellent answer, Lindsay," the focus is on the response, not the process by which it was derived. The process is important because it provides generalizable guidelines for making similar excellent responses in the future.

Other ways that teachers can treat students' accurate responses include feedback statements that paraphrase, elaborate, or clarify students' responses. **Paraphrasing** entails restating what the student said or did in order to emphasize the responses and to ensure that others observed the response. An example from the reading lesson above would be the teacher stating, "That nasty lion did try to eat the poor little mouse," following a student's response, "That bad lion was going to eat 'em." **Elaboration** is feedback that uses students' responses as a core to which the teacher adds further information. For example, a student responds to the question, "Why do lions have such big claws?" by stating that "They need them to climb trees." The teacher then states, "Yes, they often hide in trees, wait for animals to walk nearby, and then they jump on them." A **clarifying response** is used to either confirm what students have said or to reformulate the response in a more comprehensible way. For instance, when asked to state why people (or the mouse and elephant) become friends, a student responds, "Well, because they sort of think they're cool and they do stuff together, you know, like that." A teacher's clarifying response would be, "So you are saying that people become friends because they are interested in doing the same kinds of things, like going to concerts or playing basketball, and enjoy doing those things with each other."

These forms of positive feedback are important because they provide information about students' responses without providing any explicit praise. Keeping in mind that gradual thinning of reinforcement is important for the maintenance and generalization of behaviors, the systematic use of combinations of academic praise and other feedback techniques is an important teacher strategy.

When students' responses are inaccurate, teachers can use the steps for corrective feedback associated with teaching low-level content using the DI model. Another set of options is to rephrase the question or request, provide additional cues to guide the student's response, or indicate to students that the response is inaccurate and help them to identify the nature of the inaccuracy. **Rephrasing** entails presenting the stimulus question in a slightly different form that may clarify the desired response or refocus students' attention. If a teacher asks, "How did the elephant use his trunk?" and the student responds, "He eats peanuts with it," the teacher may rephrase the question, "Let me ask that question a different way. In the story when the lion was coming closer, how did the elephant use his trunk?" Providing **additional cues** is synonymous with giving "hints." For example, a teachers asks, "How did the lion sneak up on the mouse?" and when the student's response is inaccurate, the teacher adds, "Remember the tall grass."

A third option for teachers is to **indicate that the response is inaccurate** and help students to determine what the correct response is. This may be done by telling students their response is inaccurate and then redirecting the question to another student or to tell the student why the response does not fit the question. For instance, in the case where a teacher asks students to state the characteristics of someone who is helpful, and a student responds, "They leave other people alone," the teacher may redirect the same or a rephrased question to another student (e.g., "What do helpful people do to help other people?") or tell the student that the response is incorrect and why (e.g., "Being helpful is judged by the things you do for others, not by the things you don't do").

CLOSING A LESSON: ENDING REVIEW   The closing review provides an end-point and summary of what has occurred during the lesson. The review cues students to the impending transition from one lesson to another. In addition, it is an opportunity for the students to conceptualize the relationships among the discrete content elements of the lesson. For instance, as part of a written expression lesson, the teacher can guide students in restating the rule for writing a complete sentence and showing two or three examples and nonexamples of the rule application.

The review component proceeds in the same way as a lesson-initiating review, either by the teacher making verbal summary statements or physical demonstrations of the target responses, or by asking a series of guiding questions to emit the responses from students. The latter is the preferred format because it increases the opportunities for students to practice responses actively. With the sentence writing lesson, the teacher might say, "When writing a complete sentence, a subject and predicate must be included. An example would be 'The dog barked' or 'The cow jumped over the moon.' On the other hand, 'The black angry dog' is *not* an example because it doesn't have a predicate." A guided review, however, would entail the teacher asking, "What is the rule for writing complete sentences?" Subsequently, examples and nonexamples would be induced.

Lesson Format for Direct Instruction and Guided Discovery Learning Approaches

To summarize the elements of this chapter, the following section is designed to show in outline form how the principles of DI and GDL can be overlayed with the procedures for presenting concepts and academic rules at each of the stages of learning. This integrated format can be used in structuring the development of lessons in a manner that incorporates the critical elements of effective instruction.

Acquisition Stage — Introduction

As described earlier, this initial stage of learning requires significant amounts of teacher time and attention directed toward planning and monitoring students' responses to target concepts and academic rules. The introduction phase of the acquisition stage is characterized by precise demonstrations and guided practice using examples only. The following sequence exemplifies this and other features of lesson development at this stage of learning:

1. Gain student attention and orient students with an outline of the activities to be completed during the lesson.
2. Link the present lesson with previous lessons by **reviewing** related concepts or academic rules previously taught.
3. During the **demonstration**, model or induce through questioning the target concept or academic rule. Use **examples only.**
4. During **guided practice**, provide extensive opportunities to respond through practice activities involving the target concept or academic rule. Use extensive prompts and cues to emit responses involving **examples only.**
   a. **Lead** or induce students in stating definition, attributes, or rule.
   b. **Lead** or induce students in identifying concept examples or applying rules to examples using signaling to lead choral responses when appropriate.
      1. Pose a question, wait 3 to 5 seconds, then call on a student for a response.
      2. Recognize a student's response by giving academic praise, paraphrasing, amplifying, clarifying, or redirecting to another student.
   c. Provide **corrective feedback** as needed.
5. For **independent practice**, provide daily activities involving examples of the target concept or academic rule that students can perform with minimal prompting or cues. Students should be able to perform tasks with **90% accuracy or better**.
   a. Give directions to complete the activity tasks.
   b. Lead the students in completing example tasks.
   c. Indicate the deadline for completing activity.
   d. Circulate and assist the students as needed.
   e. Review students' responses to activity tasks.
6. Engage students in an **ending review** to summarize the content covered in the lesson and to signal the transition to the next lesson.

Acquisition Stage — Discrimination

The acquisition stage continues with the introduction of nonexamples used to teach students to discriminate between the target concept or academic rule and other similar concepts or academic rules. Accurate discrimination responses are indicators that students are solidifying their skills. The steps are identical to those under the acquisition–introduction stage, except that **examples and nonexamples** are used during instruction.

Fluency-Building Stage

Lessons at the fluency-building stage entail independent practice activities. Teachers simply introduce the activity and monitor students' responses to a few example stimuli to ensure that they are making responses with relative degrees of speed and accuracy. To ensure that students use their time productively and that fluency is built, the following steps are suggested:

1. Gain student attention and orient students with an outline of the activities to be completed during the lesson.
2. Link the present lesson with previous lessons by **reviewing** related concepts or academic rules previously taught.
3. Provide **daily independent practice** activities that engage students in responding to examples and nonexamples of target concept or academic rule. The focus of practice is on **high rates of speed and accuracy.** Students should be able to perform tasks with **90% accuracy or better.**
   a. Give directions to complete the activity tasks.
   b. Lead the students in completing example tasks.
   c. Indicate the deadline for completing the activity.
   d. Circulate and assist the students as needed.
   e. Review students' responses to activity tasks.
4. Engage students in an **ending review** to summarize the content covered in the lesson and to signal the transition to the next lesson.

Maintenance Stage

The primary characteristic of the maintenance stage is that practice schedules are distributed over longer intervals of time. These weekly or monthly practice activities are geared to assist students in retaining appropriate levels of fast and accurate responding. As the interval of time between sessions increases, the need to conduct a brief review of the target concept or academic rule will increase. Additionally, instructional

antecedents and reinforcement should be thinned. The following steps
are guidelines for lesson development:

1. Gain student attention and orient students with an outline of the
   activities to be completed during the lesson.
2. Link the present lesson with previous lessons by **reviewing** related
   concepts or academic rules previously taught.
3. Provide **weekly or monthly independent practice** activities that engage students in responding to examples and nonexamples of the
   target concept or academic rule. The focus of practice is on **high
   rates of speed and accuracy.** Students should be able to perform
   tasks with **90% accuracy or better**.
   a. Give directions to complete the activity tasks.
   b. Lead the students in completing example tasks.
   c. Indicate the deadline for completing the activity.
   d. Circulate and assist the students as needed.
   e. Review students' responses to activity tasks.
4. **Fade out** the frequency and intensity of response antecedents and
   consequences using intermittent schedules.
5. Engage students in an **ending review** to summarize the content covered in the lesson and to signal the transition to the next lesson.

Generalization Stage

Unlike the earlier stages of learning, the steps for teaching generalization
outlined below are not taught in separate discrete lessons. Instead, these
steps are incorporated to varying extents into lessons at all previous
learning stages. The primary characteristic of generalization instruction
is that students are encouraged to use their skills in other settings and
at different times. The following suggestions are means to set the occasion for generalization: (a) use instructional antecedents and consequences that occur in other settings, (b) use materials found in other
settings for practicing target concepts or academic rules, (c) use delayed
and intermittent reinforcement schedules, (d) teach students to self-reinforce fast and accurate responding, (e) encourage other teachers to reinforce students' use of target concepts and academic rules, and (f) tell
students to use concepts and academic rules in other classrooms.

When to Use Specific Elements of Effective Instruction

The lesson-format outline and the overall discussion in this chapter deal
primarily with **what** effective teachers do. The classroom examples provided throughout the chapter are aimed at illustrating **how** effective

teachers operationalize the principals of effective instruction. Another important aspect of effective teaching deals with knowing **when** to use certain key elements. Below are some guidelines to assist developing teachers in making decisions about when they implement specific elements of effective instruction provided in the lesson-format section above.

Teaching Concepts and Academic Rules Using the DI and GDL Models

First, decisions must be made regarding when to use either of the two general models of instruction presented in the chapter. The DI model can be used with either concepts or academic rules. It is more often used with content that entails rote learning of basic facts and skills. It can be used, however, with content and learning tasks that involve high-order cognitive processes such as synthesis, analysis, and application. In the latter case, the concept definition and examples and nonexamples are given by the teacher but the students are asked to apply the concept to novel situations, thus requiring high-order cognitive processes. The GDL model, on the other hand, can be used with both concepts and academic rules but is more frequently used with concept induction. GDL is more often used with high-order content and learning tasks than for rote learning.

The second decision is when to treat content as concepts or academic rules. Concepts are ubiquitous; they are a part of all content area material including basic tool skills such as reading and math, social science, science, vocational subjects, and daily living skills. When the developing teacher is teaching categories of information, the material should be treated as conceptual knowledge. Academic rules are not so pervasive; they are associated more with basic tool skills and, to some extent, other content areas, such as auto mechanics, where a set of procedures must be followed to complete a learning task. When the subject matter entails students learning how to complete a learning task either covertly (e.g., learning strategy) or overtly (e.g., compute a math sum), the content should be treated as academic rule knowledge.

A third decision regarding the implementation of the two generic models regards the degree of precision with which developing teachers must follow the prescribed steps. In first learning to implement either model, developing teachers should start out with careful precision until they automatically carry out the steps. Then they can begin to focus more on students' responses to specific aspects of a lesson. At this point, developing teachers can make decisions about varying things, such as the number of examples presented or asking students to volunteer examples rather than the teacher giving them. Such decisions will be based on the students' familiarity with the steps in instruction as well as their interest and prior knowledge of the content.

Stages of Learning

Decisions concerning when to move students through the different stages of learning should be based on the accuracy and rate of students' independently made correct responses. In a very general sense, a criterion of 90% accuracy is a sound basis for moving students from the acquisition to fluency-building stages. Movement into the other stages should be based on speed as well as accuracy.

The rate criterion can be derived from one of two sources. The first source, peer medians, is readily available regardless of content area and grade level, but it may take a little advance work. To determine the rate for a particular response, developing teachers must sample the rate of responding of a peer group that has mastered the target response. The median rate of responding (i.e., responses per minute or some other unit of time) for the peer group is used as the criterion for mastery. The second source, published proficiency rates, can be obtained for most tool skills in reading, math, and spelling but may not be available for other content areas. Table 5.2 is a sample of rate criteria from a variety of sources.

Lesson Development

The two decision areas in lesson development most often of concern to developing teachers are frequency of reviews and mixing of low- and high-order questions. Some teachers are concerned that overdwelling on reviews may cause boredom and impede students' progress in mastering the full range of skills needed to be completed in a school year. Both are legitimate concerns that can be the dysfunctional effects of reviewing too frequently or for too long a period of time. To help avoid these potential problems, developing teachers need to remember that the review need only deal with the major points of the lesson and not all the details. Also, developing teachers can use lesson-initiating reviews judiciously. When making an important conceptual bridge between two closely related concepts or academic rules, they should engage students in a thorough review at the beginning of the lesson. When the lesson is a continuation of work on a concept or rule that was introduced earlier, developing teachers can spend less time reviewing at the beginning of the lesson. Ending reviews appear to be more crucial. Developing teachers should be less willing to cut back on these reviews.

The second area of concern deals with the mix of low- and high-order questions. To begin with, developing teachers need to be aware of a trap into which many teachers fall. When working with academically lower functioning students, many developing teachers fixate on asking low-order rote questions, believing that such students are not capable of handling high-order questions. The trap is that without instruction

TABLE 5.2 Criterion Levels for Corrects and Errors Per One-Minute Sample for Reading, Math, and Spelling Skills

PROFICIENCY RATES FOR READING SKILLS

	Says isolated Sounds (K-3)		Says Words in List (2-4)		(5-6)		(Adult)		Says Words in Text (1-3)		(4-6)		(Adult)	
	Cor.	Err.[a]	Cor.	Err.	Cor.	Err.	Cor.	Err.	Cor.	Err.	Cor.	Err.	Cor.	Err.
Koenig & Kunzelmann (1980)														
Starlin & Starlin (1973)	140	0	120–130	0					50–70	2	100–200	2	100–200	2

PROFICIENCY RATES FOR MATH SKILLS

	Addition Facts 0–9 Gr. 2–3		Sub. Facts (1–5) and Facts Top Numb. 2–9 Gr. 2–3		Add. Facts Sums and Sub. Facts Top Numb. 6–9 Gr. 3–4		Two-column Addition with Re-grouping Gr. 4–5		Two-column Subtraction with Re-grouping Gr. 4–6		Multiplies Facts Through x9 Gr. 5–6		Divides Facts Through Divisor of 9 Gr.6	
	Cor.	Err.	Cor.	Err.	Cor.	Err.	Cor.	Err.	Cor.	Err.	Cor.	Err.	Cor.	Err.
Koenig & Kunzelmann (1980)	60	–	60	–	90	–	60	–	60	–	90	–	60	–
Precision Teaching Project (Montana)	70–90	–	70–90	–	70–90	–	70–90	–	70–90	–	70–90	–	70–90	–

PROFICIENCY RATES FOR SPELLING

	Gr. 2		Gr. 3		Gr. 4		Gr. 5		Gr. 6	
	Cor.	Err.	Cor.	Err.	Cor.	Err.	Cor.	Err.	Cor.	Err.
Koenig & Kunzelmann (1980)	60–90	–	90–100	–	100–120	–	110–130	–	120–140	–

	K–Gr. 2 Independent Level		Instructional Level		Gr. 3–Adult Independent Level		Instructional Level	
	Cor.	Err.	Cor.	Err.	Cor.	Err.	Cor.	Err.
Starlin & Starlin (1973)	30–50	≥2	15–29	3–7	50–70	≥2	25–49	3–7

[a] Letters correct and errors.

SOURCE Adapted from Mercer, C. D., & Mercer, A. R. (1985). *Teaching students with learning problems*. Columbus, OH: Merrill.

and practice in answering high-order questions, these students will surely be limited in their ability to respond to questions involving comprehension, application, analysis, synthesis, evaluation, or judgment. Therefore, developing teachers should start units or segments of instruction with lower-order questions but should plan in advance the introduction of higher-order questions for students at all levels of ability once accuracy of rote responding reaches criterion. Effectively using cues and prompts can help students to respond accurately to high-order questions.

Summary

This chapter presents a variety of elements found in the effective delivery of instruction. These elements are very complex and are intricately interwoven into the fabric of teaching. They have been artificially separated and described here for purposes of analysis, but, when put into practice, they can be difficult to identify as discrete elements. Nonetheless, developing teachers who continuously analyze the instructional environment of their classrooms and their role in that environment can benefit from the application of these elements to their own instructional repertoire.

Educational researchers and philosophers continually strive to explain what makes effective instruction work. They have devised and revised a variety of instructional models. Two prominent models of instruction are direct instruction (DI) and guided discovery learning (GDL). Often these models are viewed as diametrically opposed, but in another light they can be viewed as complementary. DI offers developing teachers a set of procedures for presenting subject matter by having teachers model components of concepts or academic rules and then present examples and nonexamples. GDL generally entails presenting strong examples first and then having students deduce the concept or academic rule through a series of guided questions. Many other features of these two models are similar, such as the importance of guided practice, the development of content mastery through extensive practice, the selection of strong examples, and the need to identify essential attributes of concepts and steps for academic rules. Selecting which model to use can be guided by applicability of subject matter to the instructional steps in each model and the need to mix instructional techniques to enhance student interest.

Another important element of instruction is the type of subject matter being presented. Two categories of content and the steps for presenting them have been outlined: concepts and academic rules. Concepts are pervasive subject matter that are central to all content areas. They provide a means by which students can categorize and classify information and understand the relationships of various superordinate and subordinate levels. Academic rules are procedures used to complete academic tasks that involve covert and overt responses by students. They are also found in a variety of content areas that require problem solving and the application of conceptual knowledge.

The third element of instruction discussed in the chapter is the stages of learning. Developing teachers can benefit in recognizing that students first acquire skills in responding to concepts and academic rules through careful presentation of examples and nonexamples. Once they have acquired a degree of accuracy in working with target subject matter, fluency is built through daily practice sessions. In order for acquired skills to be maintained and not degenerate, practice sessions need to be distributed over longer intervals of time. The final stage of instruction, generalization, is focused on having students use their acquired skills in different settings and times.

The final section of the chapter is an outline of the integration of the above elements. This lesson-development format is designed for developing teachers to use in guiding students to the ultimate goal of instruction: students independently using subject matter in appropriate settings at appropriate times.

References

ALLEY, G.R., & DESHLER, D.D. (1979). *Teaching the learning disabled adolescent: Strategies and methods.* Denver, CO: Love.

ANDERSON, L.M., EVERTSON, C.M., & BROPHY, J.E. (1979). An experimental study of effective teaching in first-grade reading groups. *Elementary School Journal, 79,* 193–222.

AUSUBEL, D., NOVAK, J., & HANESIAN, H. (1978). *Educational psychology: A cognitive view.* New York: Holt, Rinehart & Winston.

BARLOW, D.L. (1985). *Educational Psychology: The teaching–learning process.* Chicago: Moody Press.

BECKER, W.C., ENGLEMANN, S., & THOMAS, D.R. (1971). *Teaching: A course in applied psychology.* Chicago: Science Research Associates.

BIEHLER, R.F., & SNOWMAN, J. (1986). *Psychology applied to teaching* (5th ed.). Boston: Houghton Mifflin.

BELKEN, G.S., & GRAY, J.L. (1977). *Educational psychology: An introduction.* Dubuque, IA: Wm. C. Brown.

BRUNER, J.S. (1966). *Toward a theory of instruction.* New York: Norton.

CARNINE, D., & SILBERT, J. (1979). *Direct instruction: Reading.* Columbus, OH: Merrill.

DESHLER, D.D., & SCHUMAKER, J.B. (1986). Learning strategies: An instructional alternative for low-achieving adolescents. *Exceptional Children, 52,* 583–590.

DUNKIN, M., & BIDDLE, B. (1974). *The study of teaching.* New York: Holt, Rinehart & Winston.

ENGLEMANN, S., & CARNINE, D. (1982). *Theory of instruction: Principles and applications.* New York: Irvington.

FISHER, C.W., BERLINER, D.C., FILBY, N.N., MARLIAVE, R., CAHEN, L.S., & DISHAW, M.M. (1980). Teaching behaviors, academic learning time, and student achievement: An overview. In C. Denham, & A. Lieberman (Eds.), *Time to learn.* Washington, DC: U.S. Government Printing Office.

GAGNE, R.M. (1970). *The conditions of learning* (2nd ed.). New York: Holt, Rinehart & Winston.

GREENWOOD, C.R., DELQUADRI, J.C., & HALL, R.V. (1984). Opportunity to respond and student academic performance. In W.L. Heward, T.E. Heron, D.S. Hill, & J. Trap-Porter (Eds.), *Focus on behavior analysis in education* (pp. 58–88). Columbus, OH: Merrill.

GREGORY, J. (1985). The concept teaching model. Unpublished manuscript.

KOENIG, C.H. & KUNZELMANN, H.P. (1980). *Classroom learning screening manual.* San Antonio, TX: Psychology Corporation.

LLOYD, J., & DE BETTENCOURT, L.J.U. (1982). *Academic strategy training: A manual for teachers.* Charlottesville: University of Virginia Learning Disabilities Research Institute.

MARTIN, J. (1979). Effects of teacher higher order questions on student progress and product variables in a single classroom study. *Journal of Educational Research, 72,* 183–187.

PALINCSAR, A.S., & BROWN, A.L. (1984). Reciprocal teaching of comprehension-fostering and comprehension-monitoring activities. *Cognition and Instruction, 1,* 117–175.

PARIS, S.G., CROSS, D.R., & LIPSON, M.Y. (1984). Informed strategies for learning: A program to improve children's reading awareness and comprehension. *Journal of Education Psychology, 76,* 1239–1252.

Precision Teaching Project. Available from Skyline Center, 3300 Third Street Northeast, Great Falls, MT 59404.

ROSENSHINE, B. (1971). *Teaching behaviours and student achievement.* London: National Foundation for Educational Research.

ROSENSHINE, B. (1976). Academic engaged time, content covered, and direct instruction. *Journal of Education, 160* (3), 38–66.

ROWE, M. (1974). Wait-time and rewards as instructional variables, logic and fate control: Part 1. Wait-time. *Journal of Research in Science Teaching, 11,* 81–94.

STARLIN, C.M., & STARLIN, A. (1973). Guides to decision making in computational math. Bemidji, MN: Unique Curriculums Unlimited.

WOLLERY, M., BAILEY, D.B., & SUGAI, G.M. (1988). *Effective teaching: Principles and procedures of applied behavior analysis with exceptional children.* Boston: Allyn & Bacon.

CHAPTER 6

Classroom Management: Promoting Discipline and Self-Control

When asked what concerns them most about upcoming student-teaching assignments, developing teachers' responses typically center on their apprehension and anxiousness about classroom behavior management. Specifically, many preservice (and, unfortunately, a large number of inservice) teachers worry about losing control of the students in their charge and about possible encounters with students who do not comply with implicit and explicit behavioral standards. Most student teachers find they are able to apply management skills learned in their university-based training programs. However, feelings of apprehension persist when student teachers move on to their own first classrooms. Surveys of beginning teachers indicate that the management and remediation of student misbehavior are among the most pressing problems reported. In a review of studies concerned with the perceived problems of beginning elementary and secondary teachers, Veenman (1984) found that classroom discipline and student motivation ranked one and two among a listing of 24 problems. These concerns are also shared by the general public; in 14 of the past 15 Gallup Polls of Public Attitudes about Public Schools, lack of discipline in schools has ranked first among the major concerns facing the public schools.

Because students with mild and moderate handicaps engage in a wider range and higher rate of problem behaviors than most students in mainstreamed settings, it is essential that prospective special education teachers become effective classroom managers. In most university-based

165

training programs for special educators, issues and strategies related to discipline and the management of classroom behavior problems receive considerable attention. Prospective special educators typically complete coursework and projects on (a) the characteristics of child and adolescent behavior problems, (b) applied behavior analysis, and (c) classroom management alternatives. The lesson that emerges is that there are no "magic bullets," formulas, or recipes to ensure appropriate student behavior.

On the positive side, however, there are a series of general strategies that, used correctly, can increase the probability of a successfully managed classroom. These general strategies provide the organizational structure for our discussion of effective classroom management. First, specific techniques and basic teacher attitudes related to the prevention of problem behaviors will be presented. Second, specific group and individual behavior-change strategies will be reviewed. Finally, guidelines for the completion of formal behavior-change efforts for individual and groups of students will be presented.

Prevention of Problem Behaviors

The key to successfully managing the high activity learning environments that serve students with mild and moderate handicaps is **prevention**. It is essential for developing and beginning teachers to be aware of the number of antecedent events related to student behavior that they as teachers can influence. Antecedent events include any expectations, attitudes, environmental conditions, or teacher behaviors that typically precede a student's response. As noted in Chapter 3, many antecedent events are associated with increased academic achievement, especially those related to the planning of instruction and the organization of a learning environment. Therefore, it is not surprising that many of the factors associated with the effective planning for instruction overlap with those associated with effective classroom management.

An Appropriate Management Perspective

The management of student behavior is not a cut and dried technical activity devoid of the human touches of empathy and emotion. Although systematic, scientifically validated techniques are applied for the purpose of maximizing student learning and social adjustment, management techniques are delivered through a series of interpersonal exchanges between teachers and students. Close examination of these exchanges reveals that several intangible (i.e., difficult to operationalize) behaviors, personal qualities, and attitudes are essential prerequisites to the teacher for the successful management of students with mild and moderate handicaps.

RESPECT FOR STUDENTS   Successful classroom managers generally like their students and respect them as individuals (Good & Brophy, 1987). Demonstrations of this affection and respect, however, need not be presented in a superficial or overly dramatic fashion. Genuine concern for the welfare of each of the students is demonstrated through (a) regular private interactions that exude warmth and a desire for knowing students individually, (b) facial gestures and body language that indicate acceptance and respect, (c) a vocal tone that shows patience and understanding, and (d) the use of enthusiasm and humor to ease tension in anxiety-filled situations. Even in the face of frequent misbehavior, effective classroom managers make it clear that students are differentiated from behaviors—students are shown they are valued even when their instances of inappropriate behaviors are not given approval.

APPROPRIATE EXPECTATIONS   Researchers investigating teachers' expectations of their students have found that students tend to live up to the expectations their teachers have for them. The professional literature is replete with examples of how such negative self-fulfilling prophecies influence academic performance. Similarly, negative expectations can have a direct influence on rates of student misbehavior. Students considered as behavior problems are more likely to act out if expectations regarding the continuation of these types of behaviors are communicated with strength and consistency. In many instances, identified problem students have little incentive to change their behavior patterns and typically conform to the negative expectations presented by significant others in their environment.

There are several implicit and explicit ways that developing and beginning teachers can communicate positive expectations of behavior. First, similar to academic programming, reasonable goals related to how students should behave must be developed. This entails knowing what behaviors are expected of students during school and class activities. Second, expectations must be communicated to students in a no-nonsense, straightforward fashion. This communication can take several forms including the (a) formulation of positively stated classroom rules, (b) the design of an overall classroom management system in which all students are treated equally, and (c) the delivery of consistent consequences for both compliance and noncompliance to the components of the management system. Furthermore, teachers need to convey that a student's acting-out history or "teachers' lounge hearsay" has nothing to do with how consequences will be applied under the current management system. Each student should be made aware that their present behavior is evaluated in relation to current standards rather than past years' rule infractions or subjective behind-the-scenes gossip.

CREDIBILITY, DEPENDABILITY, AND ASSERTIVENESS   Effective classroom managers are models of appropriate behaviors. They practice what they preach and can be counted on to be consistent and reliable in the enforcement of classroom rules and procedures. A teacher's credibility is established when (a) instances of their verbal behavior coincide with their instrumental behavior and (b) they respect and adhere consistently to their daily responsibilities within the classroom. Once correspondence between words and actions is established, students will come to depend on the teacher's verbal intentions and will test limits less frequently. Credibility and dependability, however, will not develop if a teacher chats sociably with teachers during planned activities, makes empty threats, or enforces rules selectively rather than consistently (Good & Brophy, 1987).

Effective classroom management, like effective teaching, requires that a teacher convey strong leadership qualities. This does not mean that classes of students with mild and moderate handicaps need to be taught by power-hungry, harsh, or dictatorial men and women. Strong leaders convey authority with subtlety, tact, and diplomacy, rather than through intimidation and intrusiveness. Developing and beginning teachers can convey a strong leadership presence by (a) using clear, calm, controlled, and defined statements when requesting student compliance, (b) being self-assured, confident, and consistent when delivering the consequences of a student's misbehavior, (c) not arguing with students, and, most importantly, (d) conveying to students that any problems and concerns that may arise will be addressed in an empathic and constructive manner (Weber & Roff, 1983; Westling & Koorland, 1988).

"WITHITNESS"   "Withitness" refers to a teacher's ability to be aware of students' actions and a proficiency in communicating that awareness to students (Kounin, 1970). Teachers possessing "withitness" position themselves in ways that they can readily monitor the multitude of events occurring in their classrooms. They seem to have a sixth sense or "eyes in the back of their heads" and are able to deal successfully with more than one matter at a time. The heightened sensitivity to the events in a classroom allows "with it" teachers to prevent disruptions before they grow into serious management problems.

While "withitness," per se, cannot be directly taught in methods courses, beginning and developing special education teachers can enhance their development of this important skill by (a) arranging their classrooms to allow for easy observations of all instructional activities, (b) regularly monitoring their classrooms, (c) responding to those small events and minor disruptions that often precede major behavior problems, (d) attempting to handle multiple classroom situations simultaneously, and (e) communicating to students an awareness of what is going on in and around the classroom.

Preparation

A sure way to promote disruption among students is to be unprepared for lessons or activities. Most students, particularly those with mild handicapping conditions, are likely to act out if they are not engaged in purposeful activities. Moreover, teachers who appear unprepared for the day's events present a poor model for their students. Lack of readiness on the part of a teacher signals to students that planned classroom activities are not valued and that preparation for academic work is unimportant. Not surprisingly, teachers who are consistently unprepared for lessons have difficulties motivating and managing their students.

Thorough preparation is a difficult, time-consuming task, particularly for developing and beginning teachers. Nonetheless, time spent in preparation saves both time and anguish in the long run—prepared teachers spend less time dealing with student behavior problems. Effective classroom managers prepare for their lessons and know how to keep their students on task with productive and educationally relevant work. Prepared teachers (a) have well-developed and organized lesson plans, (b) start lessons promptly and keep to a consistent schedule, (c) have student assignments ready for distribution and boardwork prepared prior to the scheduled start of lesson, (d) keep the materials necessary for a planned activity close at hand, and (e) take care of grading and recordkeeping responsibilities promptly and efficiently. Teachers highlight the importance of class activities by preparing for them and not by wasting lesson time on clerical or organizational tasks.

Physical Environment

As discussed in Chapter 3, the physical design of the classroom environment can influence the academic and social behavior of students. It is especially important to consider the relationships between physical environmental variables and behaviors of students with mild and moderate handicapping conditions. Such students are easily influenced by events that are often regarded as merely neutral in most learning situations. Teachers of highly distractible students, for example, often find it essential to arrange group lesson tables in such a way that students' lines of vision are narrowly focused in the direction of a chalkboard. As a general rule, the proper arrangement of the classroom can assist teachers in managing their students by preventing student discomfort, decreasing opportunities for disruptive behavior, increasing levels of task-oriented behavior, and facilitating the quality and quantity of social interactions among students (Paine et al., 1983). What follows is a brief description of what teachers should consider when arranging the physical environment to prevent inappropriate behavior.

ENSURE STUDENT AND TEACHER SAFETY AND COMFORT   Students, particularly those with a low tolerance for frustration, may act out if they perceive a threat to their safety or experience physical discomfort. Teachers, also affected by the physical conditions of a school or classroom, may overreact to student behaviors if faced with persistent discomfort. The physical comfort of individuals in classrooms depends on factors such as lighting, temperature, ventilation, and noise level. To ensure physical comfort in learning environments, Smith, Neisworth, and Greer (1978) recommend that (a) lighting be warm, free from glare, and at least 100A-candles where reading and other visual tasks are required, (b) room temperature be controlled to fall within a moderate range (68°–74°F) with adequate humidity, (c) circulated fresh air be available at all times, and (d) noise levels of classrooms be controlled so that the ongoing activities of one room do not disturb others.

PROVIDE SECURITY IN AND AROUND SCHOOL   It is often said that events that occur in our schools are a direct reflection of happenings in our society at-large. In the case of crime, and the fear and anxiety associated with such violations, this is an unfortunate reality. Many students possess legitimate fears about attending certain schools. To many students, schools are not places of learning, but places where they must contend with repeated threats to their safety, property, and psychological well-being. Obviously, the fear of injury or loss of property can deleteriously influence students' behaviors in the classroom. Safe learning environments are possible, however, if school administrators, teachers, parents, and students work together to promote a security-conscious philosophy.

Developing and beginning teachers can do their part by (a) following duty assignments related to monitoring student entry, movement in, and exit from school; (b) ensuring that parents are made aware of safe avenues for students to travel to and from school; (c) closely monitoring students during recess activities and reporting any strangers who may be loitering either in or around the building; (d) securing school's, teacher's, and student's valuables and reporting instances of theft, vandalism, and property destruction; and (e) delivering immediate and potent consequences to those students who break the rules. Most importantly, however, teachers should educate students to be security conscious both in and out of school. Furthermore, specific school and class policies regarding security should be developed and transmitted to students, parents, and the community.

ARRANGE FURNITURE TO MINIMIZE DISRUPTIONS   Classroom furnishings should be safe, comfortable, durable, and age/size-appropriate for students in the class. Available classroom space should be organized to promote prosocial behavior and facilitate academic achievement. In Chapter 3, several effective classroom configurations were presented along with specific guidelines for the placement of furniture for students with mild and moderate handicaps. Important design considerations included (a) provisions for both public and private student work spaces, (b) the availability of a convenient and unobstructed view of the entire classroom, and (c) easy access to instructional materials.

Teachers of students with greater tendencies toward overactivity, distractibility, and aggression should also attend to traffic patterns within their classrooms. First, students' desks should be spaced adequately, ensuring that each student can work independently without disturbing others. Second, access to high action or activity areas (e.g., the work "in-box," the pencil sharpener, and so forth) should be designed to facilitate an easy flow of traffic. Paths to such areas should be away from major group and independent work centers, and teachers should try to limit the number of students moving to such areas at the same time. Movements within and between activities should be smooth, with little loss of positive momentum. Most importantly, the major high traffic areas should be located in different quadrants of the room. This will tend to limit the oversaturation of one part of the room and allow for the maximum use of available space.

KEEPING CLASSROOMS NEAT AND TRIM   Four good reasons exist for keeping learning environments neat and picked up. First, by taking care of and storing instructional materials in their assigned containers or areas, preparation time for lessons can be minimized. Students and teachers can begin their tasks with little need for frustrating "search" activities. Second, unsupervised high-interest materials can sway student attention from an assigned task. By storing materials, teachers limit these potential distractors that often start instances of misbehavior. Third, the storage of personal belongings prevents minor and nagging disturbances involving lost and stolen possessions. By providing adequate and secure storage of personal belongings, conflicts involving personal property losses can be minimized. Finally, students with mild and moderate handicaps tend to be unusually hard on both the hardware and consumable supplies of their classrooms. Highlighting and modeling procedures that promote respect for property can result in students demonstrating increased levels of care with instructional materials.

Rules and Procedures

Rules and procedures allow teachers to communicate the behavioral standards and expectations of the classroom environment to their students. Rules identify, define, and operationalize a teacher's specific conceptualization of acceptable behavior; procedures delineate the steps necessary for the successful and appropriate completion of an activity, task, or operation. Concise and unambiguous rules and procedures serve as discriminative stimuli for appropriate classroom behavior. When planned and implemented correctly, both rules and procedures can serve to guide, motivate, and remind students to adhere to stated standards. The research literature is clear in its support of the use of rules and procedures: teachers who establish reasonable, definable, and clearly understood rules are effective classroom managers (Weber & Roff, 1983).

As was discussed in more detail in Chapter 3, rules and procedures need to be introduced correctly and adequately maintained throughout the school year. In regard to introducing rules and procedures, developing and beginning teachers should (a) identify the specific behaviors and procedures expected of students, (b) discuss and teach rules and procedures beginning on the *first* day of school, (c) present students with a solid rationale for the rules and procedures, (d) involve students in the formulation and development of these classroom standards, (e) phrase rules and procedures positively rather than negatively, and (f) keep the number of the rules and procedures to a minimum.

By following several guidelines, the strength and integrity of agreed-upon rules and procedures will be maintained. First, rules and procedures should be posted in areas visible to students. Second, rules and procedures should be taught and practiced throughout the school year. Brief reviews of lesson rules can prompt students to adhere to the behavioral expectations specific to a particular activity. Third, teachers should model and demonstrate the correct way of adhering to school and classroom procedures. Finally, because the failure of many classroom-management systems stems from less than consistent adherence and compliance to the management system, teachers should develop a system to monitor their own performance on whether they follow the stated rules and procedures and provide consequences consistently.

The development of consequences is an essential component of successful management programs. According to Curwin and Mendler (1988), two important skills are needed for the development of effective consequences: creativity and the ability to see the logical extension of rule violations. In short, good consequences (a) are clear and specific, (b) are not punishments, (c) are natural and related directly to the rule, (d) preserve the student's dignity, (e) increase the student's motivation, and (f) promote an internal locus of control within students.

Thinking of effective consequences, however, can be problematic for developing and beginning teachers. Fortunately, there are four generic consequences that can be effective for any rule. According to Curwin and Mendler (1988) these are (a) reminder of the rule, (b) a warning, (c) developing an action plan for improving behavior, and (d) practicing appropriate behavior. Still, it takes considerable skill and practice to develop effective consequences that are not aversive. Strategies to assist developing and beginning teachers to create good consequences are found in Table 6.1.

Schoolwide Cooperation

The development of effective management procedures for students with mild and moderate handicaps is a team effort. While the ultimate responsibility for the maintenance of order in the special education setting rests with the classroom teacher, support from building administrators, regular education colleagues, and related service personnel is essential for the maintenance of successful management programs. Because most students with mild and moderate handicaps will have contact with members of the school staff, it is critical that management plans, classroom rules, and special interventions designed to foster integration into the

TABLE 6.1   Creating Effective Consequences: Five Strategies for Developing and Beginning Teachers in Special Education Settings

Strategy	Putting It to Practice
Reread and visualize the classroom rule	Close your eyes and imagine a student breaking a rule, and consider the possible scenarios resulting from the various natural consequences.
Collect effective consequences	Observe master teachers. Ask them how they respond to specific instances of rule breaking.
Ask the students	Early in the school year, have students provide input as to what they believe would be effective consequences. At the end of the year, ask students to comment on each consequence's effectiveness.
Ask parents	At IEP meetings or parent conferences, ask parents what consequences have been effective at home.
Ask yourself	Remember your own days as a student and consider what consequences helped you (a) stop misbehaving, (b) learn from the experience, (c) cooperate, and (d) not feel embarrassed, angry, or resentful.

SOURCE   Adapted from Curwin, R. L., & Mendler, A. M. (1988). *Discipline with dignity.* Alexandria, VA: ASCD.

BOX 6.1

Three Strategies for Facilitating Open Communication and Teamwork in Schools

1. Meet with the school administrators responsible for student disciplinary actions prior to the start of the school year. The agenda for this meeting should include (a) the correspondence between schoolwide discipline policies and the behavior management programs to be implemented as part of students' IEPs, (b) the proposed classroom rules, procedures, and consequences for noncompliance, and (c) suggested strategies to ensure consistency in instances when a student's behavior necessitates removal from the classroom.
2. Meet, both formally and informally, with other teachers in the building. The nature of the academic and classroom management program within the special education setting should be discussed, and issues related to the mainstreaming of eligible students should be highlighted. Arrange a mutually satisfying mode for communicating student progress throughout the academic year.
3. Alert the school support staff (e.g., psychologists, therapists, lunch-aides, and custodians) to the unique character and demands of your classrooms. Discuss provisions that will enable easy access to support services.

mainstream environment be conveyed to all relevant personnel. A prerequisite to successful collaborative and supportive working relationships within schools is clear and open communication.

Unfortunately, open communication and cooperation in school settings do not automatically happen. As with most complex social systems, schools sometimes become places where individual and immediate concerns take precedence over activities that promote communication and teamwork. Successful cooperative efforts require hard work, persistence, diplomacy, flexibility, and a genuine belief that the efforts of a team can enhance the delivery of educational services to students. Box 6.1 provides guidelines as to how beginning teachers can facilitate open communication and teamwork in their schools. Box 6.2 provides an adaptation of a classroom-behavior management form originally prepared by Grossnickle and Sesko (1985) for the National Association of Secondary School Principals. This form illustrates how all individuals involved in the education of students can work together in the management of problematic behavior within a systematic framework.

BOX 6.2

Classroom Behavior Management Form

Student Name _____

ID No. _____ Year _____

Teacher _____

Subject _____ Period _____

The above student's behavior has been disturbing the class and my ability to teach. Specifically, the problem is:

_____

_____

_____

As the classroom teacher, I have taken the following steps to correct the problem.

Step 1. An *after-class discussion* was held on _____ with the
                                                        (Date)
student regarding the above problem. The student's reaction to the problem and my suggestions for improvement was:

Favorable ☐   Unfavorable ☐   No reaction ☐

_____   _____
   (Teacher's signature)   (Student's signature)

Step 2. A *formal teacher/student conference* was held on

_____. The problem was
        (Date)   (Time)
again discussed and the student was warned that further misbehavior would result in a referral to the assistant principal. The student's reaction to my suggestions for improvement was:

Favorable ☐   Unfavorable ☐   No reaction ☐

_____   _____
   (Teacher's signature)   (Student's signature)

Step 3. A *formal behavior contract* was developed on

_____. The results of this
        (Date)   (Time)

(continued)

BOX 6.2 (continued)

effort were:

Favorable ☐   Unfavorable ☐   No impact ☐

_____   _____
(Teacher's signature)   (Student's signature)

Step 4. *Parent phone contact* was made on _____ at _____.
(Date)   (Phone no.)

The parent was advised of the problem and the steps taken thus far by the teacher to remedy the problem. The parent's support was requested. The parent's reaction was:

Positive ☐   Neutral ☐   No reaction ☐

Step 5. The following *Resource People* were consulted:
A. The department chairman made the following recommendations:

_____

_____

_____

B. The guidance counselor provided the following assistance:

_____

_____

_____

Step 6. *The problem persists.* I want this student to be seen by an *assistant principal.* Send this form and the student to 105.

_____

_____

_____   _____
(Date, time student was sent)   (Teacher's signature)

To the teacher: The assistant principal will write a referral, copies of which will be sent to you and the parent. You are urged to contact the discipline office at the end of the day to learn of the disposition of this matter.

SOURCE   Adapted with permission from Grossnickle, D. R. & Sesko, F. P. (1985). *Promoting effective discipline in school and classroom. A practitioner's perspective.* Reston, VA: National Association of Secondary School Principals.

Intervention

Although the key to successful classroom management is prevention, all students, particularly those with mild and moderate handicaps, present problem behaviors that necessitate thoughtful and effective teacher responses. In this section, we will review briefly a number of techniques that can be employed to intervene when students engage in problematic behaviors. First, we will describe generic strategies for influencing students' inappropriate behaviors. This will be followed by discussions of specific individual and group management alternatives.

Influencing Behavior

In most cases, interventions that are successful in managing and remediating student misbehavior involve both the strengthening and reducing of different behaviors. Management programs designed to reduce or eliminate problem behaviors alone may be ineffectual because they do not directly teach or strengthen appropriate behaviors. Because a student may not be aware of, or proficient enough in, a correct mode of functioning in the classroom, the reduction or elimination of one series of problematic behaviors may lead to a situation where other negative behaviors replace the initial problem behaviors. Clearly needed are dynamic management interventions that simultaneously strengthen and weaken specific student target behaviors. While techniques that increase and decrease student behavior are presented separately, it is critical that they be applied in a logical and dynamic fashion.

INCREASING BEHAVIOR   When we speak of increasing behavior, we are referring to the process of **reinforcement**. Positive reinforcement occurs when the contingent **presentation** of a positive environmental consequence results in corresponding increases in the frequency or intensity of a target behavior. Negative reinforcement, sometimes confused with punishment, occurs when the contingent **removal** of an unpleasant or aversive event results directly in the increased frequency of a targeted behavior. Whether positive or negative, reinforcement, by definition, always refers to an increase in a behavior's frequency or intensity. Therefore, praise, tokens, and free-activity time will not always function as reinforcement. To be a reinforcer, an item, event, or activity must serve to increase the strength or intensity of a behavior. For new and developing teachers, this functional definition of reinforcement highlights the need to identify potential items and events that possess the greatest likelihood of increasing an individual student's appropriate behaviors.

According to Kazdin (1975), the effectiveness of reinforcement depends on several major factors including (a) the delay between performance of a behavior and the delivery of a potential reinforcer, (b) the magnitude of a reinforcer, (c) the quality of a reinforcer, and (d) the schedule for reinforcer delivery. In delivering positive reinforcers, developing and beginning teachers should ensure that reinforcers are delivered in close proximity to the target behavior. If the delivery of a reinforcer does not closely follow the target behavior, there is a risk that behaviors other than the target behavior will be reinforced inadvertently. The magnitude or amount of reinforcement also influences the level of change in a target behavior. Quite simply, the greater the amount of a reinforcer delivered for the presentation of a behavior, the more frequent that response will be on future occasions. This relationship between amount of reinforcement and behavioral intensity, however, is limited. Too much reinforcement can easily lead to satiation, a condition whereby reinforcers lose their potency. Teachers can combat satiation by using a variety of potential reinforcers in their classroom settings.

When we speak of reinforcement quality, we are referring to a student's reinforcer preference. In general, students will work with greater intensity if their efforts are recognized with items, behaviors, or events they value. Developing and beginning teachers can determine students' reinforcer preferences through direct observation or administering a reinforcer preference survey. A complete listing of items that may be included on a preference survey are found in Box 6.3.

Schedule of reinforcement refers to a specific arrangement by which reinforcers are delivered. Continuous reinforcement is an arrangement in which reinforcers are delivered after each instance of a target behavior. When reinforcement is delivered after only some instances of a target behavior, the schedule is considered intermittent. The nature of classroom events necessitates the use of intermittent-reinforcement schedules as they reduce the risk of reinforcer satiation and promote long-term behavior maintenance.

The most common types of intermittent-reinforcement schedules are **fixed-interval (FI)**, **variable-interval (VI)**, **fixed-ratio (FR)**, and **variable-ratio (VR)**. On FI schedules, reinforcers are delivered at prearranged, unvarying intervals of time. On VI schedules, reinforcers are delivered at prearranged, varying intervals that average a certain number of minutes. On a VI:15 schedule, for example, an average of 15 minutes would pass prior to the delivery of a reinforcer. For any given occasion, the interval would be more or less than the specified 15-minute interval. An FR schedule delineates the precise number of behaviors a person must perform to receive a reinforcer. In an FR:20 schedule, a student would earn a certain number of minutes on the computer for every 20 problems completed during a seatwork activity. With the VR schedule, the number of responses necessary to receive reinforcement would vary from occasion to occasion and reflect an average number of responses desired of the student.

BOX 6.3

Possible Items for a Reinforcer Preference Survey

JOB REINFORCERS

- Passing out paper, pencils and so on.
- Taking a note to the office
- Erasing the chalkboard
- Helping the teacher with a project
- Managing the class store
- Shopping for the class store
- Helping in the cafeteria
- Assisting the custodian
- Distributing and arranging reinforcers
- Watering the plants
- Running the ditto machine
- Stapling papers together
- Feeding the fish or other animals
- Giving a message over the intercom
- Taking the class roll
- Serving as secretary for class meetings
- Raising or lowering the flag
- Carrying the wastebasket while other children clean out their desks
- Using the overhead projector
- Recording own behavior on a graph
- Teaching another child
- Helping the librarian
- Telling the teacher when it is time to go to lunch
- Sharpening the teacher's pencils
- Adjusting the window shades

TANGIBLE REINFORCERS OTHER THAN FOOD

- Tickets to games or movies
- Personal grooming supplies
- Toys and games from the class store
- Colored chalk, pencils, or felt-tipped pens

SOCIAL REINFORCERS

- Receiving verbal praise
- Having photograph displayed

(continued)

BOX 6.3 (continued)

- Getting personal time with the teacher, aide, counselor, or principal
- Having work and projects displayed
- Participating in show and tell
- Clapping and cheering by others when successful
- Being leader or organizer of an event
- Getting a hug, a handshake, or pat on the back
- Sitting next to the teacher at lunch
- Playing with a classmate of choice
- Sitting and talking with a friend (adult or child)

CONSUMABLE FOOD REINFORCERS

- Raisins
- Crackers
- Cookies
- Popcorn
- Potato chips
- Peanuts
- Gumdrops
- Jelly beans
- Small candies
- Juice
- Soda
- Ice cream
- Lollipops

REINFORCING ACTIVITIES

- Reading books, magazines, and comic books
- Writing on the chalkboard with white or colored chalk
- Getting free time for self-selected projects
- Making things, such as kites, model cars, and airplanes
- Making bead jewelry
- Playing games (e.g., Monopoly)
- Doing puzzles
- Singing
- Finger painting
- Playing with puppets
- Drawing
- Reading with a friend
- Studying with a friend
- Tutoring younger children
- Eating lunch at a restaurant

BOX 6.3 *(continued)*

- Decorating a designated area of the room in own style
- Taking field trips
- Going on outdoor walks
- Watching a movie
- Watching television
- Listening to music
- Doing a project of own interest
- Using the tape recorder or phonograph
- Getting extra recess
- Going home early
- Taking a class pet home for the weekend
- Going on a trip to a fair or museum
- Using a typewriter
- Doing "special," "the hardest," or "impossible" teacher-made arithmetic problems
- Reading the newspaper
- Reading or drawing a road map
- Listening to the radio with earplugs
- Going to the library
- Doing a science experiment
- Weighing or measuring various objects in the classroom

Alternative procedures for increasing students' levels of appropriate behaviors range from the contingent delivery of edibles to the contingent awarding of tokens or free-activity time. Because students with mild and moderate handicaps have individual and often unique needs, it is important that teachers apply the procedures with the knowledge that outcomes will typically vary from student to student. Table 6.2 summarizes some of the more common procedures for increasing appropriate student behavior.

DECREASING BEHAVIOR   Students with mild and moderate handicaps present a number of problematic behaviors that need to be reduced or eliminated. Three types of procedures exist for the systematic reduction of problematic behaviors: extinction, differential reinforcement, and punishment. Extinction is a process that decreases the strength and intensity of behavior by withholding reinforcement previously given to the behavior. The most common and productive application of extinction is the planned ignoring of minor inappropriate behaviors (e.g., the tapping of a pencil on a desk) that had been reinforced previously through teacher attention. High-intensity problematic behaviors such as tantrumming, fighting, and noncompliance require the use of stronger behavior-reduction techniques.

TABLE 6.2   Procedures for Increasing Appropriate Behaviors

Type	Definition	Advantages	Disadvantages
Edible	A primary reinforcer. Potency varies as a function of deprivation and satiation.	Potency with students who possess severe handicaps. Useful in establishing reinforcing properties of other events (e.g., praise, smiles, and so forth).	Delivery disrupts classroom functioning. Difficult to dispense in busy classroom settings. Need to be constantly aware of student allergies.
Praise and Attention	Conditioned social reinforcers that can be delivered verbally and nonverbally (e.g., smiles, winks, physical contact).	Easily and quickly administered. Unobtrusive during classroom activities. Little preparation required.	Because the reinforcement value of praise and attention need to be learned, some individuals may not respond. Limited potency with inappropriate behaviors that have high secondary reinforcing properties (e.g., theft, substance abuse).
High Probability Behaviors	The preferred activities of students can be used as reinforcers for lower probability behaviors.	Schools have large numbers of desirable activities available. Powerful and cost free. Low probability of satiation.	Difficulty in delivering activity reinforcers immediately. Disruptions may occur during transitions between activities. Delivery mode tends to be all or none; little opportunity to portion out activities.
Performance Feedback	Using the knowledge of progress or results to reinforce a target behavior.	Easily initiated in settings where performance criteria are explicitly stated. Low cost and motivating.	Effectiveness of feedback alone has been equivocal.

TABLE 6.2 (*continued*)

Tokens	Conditioned, generalized reinforcers whose strength is derived from items, activities, and desirable consequences they present.	Combat satiation in that a number of backups can be employed.	Require effort in record keeping and other management activities.
		Easily dispensed.	Fading of tokens often neglected.
		Serve to bridge the period of time between the occurrence of a behavior and the delivery of a primary reinforcer.	
		Allow for gradations of reinforcement.	

Inappropriate classroom behaviors can be reduced indirectly by the creative use of reinforcement contingencies. By employing differential reinforcement of low rate of behaviors (DRL), teachers can reduce the frequency of a problem behavior by reinforcing a student for keeping the targeted problem at or below a particular level. Another technique, differential reinforcement of other behavior (DRO), involves the reinforcement of any behavior except the behavior to be reduced. To receive a reinforcer under a DRO schedule, the student must refrain completely from performing the behavior targeted for reduction. Thus, other behaviors are developed to replace the problematic behaviors being reduced or eliminated. The most stringent differential-reinforcement technique is differential reinforcement of appropriate behaviors incompatible with a targeted behavior (DRI). The power of DRI is that students cannot engage in problematic behaviors if those behaviors are operating under contingencies to promote behaviors contradictory to the problem behavior. Because a behavior such as correctly completing seatwork cannot occur simultaneously with running around the classroom, the reinforcement of seatwork completion could result in the reduction of the room-running behavior.

Punishment, the manipulation and delivery of consequences designed to decrease the strength or intensity of a target behavior, typically takes one of two forms: the presentation of an aversive consequence or the removal of a previously earned reinforcer. Three common punishment techniques are reprimands, response-cost, and time-out. These techniques are described in Table 6.3.

TABLE 6.3   Three Commonly Used Punishment Techniques

Type	Definition	Advantages	Disadvantages
Reprimand	A verbal statement or nonverbal gesture that expresses disapproval.	Easily applied with little or no preparation required. No physical discomfort to students.	Sometimes not effective. Can serve as positive reinforcement if this is a major source of attention.
Response cost	A formal system of penalties in which a reinforcer is removed contingent upon the occurrence of an inappropriate behavior.	Easily applied with quick results. Does not disrupt class activities. No physical discomfort to students.	Not effective once student has "lost" all reinforcers. Can initially result in some students being more disruptive
Time out	Limited or complete loss of access to positive reinforcers for a set amount of time.	Fast acting and powerful. No physical discomfort to students.	Difficult to find secluded areas where students would not be reinforced inadvertently. May require physical assistance to the time-out area. Overuse can interfere with educational and prosocial efforts.

Promoting Self-Control and Problem Solving

SELF-CONTROL   The ultimate goal of any classroom management effort should be the development of student self-management. Students who are able to control their own behaviors independent of external agents in situations requiring delays in gratification, problem-solving skills, and conflict resolution are better prepared to meet complex societal demands. Self-control procedures allow students to assume a larger role in many aspects of their classroom behavior management programs. According to Hallahan, Lloyd, and Stoller (1982), most self-control programs include three major components: self-assessment, self-recording, and self-determination of reinforcement. First, a student examines his or her own behavior and decides whether a target behavior (or series of target behaviors) was performed. This is followed by self-recording, a process in which a student records objectively the results of the self-assessment. Finally, in the process of self-determination of reinforcement, a student determines the nature and amount of reinforcement he or she should receive for the performance of the target behavior.

Self-monitoring, a combination of self-assessment and self-recording, should be employed regularly by developing and beginning teachers. Its use increases the probability that maintenance of intervention efforts will occur. According to Hallahan et al. (1982), materials needed for a self-monitoring program include (a) a self-monitoring cuing tape, (b) a self-monitoring card, and (c) an assigned task that a student can work on while self-monitoring. The procedure is introduced by informing an individual or small group of students that it is important to keep track of the occurrence and nonoccurrence of a target behavior. The student is then introduced to the cuing tape, tape recorder, and the self-monitoring card. Every time the student hears the tone of the cuing tape, she is to ask covertly, "Was I engaging in the target behavior?" and to mark the monitoring card appropriately. The procedures should be modeled and practiced initially to ensure that students can reliably differentiate between the occurrence and nonoccurrence of the target behavior. Once the procedure succeeds in teaching students to monitor and record their own behavior, procedures designed to teach the self-determination of reinforcement can begin.

Upon reaching an acceptable level of performance, it will become necessary to wean the student from the external aspects of the procedure. Hallahan et al. (1982) recommend that the process begin by removing either the tape or self-monitoring card. If, however, student performance begins to deteriorate, there should be no hesitation to resume using the external prompts as part of a modified maintenance strategy.

PROBLEM SOLVING   Many students possessing mild and moderate handicaps are deficient in their ability to solve interpersonal problems. The goals of problem-solving programs are to teach children (a) to be sensitive to interpersonal problems, (b) to develop the ability to generate alternative solutions to problems, and (c) that effects of one person's behavior affects the behavior of others.

Successful problem solving consists of several components—each of which can be taught directly to students who exhibit inappropriate patterns of behavior. The following list of these components has been gleaned from several sources, including D'Zurilla and Goldfried (1971) and Spivack and Shure (1982). Suggestions on how to apply these components are also provided.

1. *Develop a general sensitivity or orientation to the problem.* Students need to be instructed and given the opportunity to practice recognizing that interpersonal problems exist. This can take the form of role playing or examination of case studies in which problems appear.
2. *Articulate the specifics of a problem.* Students need to practice identifying the specific troublesome aspects of problem situations. For example, this could involve the task-analyzing of hypothetical conflict situations.

3. *Develop step-by-step procedures for solving the problem.* Students require models and practice opportunities in the ordering of events that could lead to a problem's solution. For example, case studies and hypothetical problem situations that require several steps for possible resolution can be practiced through role playing and group discussion activities.

4. *Generate a set of alternative strategies to approach a problem.* Using the ordered steps necessary for problem resolution, students need to be able to generate alternative solutions to the presenting problem. Through brainstorming sessions, students should be encouraged to think of all types of possible strategies that could result in problem resolution. This component of the process should not be neglected; there is considerable evidence to suggest that the capacity to generate alternative solutions to problems is positively related to increased problem-solving ability and social adjustment throughout the life span.

5. *Consider the consequences of each of the generated alternatives.* Once the set of possible alternatives has been listed, students should be encouraged to identify the possible consequences for each. This can be structured by having students relate what the worst and best scene scenarios could be for each. This is a critical step. It requires students to project beyond the presenting problem and determine what might happen if a particular alternative is chosen.

6. *Decide on a course of action.* Based on a thorough consideration of alternatives, students are to choose the best alternative for solving the presenting problem.

7. *Verify whether the selected alternative achieved the desired outcome.* Students should be made aware that the initial choice of a solution may not always resolve the problem as anticipated. It may be necessary to consider another alternative.

In terms of efficacy, self-monitoring and interpersonal problem-solving techniques show great promise for teaching appropriate behaviors to students with mild and moderate handicaps. These proactive activities can be employed for intervening with problem classroom behaviors.

Individual Behavior-Change Procedures

When a student's inappropriate behavior patterns cannot be prevented, many teachers employ individual behavior-change procedures. While these often involve considerable amounts of time for planning and monitoring, the initial effort is usually rewarded by increases in appropriate classroom functioning. A step-by-step sequence of activities for implementing individual behavior-change procedures follows.

Rationale and Current Intervention Efforts

Two important concerns should be addressed before the implementation of formal behavior-change procedures. First, the teacher should know why a formal change procedure is necessary. Second, details of previous (and presumably unsuccessful) behavior-change efforts involving the student should be known. In addressing concerns related to the rationale, developing and beginning teachers should be able to readily cite why changing the observed problem behavior is necessary. If the change procedure is to be implemented, the benefits of the effort should be readily interpreted as being of social and educational relevance to the student. A listing of previously unsuccessful behavior-change efforts is necessary to assist in planning for intervention—there is no need to repeat strategies found to be unsuccessful.

Pinpointing a Target Behavior

Educators frequently characterize the inappropriate behaviors of their students in general (e.g., hyperactive, lazy, aggressive) rather than specific terms. These descriptions are not especially useful for individual behavior-change programs. Specific valid and reliable behavioral pinpoints are necessary. The pinpointing process involves moving from general to specific descriptors of behavior. For example, hyperactivity (a general descriptor that would vary from observer to observer) is not a good pinpoint; out-of-seat behavior would be a more useful and reliable descriptor of the problem behavior. A good rule of thumb when developing behavioral pinpoints is to ensure that targeted behaviors (a) are overt, (b) are easily observed, and (c) contain movement. Several individuals observing a student should be able to agree whether or not a target behavior did or did not occur.

Selection of an Observation and Recording Procedure

Once an appropriate target behavior has been pinpointed, a convenient method for observing and recording the behavior should be selected. Alternatives range from labor intensive continuous-recording systems to more time-efficient systems such as behavior sampling (Table 6.4).

Record Baseline Measures of Targeted Behavior

Once decisions have been made on the pinpointing and recording of behavior, a baseline measure of a targeted behavior must be obtained. Baseline refers to the level or intensity of a behavior prior to the intro-

TABLE 6.4   Alternatives for Observing and Recording Behavior

Format	Purpose	Advantages	Disadvantages and Cautions
Continuous recording	Narrative description of behavior allows specification of conditions in which behavior occurs. Can provide general information that will assist when seeking a more formal and objective recording alternative.	Provides a broad-based subjective account of a problem behavior's antecedent and consequent conditions. A useful diagnostic approach to determine the possible environmental interactions that elicit and maintain behavior.	Requires continuous attention and considerable time. Subjective nature can result in reduced accuracy.
Permanent product	A physical product of a behavior can be translated into numerical terms and provide a direct measure of an effect of a behavior. Examples include student worksheets, time-clock records, and videotapes.	Direct observation of student not necessary. Typical practice in most classroom settings. Tangible product allows for review at varying intervals.	Not practical for many behaviors in the social/emotional domain.
Event recording	A simple frequency count of discrete behaviors (e.g., number of swear words, number of times talking-out, and so forth) during a predefined period of time.	Useful with behaviors that have clear beginning and ending parts. Easily recorded with either a checklist, bead counter, or pencil-stroke procedure.	Not useful for long or varying duration behaviors. Requires considerable attention during the predefined observation period. Lower accuracy with very high-rate behaviors.

TABLE 6.4 (*continued*)

Duration recording	A record of how long a behavior occurs within a given time period. Can be used to record the total length of time for each occurrence of a behavior as well as response latency.	Most useful for low-frequency behaviors of moderate to long duration.	Usually used with only one student. Not useful for high-rate behaviors of short duration. Requires continuous attention during observation period and the use of a stopwatch.
Interval recording	A determination of whether or not a behavior occurred within specified time intervals (observation period is divided into smaller, equally sized intervals).	Applicable to a wide range of behaviors and can be used with multiple students. Provides estimates of both frequency and duration of behaviors. Provides information about student behavior across time intervals.	Difficult for teachers to use while instructing students. Length of interval must be appropriate for the behavior targeted.
Momentary time sampling	An on-the-spot determination of whether or not a behavior occurred immediately following specified time intervals.	Allows teaching and data collection to occur simultaneously. Applicable to a wide range of behaviors and can be used with multiple students.	Length of interval must be appropriate for the behavior targeted. Not useful for low-frequency and short-duration behaviors.

duction of an intervention procedure. Data recorded under subsequent intervention phases are compared to the baseline data. There are no general rules as to how long baseline data should be collected. The amount of time will vary according to the behavior pinpointed. Baseline data should continue to be collected until a stable trend is noted. Stability is characterized as the lack of a significant slope in the data and only moderate variability in daily observations. It should be remembered, however, that many aggressive and destructive behaviors require rapid intervention. In such cases, short baseline periods are the only practical course of action, even though they lack the predictive power of longer baseline periods.

Goal Setting

Once the presenting problem has been pinpointed and the baseline data recorded, a goal or set of goals for the intervention should be set. Without goals, teachers would be unable to ascertain if, when, or how well their interventions succeeded. Two of the more common methods for setting behavior management goals are the use of normative data guidelines and consulting previous performance records.

NORMATIVE DATA GUIDELINES   Normative data guidelines attempt to bring students' problem behaviors into line with least restrictive or regular environmental expectations. Therefore, social-emotional goals for students with mild and moderate handicaps should, in most cases, approximate or even match behavioral frequencies found in chronological age-appropriate regular classroom settings. To obtain such data, developing and beginning teachers can observe regular classrooms and collect behavioral frequencies of various prosocial and inappropriate target behaviors. These frequency counts can be used as terminal goals for the students in the special education settings. Such an approach to goal setting is consistent with the goal of normalization and can facilitate the process of returning students to least restrictive educational settings.

PREVIOUS PERFORMANCE GUIDELINES   For certain behavior problems, it is reasonable to expect student performance to match previous intervention outcomes. For example, if a student reduced the rate of hitting others by 80% under a particular contingency management program, it would be reasonable to expect the same goal could be attained with another target behavior (e.g., out-of-seat behavior) under the same or slightly modified management program.

Administration of the Intervention

When selecting an individual or set of intervention procedures, it is important to record all components of the program and to note all environmental changes that accompany the implementation of the procedures. Such precision will produce a resource bank of possible treatment alternatives and facilitate the replication and utilization of successful approaches.

To facilitate the precise recording of a program's components, many educators use behavioral contracts to specify joint agreements between themselves and their students. These contingency contracts list the specific behaviors the contracting parties should emit and the consequences that will result. Contracts are advantageous in individual behavior-change programs because they allow students to work at individualized rates and involve students in the planning of interventions. According to Hall and Hall (1982), contracts should always (a) be stated in positive terms, (b) be designed to promote success (e.g., reward small gradations of change), (c) provide frequent and immediate reinforcement, and (d) be the result of mutual negotiation between teacher and student. The physical body of the contract should contain:

1. The dates the contract is to begin, end, and/or be renegotiated.
2. A clear specification of the behavior or behaviors targeted for intervention.
3. The consequences (i.e., rewards) for meeting the terms of the contract.
4. A listing of who is to provide the consequences.
5. A signature of all parties involved in the contract.

A sample contract is found in Figure 6.1. For more detail on the construction of contracts, consult Hall and Hall (1982), Homme (1977), or Kazdin (1975).

Continuous Analysis of Results

Because data are collected throughout the intervention period, evaluation and interpretation of results are relatively straightforward. By merely "eyeballing" the continuously measured performance of the student in contrast to the goal of the intervention, an assessment of the treatment program's effects can be completed. If the treatment is on a successful course, then it should be continued; if it seems unsuccessful, it should be modified or alternative intervention procedures should be considered.

Follow-up and Maintenance Procedures

Once a treatment goal has been achieved, two interrelated programming activities need to be completed to ensure that the positive outcomes maintain and generalize to nontreatment settings. First, there should be a gradual removal or fading of all external and artificial treatment components. Rapid and unsystematic removal of external treatments will

This is a contract between _____ and _____ .
                                    Student's Name   Teacher's Name

The student _____ agrees to work on the following behaviors:

  1. _____

  2. _____

  3. _____

If I meet the above conditions, I will get from the teacher:

_____

_____

_____

_____

as a special reward. If the terms of the contract are not met by the student, all rewards will be withheld.

Signatures and date

_____   _____
            Student   Date

_____   _____
            Teacher   Date

_____   _____
            Witness   Date

We will review this contract on _____ to reevaluate it.
                                      Date

FIGURE 6.1   Sample behavioral contract.

usually result in the return of inappropriate behaviors. Second, maintenance probes should be scheduled at regular intervals to assess the success of the fading procedure. If the probes indicate a significant loss of treatment gains, intervention procedures with modified maintenance plans will need to be reintroduced.

Group Behavior-Change Procedures

In addition to individual behavior-change strategies, a number of group or whole-class management alternatives are available. Three such procedures, token economies, class contingencies, and level systems, are described below.

Whole-Class Token Economies

A system that employs tokens is referred to as a token economy. In such a system, tokens function in ways very similar to currency in our own national economy. Tokens are used to purchase available backup reinforcers, which can include treats, trinkets, activities, and privileges. Token economies have been implemented in special education, remedial, and regular classroom environments and have been successful in changing a variety of inappropriate classroom behaviors. Token systems have also been successful in improving academic performance and raising standardized test scores.

Unfortunately, it is beyond the scope of this chapter to provide all of the specifics necessary to design and implement a successful whole-class token economy. It would be useful, however, to review several general guidelines prepared by Slavin (1986).

First, the specific behaviors that will be targeted for reinforcement need to be decided on and articulated clearly. In general, these targeted behaviors should be similar in content to the stated rules, procedures, and behavioral standards of the classroom.

Second, a logistically appropriate point system needs to be developed. A range of alternative schedules for the systematic delivery of points is available. In some environments, teachers can wait till the end of an instructional period before awarding earned points; in other settings, the behavioral characteristics of the students require that points be awarded more frequently. Similarly, there are a number of alternatives for the recording of points. In some instances, students are able to keep track of their own points, while in others recordkeeping must be the responsibility of the teacher.

Third, a selection of backup reinforcers needs to be developed. Each of the selections should be assigned a price, with many items being small enough that a student can earn a tangible backup in one day. There should also be a number of highly desirable big awards that require the saving of points over time.

Fourth, a response cost system that deducts points for specific instances of misbehavior should be considered. While such a system is not necessary for routine and minor instances of misbehavior, it could be

very effective in reducing instances of disruptive and aggressive behaviors.

Finally, plans must be made for the eventual fading of the extrinsic
controls. The outcome of a behavior modification program is considered
successful only when appropriate behaviors occur without artificial points
and nonnormative backup reinforcers.

Whole-Class Contingencies

Although they are less systematic than token economies, class contingencies can be used to promote and maintain appropriate classroom
behavior. In class contingency situations, the entire class receives consequences based on the behavior of its group members. Several types of
informal, whole-class contingencies can be used. For example, teachers
can put marbles, chips, or paper clips in a canister whenever they catch
students engaging in a targeted appropriate behavior or remove one of
the objects if a rule is violated (Mastropieri & Scruggs, 1987). When the
receptacle is filled, the whole class could share in a group reward such
as a party or field trip. In a second type of whole-class program, an
individual disruptive student could be made responsible for the earning
of reinforcers for the entire class of students based on his or her performance alone (Kazdin, 1975). In such an instance, all members of the
class would share in the benefits when one troublesome student behaves
appropriately.

The Good Behavior Game, originally formulated by Barrish, Saunders,
and Wolf (1969), is a formal group contingency program that has had
a long history of reducing disruptive behaviors. The game is implemented in four steps.

1. The classroom rules are stated, and the class is divided into two teams.
2. The teacher awards negative marks whenever any member of a team
   engages in a prespecified inappropriate behavior.
3. The team with the lowest number of marks is declared winner for
   the day and is given some form of reinforcement.
4. The losing team is required to do some extra work and/or forfeit a
   privilege.

It is generally believed that group contingencies work because group
members encourage one another to do the things required to earn the
reward. Overenthusiastic encouragement can, in some cases, get out of
hand. Developing and beginning teachers who employ group contingencies should ensure that peers do not use coercive or threatening means
to pressure others into behaving appropriately.

Level Systems

A level system is a group management alternative that accommodates the differing entry level behavioral skills of students within a learning environment. The system is an organizational framework within which varying intensities of management alternatives are applied. At each level of a particular system, there are specific expectations and corresponding privileges that can be earned for meeting the expectations. Students' points of entry into a system and their progress through the levels depends on the intensity of their presenting problems as well as progress through the various levels of the system (Bauer, Shea, & Keppler, 1986). The system serves to shape student behavior gradually by providing opportunities for movement through varying intensities of expectations and management alternatives. The ultimate goal of most level systems is self-management.

Level systems are flexible and can be applied in resource, self-contained day-school and residential settings (see, for example, Braaten, 1979; Mastropieri, Jenne, & Scruggs, 1988). Developing and beginning teachers can employ these systems with both elementary and secondary students. Bauer et al. (1986) have provided guidelines for the planning and implementation of levels systems (Box 6.4).

Summary

In this chapter, we covered a range of issues related to the area of classroom management. Our goal was to provide a series of strategies that could be used to promote discipline and self-control. We began by noting that there are no magic bullets, formulas, or recipes that guarantee appropriate student behaviors in classrooms for mild and moderate students. The management of classrooms involves strategies and procedures designed to increase the probability that classrooms run effectively and efficiently.

The following strategies to prevent discipline problems were presented: (a) the development and maintenance of an appropriate management perspective, (b) teacher readiness, (c) the design of the physical environment, (d) the development of rules and procedures, and (e) the coordination of schoolwide cooperation.

Procedures for intervening with student misbehavior were presented with special emphases on methods for increasing and decreasing behavior. Strategies for promoting self-control were also provided. Step-by-step guidelines were provided for the completion of individual behavior-change efforts and the chapter concluded with a brief overview of three group behavior-change alternatives.

BOX 6.4

Guidelines for the Planning and Implementation of Levels Systems

Step 1: Determine the entry-level behaviors of the students with whom the system is to be applied.

Step 2: Determine the terminal behavior expectations for the students.

Step 3: Formulate at least two but no more than four sets of behavioral expectations which seem to be appropriately graded steps between those expectations described in steps 1 and 2. Label each of the steps level 1 through level "x".

Step 4: Consider the inclusion of a transition level. This would allow for part-time placement at a higher level for a portion of the school day.

Step 5: Determine the privileges appropriate for students at level 1 and for students ready to terminate the program.

Step 6: For each of the levels developed in step 3, list corresponding privileges that would be appropriate. Ensure an equal distribution among the levels and remember to reduce the amount of direct supervision as students progress through the levels.

Step 7: Consider the following logistical concerns:
a. How, when, and at what frequency will a student's level status be reviewed?
b. Who will review a student's status?
c. How will self-monitoring procedures be implemented?

Step 8: Determine how to facilitate communication among the many individuals (e.g., parents, administrators, related service personnel, etc.) involved in the student's education in the levels system.

SOURCE   Bauer, A. M., Shea, T. M., & Keppler, R. (1986). Levels Systems: A framework for the individualization of behavior management. *Behavioral Disorders, 4,* 211–218. Reprinted with permission.

References

BARRISH, H. H., SAUNDERS, M., & WOLF, M. M. (1969). Good behavior game: Effects of individual contingenices on disruptive behavior in the classroom. *Journal of Applied Behavior Analysis, 2,* 119–124.

BAUER, A. M., SHEA, T. M., & KEPPLER, R. (1986). Levels systems: A framework for the individualization of behavior management. *Behavioral Disorders, 12,* 28–35.

BRAATAN, S. (1979). The Madison School program: Programming for secondary level severely emotionally disturbed youth. *Behavioral Disorders, 4,* 211–218.

CURWIN, R. L., & MENDLER, A. N. (1988). Discipline with dignity. *Alexandria, VA: Association for Supervision and Curriculum Development.*

D'ZURILLA, T., & GOLDFRIED, M. (1971). Problem-solving and behavior modification. *Journal of Abnormal Psychology, 78,* 101–126.

GOOD, T. L., & BROPHY, J. E. (1987). *Looking into classrooms* (4th ed.). New York: Harper & Row.

GROSSNICKLE, D. R., & SESKO, F. P. (1985). *Promoting effective discipline in school and classroom: A practitioner's perspective.* Reston, VA: National Association of Secondary School Principals.

HALL, R. V., & HALL, M. C. (1982). *How to negotiate a behavioral contract.* Lawrence, KS: H & H Enterprises.

HALLAHAN, D. P., LLOYD, J. W., & STOLLER, L. (1982). *Improving attention with self-monitoring: A manual for teachers.* Charlottesville, VA: Learning Disabilities Research Institute, University of Virginia.

HOMME, L. (1977). *How to use contingency contracting in the classroom.* Champaign, IL: Research Press.

KAZDIN, A. E. (1975). *Behavior modification in applied settings.* Homewood, IL: Dorsey Press.

KOUNIN, J. S. (1970). *Discipline and group management in classrooms.* New York: Holt, Rinehart, & Winston.

PAINE, S. C., RADICCI, J., ROSELLINI, L. C., DEUTCHMAN, L., & DARCH, C. R. (1983). *Structuring your classroom for academic success.* Champaign, IL: Research Press.

MASTROPIERI, M. A., JENNE, T., & SCRUGGS, T. E. (1988). A level system for managing problem behaviors in a high school resource program. *Behavioral Disorders, 13,* 202–208.

MASTROPIERI, M. A., & SCRUGGS, T. E. (1987). *Effective instruction for special education.* Boston: College-Hill.

SLAVIN, R. E. (1986). *Educational psychology: Theory into practice.* Englewood Cliffs, NJ: Prentice-Hall.

SMITH, R. M., NEISWORTH, J. T., & GREER, J. G. (1978). *Evaluating educational environments.* Columbus, OH: Merrill.

SPIVACK, G., & SHURE, M. B. (1982). The cognition of social adjustment: Interpersonal cognitive problem-solving. In B.B. Lahey & A.E. Kazdin (Eds.), *Advances in clinical child psychology* (vol. 5.). New York: Plenum.

VEENMAN, S. (1984). Perceived problems of beginning teachers. *Review of Educational Research, 54,* 143–178.

WESTLING, D. L., & KOORLAND, M. A. (1988). *The special educator's handbook.* Boston: Allyn & Bacon.

WEBER, W. A., & ROFF, L. A. (1983). A review of the teacher education literature on classroom management. In W. A. Weber, J. Crawford, L. A. Roff, & C. Robinson (Eds.), *Classroom management: Reviews of the teacher education and research literature* (pp. 7–43). Princeton, NJ: Educational Testing Service.

CHAPTER 7

The Paperwork

Although there may be some local differences in format and content, required documentation and paperwork involved in special education are very similar nationwide. This chapter summarizes typical documentation.

Dislike and stress appear to be major potential problems confronting developing and beginning teachers when they are asked to complete paperwork. However, most experienced members of the profession can confirm: Managing classrooms successfully entails careful, written records on students and on actions demonstrated by teachers. Effective paperwork is one key to survival for many teachers.

A major thrust of the chapter is the documentation necessary in the referral process of special education and the flexible role of the special educator. Special educators function as **consultants** when students with mild to moderate handicaps are educated in the mainstream, and as **direct-service providers** when students meet the criteria for formal placement into specialized programming. Additionally, IEPs and IEP meetings are discussed in this chapter as legal plans parents and professionals develop together. A discussion of specific behaviors of classroom teachers before, during, and after the IEP meeting is intended to promote the IEP as a working document.

The chapter ends with suggestions to help developing and beginning teachers write reports about the students' progress. Continuous communication with parents and significant professionals is an important means of maintaining quality programs and services to students.

Simulated Case Example

A fictitious student named Lindsay Christopher, age 9, will be followed throughout the chapter using examples of required paperwork. Starting with pertinent data from her regular class setting, examples of the kinds of data professionals may collect will be illustrated. Beginning and developing teachers will be able to note the types of data useful to parents and professionals as Lindsay progresses through the referral process. Background information (Box 7.1) is included to help beginning and developing teachers gain insights into Lindsay's needs.

Developing Useful Paperwork: A Rationale

There can be no doubt that when teachers enter the classroom for the first time, many hours are spent in developing and maintaining written data. Long hours are used in recording student behaviors or in planning classroom events. Special education paperwork includes: (a) screening data, (b) written records of individual student progress, (c) observation records, (d) assessment results, (e) cumulative school files, (f) health and sensory notations, (g) IEPs, (h) written inquiries and responses to parents, guardians, regular classroom teachers, or others, and (i) lesson plans, or unit teaching summaries. The use of effective paperwork requires time, effort, and patience. There is a bright note: as experience develops, teachers may find demands minimized considerably. Once teachers are in the habit of using paperwork effectively, stressful tasks will be made easier.

Although tedious and time-consuming, written products are important for a compelling reason: Federal law requires written documentation by professionals on students with special needs (Education for All Handicapped Children's Act [EHA], 1975; Federal Register, 1975). Involvement in legal responsibilities of paperwork, however, can be stressful to teachers (Barner, 1982; Morsink, 1982). Some stress and conflict may be inevitable; however, the time spent developing and using paperwork should not be considered wasted time. Accurate, written information helps to create a conducive learning environment for students and a more organized workplace for adults. The development and maintenance of paperwork can also sharpen teachers' instructional, management, communication, and consulting skills. Maintaining paperwork helps professionals to make educational decisions about students and about classroom happenings. Paperwork has multiple uses to professionals working with students with special needs:

• Professional observations, analyses, and judgments in order to make educational decisions for students.

BOX 7.1

Background Information on Lindsay Christopher

Lindsay is a well-mannered, attractive youngster presently attending a third grade classroom in a large urban school. Lindsay recently transferred from another school district in the state. As of this time, few prior school records were available. School officials from her previous school did send an incomplete cumulative record of her kindergarten experience. Former professionals indicated her normal progress in kindergarten. However, no data were received describing her school progress during the last 2 years when she attended grades 1 and 2.

During the current school year, Lindsay is considered a potential candidate for special education because of problems in reading comprehension and study skills. On the Cromer Achievement Test, given by her present teacher, Ms. Marshall, Lindsay performed at 3.7 in mathematics, 1.9 in reading, and 3.3 in spelling. Chapter tests from the Universal Reading Series, level 3, were provided by her teacher. Lindsay had not mastered the first group of objectives from chapter 1 of this reading series suggesting to Ms. Marshall some of her difficulties in reading comprehension.

Lindsay's speech and language development appear to be adequate for a child of her age. Ms. Marshall reported, also, Lindsay's near-perfect handwriting skills and her love of drawing. Lindsay's motor development is adequate for a child in the third grade. She is able to run, jump, skip, and hop as most children her age. She competes satisfactorily in physical education with her classmates and performs exceptionally well in swimming. Lindsay's medical history is unnotable.

In the classroom, Lindsay neither begins on time nor completes assignments in reading. Other subject area requirements do not appear to pose problems to her. She continues to perform well in mathematics and spelling, although assignments in social skills and science are beginning to contain more required reading skills than previously. Ms. Marshall reported to her principal that she fears Lindsay is falling further and further behind her classmates as the school year continues.

- Varied explanations of variables, trends, and patterns appearing in students' past schooling, home, or community, providing clues to present behaviors.
- Determination of the most effective and efficacious way to instruct and manage students in the LRE.

- Modifications of curriculum, strategies, or programs.
- Explanation of links between the regular class placement and special education placement based on students' present education abilities.
- Continual verification of students' needs to remain in or exit from special education and related services.
- Accounts of actions in the classroom (e.g., lesson planning and unit planning as discussed in Chapter 4).
- Communication efforts with other professionals and parents.

Examples of potential problems confronting the teacher in completing paperwork and solutions to these problems are presented in Box 7.2. If implemented early in the novice teacher's career, these suggestions may reduce the time, effort, and stress associated with completion of paperwork.

Dilemma in Providing Services

In the 1980s, researchers reported a large number of students exhibiting academic and behavioral difficulties in public school settings (Ysseldyke & Algozzine, 1984). Special educators are being asked to serve increasing numbers of these students each year (Algozzine, Ysseldyke, & Christenson, 1983; Ysseldyke & Algozzine, 1984). The role of the special educator is evolving to include dimensions both of direct-service provider and consultant (Schulz & Turnbull, 1984). It is questionable whether special educators can and should serve all students affected with learning and behavioral problems under direct services (i.e., instructing students in pull-out programs from the regular class).

Reformers of special education of the late 1980s called for a new look at the way services are provided to students with special needs and at the process of documenting students' needs to be removed from the regular classroom. One reform movement is the REI. Proponents of REI suggest students with mild to moderate handicaps can be served better in general education classrooms. Funding would need to be redistributed fairly so that monies and services are redirected toward needs of students where they are placed. While the REI is not adopted by all professionals in special education (Braaten et al., 1988), the implementation of the REI can be viewed as a unique opportunity to instruct diverse populations of students in nonrestrictive settings (Maheady, 1988). If the REI reform movement comes to fruition in the 1990s, the role of the special education teacher will change.

A major duty of the special educator will be as consultant rather than solely as direct-service provider (Graden, Casey, & Bonstrom, 1985; Graden, Casey, & Christenson, 1985; Schulz & Turnbull, 1984). Consultant services include special education teachers and regular education teachers working together and with other professionals under a team-

BOX 7.2

Problems in Completing Paperwork and Potential Strategies to Prevent or Remediate Problems

1. **Unawareness of required forms, data collection, paperwork, and so forth**.

   Potential strategy: Take the time to become familiar with the content on forms prior to completion. Read directions in advance of completion. Be aware of and plan for required due dates, necessary signatures, and so forth.

2. **No plan for handling paperwork**.

   Potential strategy: Develop a plan to screen, consolidate, and prioritize the completion of forms. Use trial and error strategies in the implementation process. If problems arise, revise the plan with input from administrators, experienced special education teachers, and regular classroom teachers. Use self-evaluation techniques.

3. **Unavailability of factual information**.

   Potential strategy: Be prepared. Study past cumulative files, grade records, health histories, attendance files, and so forth of students. Talk with parents. Obtain information from the home, community, and former teachers. Store obtained facts in an accessible location for later use during school-based committees, case conferences, and so forth.

4. **Lack of time to complete paperwork**.

   Potential strategy: Find the time. Complete a daily schedule, doing paperwork in a specified time slot. Work as a team. Elicit help from others (e.g., more experienced colleagues) to complete paperwork. Ask paraprofessionals to complete demographic information or any data not requiring confidentiality. Write down and make only written decisions paraprofessionals can't.

5. **Inadequate notice to/from others contributing to written product**.

   Potential strategy: Ask for a written request for expected contributions and materials. Request written due dates if not given. Encourage others to specify notices in writing at all times. Provide an outline of required information when soliciting data from others.

6. **Unrealistic priorities.**

   Potential strategy: List what needs to be done first, second, and so forth. Put first things first. Resist unnecessary change.

(continued)

BOX 7.2 (continued)

7. **Overplanning**.
    Potential strategy: Monitor paperwork continually. Plan less (e.g., allow transition time for teachers and paraprofessionals). Write down only essential data. Use a tape recorder in lieu of writing whenever possible.

8. **Lack of policies and procedures for completion**.
    Potential strategy: Clarify your role with administrators and other teachers for completing paperwork. Ask many questions. Persist. Be diligent.

9. **Lack of skills for improving paperwork**.
    Potential strategy: Set and realize deadlines. Use cues to remind yourself when paperwork is due (e.g., write out short, daily to-do lists to yourself). Self-monitor progress. Solicit feedback from others. Self-evaluate. Attend workshops and professional conferences for updated information.

10. **Lost data**.
    Potential strategy: Keep a copy of all written data turned in to others in an accessible location. Initial and date all copies. Throw out all unnecessary, outdated copies.

11. **Lack of motivation to complete paperwork**.
    Potential strategy: Become aware of the impact of your own teacher effectiveness on students, parents, peers, and so forth. Seek individual causes for lack of motivation and self-correct.

12. **Inadequate maintenance and storage of paperwork**.
    Potential strategy: Keep a copy of all written data in an accessible location. Set up a realistic filing system. File important documentation immediately. Computerize as much as possible. Use a tape recorder in lieu of written documentation whenever possible.

model approach. Consultant services depend heavily on prereferral planning, cooperation, and data collection of accurate documentation from a variety of sources.

Prereferral Process

Prereferral consists of procedures for problem solving (consultation) and intervention as the first step of special education referral. It provides assistance to students and their teachers in the regular class, where the problems first arise. The actions of prereferral were identified by Graden and co-workers (Graden, Casey, & Bonstrom, 1985; Graden, Casey, &

Christenson, 1985) as a logical first step in professional efforts to help students remain in the LRE.

Important questions, based on the work of Cartwright, Cartwright, and Ward (1981) and posed by multidisciplinary team members, may be helpful to new teachers to determine appropriate prereferral strategies for students exhibiting mild to moderate problems. These questions can help to guide the types of data and written products teachers will collect. Examples are:

- Under what conditions does the student seem to have the most trouble?
- What specifically are the student's problem areas?
- What specifically are the student's strengths?
- How does the student learn best (e.g., independently, in small groups)?
- Does the student display both academic weaknesses and problem behaviors?
- What has been tried thus far by professionals?
- Are current approaches successful? Why or why not?

Written documentation can be collected to help professionals specify students' strengths and weaknesses. Effective beginning and developing teachers will consult with regular classroom teachers and other professionals in prereferral attempts. In the case example, prereferral questions were posed to Lindsay's classroom teacher, Ms. Marshall (Box 7.3). Ms. Marshall provided important clues in specifying some of Lindsay's strengths and weaknesses in the regular classroom setting.

Paperwork in the Referral Process

The referral process includes a comprehensive collection of documentation from many sources including data of present progress in the current educational setting, prior school records, sensory screening results, both formal and informal observations, assessments, and past health records. Among relevant data required to refer a student for a change in educational placement is evidence the student was provided the full opportunity to remain in the LRE, the setting closest to the regular class (EHA, 1975; Federal Register, 1977). To remove a student from instruction with mainstream students for even part of the day, written data are required to establish the need for a change in placement and the type of instruction the student receives.

Written documentation of prereferral is actually the first step in the formalized referral process of special education (Gloeckler & Simpson,

BOX 7.3

Prereferral Questions on Lindsay Christopher

Lindsay's teachers were asked to answer prereferral questions about her classroom progress. This is what her teacher, Ms. Marshall, wrote:

1. **Under what conditions does the student seem to have the most trouble?**

   Lindsay demonstrates problems during independent study periods and unstructured class time. She also has noted difficulties with reading, especially when asked to complete read and answer sheets.

2. **What specifically are the student's problem areas?**

   Lindsay's main problem appears to be self-management. She just doesn't seem to want to try in reading. However, I'm not sure she has the ability to comprehend the tasks required of her. Perhaps the assignments are too difficult. She lacks many reading comprehension skills for a child in the third grade.

3. **What specifically are the student's strengths?**

   Lindsay demonstrates strong skills in basic mathematical operations. She has excellent abilities in spelling. However, none of these tasks has required much reading so far. Another strength I notice is how well she gets along with peers and adults. I think she really does try to please others.

4. **How does the student learn best (e.g., independently, in small groups)?**

   Lindsay appears to learn best in small groups. I've noticed she does well when she works with a classmate. She also works well in one-on-one situations with adults. I just can't always have someone there to work with her.

5. **Does the student display both academic weaknesses and problem behaviors?**

   Her main problem areas appear to be reading comprehension and completion of independent work.

6. **What has been tried thus far by professionals?**

   Lindsay has worked with minimal success with our classroom paraprofessional. School volunteers have tried also to tutor her. It seems she would rather socialize with them than complete her tasks.

7. **Are current approaches successful? Why or why not?**

   Unknown at this time.

BOX 7.4

Data of the Completed Referral Process

PRESENT EDUCATION-SETTING DOCUMENTATION

- Data of students' deviations from the norm of classroom behaviors.
- Data collection by professionals and parents from the home, school, or community.
- School-based planning meeting results.
- Prereferral strategy-implementation results.
- Professional observations.
- Case study conference results.

TESTING DATA

- Sensory-screening results.
- Consent for individualized testing by parents.
- Complete battery of tests.
- Explanation and interpretation of formal testing in a written report.
- Written results of eligibility meetings determining educational placement.

INDIVIDUALIZED EDUCATION PLANS

- Consent for placement by parents.
- Initial placement IEPs.
- Annual updated IEPs.
- Results and implications of reevaluations.

1988). The completed referral process should include data related to (a) the present education setting, (b) testing, and (c) individualized education plans. Box 7.4 is included to delineate components of the completed referral process. Each of the areas of the completed referral process will be explained below through typical actions of school professionals. Examples of required paperwork are provided in each section.

Beginning and developing teachers should note that the forms and content of required paperwork may differ slightly from school district to school district. Names of meetings and professional teams (e.g., school-based committee meetings, educational-planning teams) may differ from locale to locale. However, professional team members completing effective paperwork share the common theme: providing evidence the student is served in the educational setting best suited to his or her needs.

Present Education Setting

Students may deviate from others in cognition, language, self-help, motor, behavior, social-emotional skills, or other domains. The teacher's task is to begin to discern whether students who display deviations require specialized assistance.

Deviations from the Norm

In many school systems, regular classroom teachers complete similar tasks as they go about the daily challenges of implementing instruction and managing the behaviors of students. Most teachers observe students and measure progress through teacher-made materials, chapter tests, student-made products, commercially prepared assessment devices, academic rating scales, or behavioral checklists. Every teacher observes and assesses each student daily either by formal methods (e.g., checklists, rating scales, tests) or by informal methods (e.g., discussions with past teachers, unstructured comments). Effective teachers are able to discern their students' patterns of normal behaviors (Cartwright et al., 1981). Through assessment and observations of all students, teachers begin to note those displaying some variations from others in learning tasks, social behaviors, organizational skills, attention to tasks, study skills, developmental milestones, or cultural expectations. If teachers are familiar with students' backgrounds, they use data that are continually being generated in the classroom, home, and community to identify and screen out students suspected of low ability, learning difficulties, or problem behaviors. Concerned teachers may examine data in the student's cumulative folder in order to discern grade levels repeated, school achievement, past test results, anecdotal information, and attendance patterns (Gloeckler & Simpson, 1988). Other teachers may talk with parents and community personnel involved with the student and family. Individuals whose behaviors differ greatly from the norm may require more formalized observations and evaluations. When deviations are noted frequently, over time, and to such an intensity the teacher believes the student is in danger behaviorally or academically, other professional judgment is required. More data need to be generated on the targeted student in order to make appropriate educational decisions (Cartwright et al., 1981). As an example, Figure 7.1 shows paperwork collected from Lindsay's home, community, and school that are useful in educational screenings.

Data Collection by Multi-Professionals

An educational planning team (EPT) is typically necessary when evidence is found indicating that an individual stands out from his or her peers. The team may be called by a host of titles, but the intent of professionals

Home

Complies with parental demands?	yes
Demonstrates good rapport with siblings?	yes
Completes chores routinely?	no
Displays self-help skills?	yes
Are developmental milestones on time?	yes
Demonstrates adequate health/nutrition?	yes

School

Displays academic weaknesses?	yes
Has problem behaviors?	no
Demonstrates adequate organization skills?	no
Demonstrates adequate study skills?	no
Displays adequate social-emotional development?	yes
Displays adequate speech/language skills?	yes
Has adequate motor abilities?	yes

Community

Frequents social organizations?	yes
Demonstrates leisure-time activities?	yes
Uses community resources?	yes
Complies adequately with neighborhood peers?	yes
Complies with community norms?	yes
Has and uses a support system?	yes

Comments: Parents' report: Lindsay does not always fulfill her family responsibilities at home. She sometimes completes household chores haphazardly. She will complete adequately if offered a reward. She needs to be reminded often. She doesn't always remember what her home chores are.

School social worker's report: Lindsay appears to function adequately in her community setting. She demonstrates no major problems with peers, neighborhood organizations, and community groups.

Teacher's report: Lindsay's organizational and study skills are of concern. She doesn't complete required assignments and rarely brings in homework papers.

Darby Olsen, Social Worker
February 1, 1990

Mr. Thompson, Counselor
February 1, 1990

FIGURE 7.1 Home, school, and community data of Lindsay.

is to discover more information on the target student differing in important ways from other students. The team of multidisciplinary professionals may include principals, counselors, school psychologists, educational diagnosticians, specialized subject-area teachers, nurses, therapists, special education teachers, or other teachers and administrators. The purposes of an EPT meeting are twofold: (a) to generate classroom strategies (i.e., prereferral strategies) to help the student remain in the present setting, and (b) to determine observation schedules needed to verify the student's progress toward the regular classroom goals and prereferral objectives.

Prereferral Strategy Implementation

Strategies are implemented by the regular classroom teacher with consulting help by the special education teacher, psychologist, administrator, clinician, counselor, or others. A functioning multidisciplinary team shares rights and responsibilities in the efforts to help the student succeed with prereferral strategies. Rights pertinent to regular teachers and special education teachers (based on Schulz and Turnball, 1984) include:

- The opportunity to attend all meetings in which educational decisions are made affecting the student and professionals involved with the student.
- A chance to select appropriate content, methodology, or objectives from a program to use in assessment or instructional activities implemented in prereferral attempts.
- Access to all specialized materials, equipment, and curricula that would make instruction and management easier in the regular classroom setting.
- Participation in baseline data collection, strategies implementation, and teaching modification monitoring.
- Input and feedback into all learning strategies and behavioral management steps devised as prereferral strategies.
- Assistance in acquiring resources and extra classroom helpers, including parents, volunteers, aides, specialized itinerant help, or peer tutors.

Responsibilities of professionals to prereferral implementation should be recognized also and include:

- Demonstrated competency in given specialization areas.
- Display of effective organization of the learning environment.
- Ongoing observation of and data collection on strategies and management steps.
- Continual and objective assessment.
- Individualization based on students' needs.

- Attempts to make baseline data collections, prereferral strategies, observations, and other teaching modifications relevant so that students with special needs are a part of all regular class activities.
- Monitoring of student's academic and social-emotional requirements over time.
- Consultation efforts including input of parents and professionals.

Together with other team members, the special education teacher helps to determine the success of attempts to remediate within the current setting. Schulz and Turnbull (1984) recognized the importance of teaming attempts. A team approach means special educators, regular teachers, principals, counselors, school psychologists, librarians, therapists, paraprofessionals, students, parents, community volunteers, and professional/consumer organizations all have opportunities in planning and implementing strategies to help students remain in the mainstream with normally functioning peers. Emphasis is directed to coordinate and monitor all involvement carefully in order to maximize the ultimate benefit to students. Coordination, communication, and cooperation are keys to shared strategy implementation and successful programming.

The developing special education teacher and other team members may be called on to assist the regular classroom teacher to devise and implement strategies such as those listed in Box 7.5. Examples of applied activities of the teacher are listed under each strategy.

Examples of components of the paperwork used in prereferral strategies are illustrated on Figure 7.2. On this form, modifications in prereferral strategies are planned with implementers collecting data on Lindsay's baseline level. There is a space to monitor modifications every day of the week for 6 weeks. Professionals at Lindsay's school discovered the necessity to review her educational program at the end of the 6-week period. Prereferral modifications of teaching strategies were not enough to remediate her problems in independent study skills and reading comprehension. Teaming efforts must be intensified for her, and more formal data are required. As in Lindsay's and other students' cases, observations of the strategies by professionals other than the regular classroom teacher (e.g., special education teacher, psychologist, counselor, principal) help to provide evidence of objective modifications in teaching or changes in procedures. Observations may indicate, also, students require more help by specialists than can be provided in the present setting.

Professional Observations

Professionals who observe students with learning and behavioral problems highlight data on the appropriateness of the current setting. When many strategies have been tried, professionals familiar with the students

BOX 7.5

Prereferral Implementation Strategies

1. Special modifications in teaching strategies.
   - Team teach with peers often, especially in individual areas of expertise.
   - Write the homework assignments on the blackboard and have students copy into their notebooks. Make sure the directions are clear.
   - Team students (peer tutoring) who have complementary strengths and weaknesses. The entire class can begin independent study at the same time using this buddy system.
   - Let some students listen to taped reading assignments while others work on computerized assignments or read from texts. Change groups so all students experience a variety of teaching modes.

2. Changes in classroom materials.
   - Break the work into short assignments. Place a marker over distracting pictures or other stimuli.
   - Use audiovisual equipment with students as often as possible.
   - Raise the stimulus value of elements to be learned: any novel emphasis will help (e.g., color coding, emphatic use of voice, animation of materials).
   - Block off sections of work the student has completed so that she is aware of where the assignment is on the page.
   - Encourage the use of a typewriter for students whose writing is slow and labored.
   - Prerecord the classroom material to assist the slow reader.

3. Varying evaluation/schedules to be used.
   - Adjust grades so that the student is not constantly experiencing failing marks.
   - Consider alternatives to grades such as rewards for conduct, effort, and so forth.
   - Count intermittent scores on academic tests.
   - Eliminate lowest and highest scores occasionally and go with average scores.

4. Modified curricula.
   - If students are required to take notes in class, provide an outline of general topics, so that students can keep notes in order.
   - Allow slow learners to complete work at their own pace.

BOX 7.5 *(continued)*

> • Integrate subject areas students succeed in (e.g., let students draw the answer rather than write it if art is a strong subject for students).

5. Identification of effective assessment techniques for learning weaknesses and problem behaviors.
   • Consider that spelling and grammar need not be the basis for grading if mastery of the content is the objective.
   • Draw lines on or fold worksheets and tests to divide them into various sections by types, questions, or problems.
   • Use a variety of formal and informal assessment techniques.
   • Consider curriculum-based assessment rather than standardized assessment.

6. Behavior management plans specific to the student's observed problems.
   • Set up contingency contracting: the completion of X before the student is able to do Y.
   • Devise a token economy or point systems: students earn tokens that are exchanged for specific rewards.
   • Use time-out: the removal of the student from an apparently reinforcing setting to a presumably nonreinforcing setting for a specified and limited period of time.

can help to determine the success of prereferral planning. These individuals can provide an objective perspective to the students' opportunities to meet the classroom teachers' or parents' expectations. An appropriate observer may be an administrator, school psychologist, school counselor, or another teacher familiar with the target student.

In each observation, the selection of a valid data collection procedure should be matched to the student's needs. Data should be collected through systematic procedures ensuring replicability and use of discrete behaviors. This means that areas of strengths and problem behaviors of students are specified (i.e., defined in observable terminology for use by professionals). Efficient and consistent observation procedures ensure that the behaviors were actually observed. To increase the likelihood of interrater reliability, two or more observers must agree on the behaviors that occurred (Cartwright et al., 1981).

The use of a stop watch or clock to time observations and a graph of the results may help to produce evidence of strategy effectiveness. Tangible products also can be observed and measured systematically for clues to the target student's strengths or problem areas including the student's organization or study skills, appropriateness of the teacher-

Student's Name _Lindsay Christopher_ Teacher _Ms. Marshall_

School _Howard Elementary_ Birthdate _May 14, 1982_

Date _March 9, 1990_ Subject area _Reading_

Modification(s) in (circle):   (Teaching strategies)   Classroom materials
                                 Evaluation schedules   Curriculum
                                 Assessment   Behavior management
                                 Other

Describe modification(s):   * _Peer tutoring with another student to aid in_
                                 Lindsay's reading skills.

Reason for prereferral: * _Lindsay cannot complete classwork independently._

Target student's baseline   * _4/5 times Lindsay does not turn in reading compre-_
level in problem area: _hension materials when asked to do so._

Student progress (describe):   _Lindsay's progress has been minimal. Tom W._
                                 (peer) has been assigned to help her complete
                                 reading comprehension papers.

Modification	Week 1	Week 2	Week 3	Week 4	Week 5	Week 6	Comments
M	R=62% P	R=59% P	—	—	—	R=60% P	_Papers turned in on Monday with teacher's cue. (Accuracy is low — 60%.)_
T	R=40% P	absent	R=60% P	R=50% P	—	—	_Accuracy is low, x̄ = Papers turned in 3/6 times._
W	R=10% P	—	R=5% P	—	—	—	_Comprehension problems noted._
T	—	—	—	R=62% P	—	—	_Low turn-in rate; 62% accuracy rate._
F	R=50% P	—	—	—	absent	—	* _Lindsay has not responded to peer tutoring strategy/less work requirements._

Professional's name/title   _Ms. Marshall - Teacher,   Mr. Thompson - Counselor_
                                 Ms. New - Special Education Teacher

$P =$ _Paper completed and turned in_

$R =$ _Accuracy rate (percentage of correct comprehension questions) for independent work_

FIGURE 7.2   Prereferral strategies implemented in Lindsay's regular classroom.

BOX 7.6

Methods of Observations on Lindsay

A. Record of student's permanent products (e.g., worksheets, artwork, and so forth):

___✓___ 1. Collect and keep a record of these products.

___✓___ 2. Systematically analyze the quality of student's products.

___✓___ 3. Engage in error analysis (i.e., systematic analysis of the kinds of errors students make).

Comments: *During a 6-week period, work samples were collected 10 out of 64 times (30% of total work required). Accuracy rate, reported by Ms. Marshall, was in the low range (62%). Most errors were reported to be careless errors, although reading comprehension problems were noted. Ms. Marshall suspected that the reading material may be too difficult for Lindsay. Motivation may also be a problem.*

B. Anecdotal records:

___✓___ 1. Write down recollections of the occurrence of specific behaviors.

___✓___ 2. Keep a log of teacher's comments.

Comments: *Ms. Marshall keeps a daily log of Lindsay's progress. Lindsay appears to socialize during peer-tutoring sessions rather than attend to assignments. She is reported to be off-task for more than 70% of the independent reading time. When given one-on-one instruction she often completes the reading assignments accurately (if instruction provided by her teacher is a direct instruction format). This last observation of successful direct instruction was observed by Ms. New, special education teacher.*

C. Frequency counts:

___✓___ 1. Record the frequency of observable behaviors.

___✓___ 2. Record the extent to which other students exhibit same behaviors.

___✓___ 3. Compare target student's behaviors to others.

Comments: *Relative to other students, Lindsay's independent study skills are off-target (average observation was 8 out of 12 times she did not complete and organize work). Independent reading assignments completed only 4/14 trials. Accuracy rates reported to be 85% when direct instruction was provided by Ms. Marshall. (Observations were reported by Ms. New, special education teacher.)*

D. Duration recordings:

___✓___ 1. Gather data on the occurrence of the behavior by recording the length of time it persists.

___✓___ 2. Indicate initiation time and ending time of behavior.

Comments: *Off-task behavior during peer-tutoring sessions averaged 28 minutes out of 35 minutes during a 6-week period. Lindsay was observed to be off-task for group reading instruction 73% of the time and 90% of independent seatwork. She*

(continued)

BOX 7.6 (continued)

was observed to be on-task 85% of time during one-on-one instruction with her teacher. Initiation and ending time for direct-instruction reading was reported by Ms. New (special education teacher).

E. Time samplings:
    ___√___ 1. Measure the number of times a behavior occurs after a preset observation period.
    _____ 2. Measure the number of times a response occurs after a preset observation period.

Comments: *Lindsay appears to complete reading tasks 85% of the time during a direct-instruction format by Ms. Marshall. She cannot work independently on these same reading tasks. Apparently she has begun to recognize some of the required vocabulary, but as observed by Ms. New, she cannot apply vocabulary words to independent reading tasks.*

SOURCE   Adapted from Algozzine, B., Ysseldyke, J., & Christenson, S. L. (1983). An analysis of the incidence of special class placement. The masses are burgeoning. *Journal of Special Education, 17,* 141–147.

made product, or the student's approach to problem solving. Methods of observations include: (a) record of student's permanent products, (b) anecdotal records, (c) frequency counts, (d) duration recordings, and (e) time samplings (Ysseldyke & Algozzine, 1984).

The use of paperwork, such as that shown in Box 7.6, helps teachers to define steps to each of these methods of observations. Developing and beginning teachers of special education may be asked to observe and/or to help other members of the multidisciplinary team observe the student's progress. Box 7.6 is used to highlight Lindsay's data. Ms. Marshall's suggestions to operationalize the methods of observation are delineated on the box. Both Lindsay's teachers and her counselor, Mr. Thompson, collected data and examined written products to verify Lindsay's strengths and weaknesses in the regular classroom setting. Ms. New, the school's special education teacher, participated actively in Lindsay's observations.

Case Study Conference Results

When observations are completed, professionals meet with parents in a case study conference or similarly titled meeting to analyze the data and discuss the student's current functioning. Parents should be involved in all meetings when educational decisions are made (EHA, 1975; Federal Register, 1977). It is important they are aware of educational conferences when evidence is provided promoting the student's progress in the present educational setting. The purposes of this updated team meeting are to: (a) analyze the prereferral strategies, (b) discuss the results of all classroom observations; (c) review new data collected since the initial

---

SCHOOL DATA

Academic documentation	**Behavioral progress data**
Prereferral data	Behavioral ratings
Classroom strategy results	Social–emotional progress reports
Observations by multiple professionals	Observation reports of attention to task
Previous formal/informal assessments	Data reports of rapport with others

FAMILY DATA

Parental observation notations	Family member observations
Interaction with other reports	Child behavior scale ratings by parents, siblings, other family members

COMMUNITY DATA

Interaction with neighbors' observations	Involvement in community reports
Access to community functions data	Habilitation plans
	Social worker's checklists

FIGURE 7.3   Data relevant to the case study conference.

educational planning team meeting; (d) elicit the parents' perceptions of their child's functioning and needs; (e) decide whether the student is to be provided individualized testing and continue in the formal referral process; (f) secure the parents' written permission if the student is to be a candidate for formal testing; and (g) complete the formal referral application as warranted for student's testing, signed and dated by referring professionals and/or parents.

Examples of data collected relevant to the case study conference are illustrated in Figure 7.3. School academic documentation is highlighted as are behavioral data from the school, home, and community.

An example of the paperwork used for a formal referral application is illustrated in Fig. 7.4. On this application, referring individuals and their titles should be described. The reason for referral and the results of prereferral strategies and observations are summarized. Additionally, recommendations for follow-up and testing must be targeted. In Lindsay's case, information from prereferral strategies and results of professional observations verify the need to test her further by professionals including the school psychologist and or the educational diagnostician.

Name *Lindsay Christopher* _____ Birthdate *May 14, 1982*

Class *3* _____ Parents *John & Mary Christopher*

Address/Phone *62 Sandlewood Dr. / 472-0765*

Teacher *Ms. Marshall*

Referring individuals:

Name	Title	Date
Jane Marshall	*Classroom Teacher*	*May 2, 1990*
Terri Thompson	*Counselor*	*May 2, 1990*
Betsy New	*Special Education Teacher*	*May 2, 1990*

Reason for referral:

Lindsay demonstrates problems in following directions, motivation, and independent study skills. She may have a reading problem — especially comprehension of 3rd grade material.

Results of prereferral strategies:

Strategy

1. *Peer tutoring was unsuccessful. During a 6-week period, she turned in only 10 assignments completed independently (highest accuracy rate = 62%).*

Strategy

2. *Amount of reading assignments required was reduced — she still did not turn in organized, completed work.*

Results of observations:

Work may not be motivating for her or assignments may be too difficult. Her reading level may be too low to complete requirements. She can comprehend, apparently, in a direct instruction, one-on-one format with her teacher.

Recommended follow-up and testing:

It is recommended that she be tested by Dr. Weiss, the psychologist, to determine whether Lindsay has a learning problem (especially in reading).

FIGURE 7.4   Lindsay's formal referral application.

Summary of Present Educational-Setting Documentation

Much paperwork is required before students with mild to moderate handicaps may leave the regular class. Necessary steps of comprehensive data collection, initial parental contact, and completion of the referral form must be accomplished (Gloeckler & Simpson, 1988). During the student's time in the current setting, the special education teacher assumes the role of consultant, assisting in prereferral strategies and observations. Many students with mild to moderate handicaps are provided instruction with their normally functioning peers. When students still require more specialized help, the collection of comprehensive information helps professionals to initiate a change in educational placement for students requiring the direct service model of special education. These students continue in the formal referral process because evidence has been provided that the regular class setting may not be the LRE for that student. Through an initiation of formalized testing, the student continues to be monitored for specialized help. Test results provide additional evidence of the need for special education and related services.

Formalized Testing

Relying on the analysis of regular class data discussed during a student's case study conference, professionals may indicate the success of prereferral strategies. That is, educators, psychologists, counselors, or others may be able to document mastery of academic objectives or a decrease in inappropriate behaviors. Parents may confirm the success of prereferral attempts through home observation. This student does not need to continue in the formal referral process. However, despite prereferral strategies and observations, another student may continue to demonstrate low ability, problem behaviors, or academic difficulties. At this point, professionals should acquire the parents' written permission to test the student formally. With parents fully aware of the decision to test, the formal referral process of special education is in operation. (If parents refuse to sign their permission, school officials resort to the mediation and hearing procedures as detailed in Chapter 2.) An example of the required paperwork for permission to test Lindsay is included in Figure 7.5. As can be seen, Lindsay's parents were involved in the decision to test her formally. The reasons for testing Lindsay and the names of specific tests to be used with her are marked clearly on the form for her parent's perusal and consent.

Collection and Results of Sensory Screenings

Prior to official testing by the school psychologist or other evaluator, sensory data on the student is collected, including health, hearing, vision,

Student's name *Lindsay Christopher*

Parent/guardian's name *John & Mary Christopher*

Parent/guardian's address *62 Sandalwood Dr.*

Birthdate *May 14, 1982*   Parent's phone *492-0765*

Class *3*   Teacher *Ms. Marshall*   Date *May 4, 1990*

Reason for testing

Level of class assignments may be too difficult for Lindsay. Teacher suspects a learning problem in reading (reading comprehension may be too low to complete assignments). Classroom strategies reported to be unsuccessful. Observations verified low accuracy rates and incomplete assignments; off-task behavior observed to be high. On-task behavior and higher accuracy rate during direct instruction with teachers.

Check all test types to be given/name of tests

	Types	Name
Ability	√	*Wechsler Intelligence Scale for Children —Revised*
Achievement	√	**Woodcock Johnson Psychoeducational Battery*
Social–emotional	√	*Achenbach Behavioral Scales*
Process	√	*Developmental Test of Visual Perception*
Adaptive behavior		
Others	√	*Brigrance Diagnostic Inventories (Reading)*
		Gates - McKillop Reading Diagnostic Test

Other comments **Only the educational component of the Woodcock Battery will be given.*

Student's name *Lindsay Christopher*

___√___   I give permission to test my child *Lindsay*   .
            I understand I will be informed of all results. I have been given
            procedural safeguards.

_____   I do not give permission to test, I have been given procedural
            safeguards.

_____   I wish to have another meeting prior to granting my permission
            to test my child.

Parent/guardian's signature *John Christopher*   Date *May 5, 1990*

FIGURE 7.5   Permission to test Lindsay.

or speech and language screenings (EHA, 1975; Federal Register, 1977). If the student fails any of the sensory or health screenings, more data must be obtained from health professionals (e.g., if the student fails the hearing screening, an audiometric report by a certified audiologist is pertinent; if the student fails the vision screening, such as the Snellen Chart screening, a report from an ophthalmologist or optometrist is in order). These data are important for a number of reasons: (a) evaluators must give the correct test matched to student needs; (b) sensory impairments may be the major reason for the student's difficulties, suggesting a different interpretation and explanation of test results; (c) the discovery of a sensory impairment as the student's primary handicapping condition may yield different educational placement options; and (d) the discovery of a sensory impairment may suggest different goals/objectives on the IEP.

An example of the paperwork used in the collection of Lindsay's sensory data is found in Figure 7.6. Upon close examination of this required paperwork, the teacher is able to confirm that Lindsay has no sensory impairment. This information now is used to substantiate Ms. Marshall's data from previous reports. Vision, hearing, speech and language, and overall health appear to be in the normal range.

Consent for Individualized Testing

Prior to testing, parents must be assured of their procedural safeguards (explained in detail in Chapter 2). When all pertinent sensory data are collected and parents have signed the necessary paperwork giving their permission to test, the evaluator provides the student with the individually administered battery.

Individualized Battery

The purpose of the formalized testing situation is to link identification and intervention. Teachers need specific data to describe the student's strengths and to help refine appropriate instructional strategies and techniques (Cartwright et al., 1981; Ysseldyke & Algozzine, 1984). Assessment must be multifactoral, examining all areas of functioning. Through assessment, the guidelines for appropriate instruction begin.

Testing Requirements

Testing is to be completed in the student's native language with all testing materials sensitive to the student's abilities. Examples of tests that may be included in an individualized battery are included in Box 7.7. Teachers may be asked to complete part of these instruments (e.g., to complete a behavioral rating, to write down anecdotal information used by the psychologist in the test interpretation), or the instruments may

Student's name *Lindsay Christopher*   Class *3*
Birthdate *May 14, 1982*   Teacher *Ms. Marshall*

1. Vision screening

    Distance acuity results *20/20 (ℓ)   20/30 (r)*

    Measure *Snelling*   Given by *Ms. Parkens (nurse)*   Date *Oct. 2, 1989*

    Field vision results *Adequate*

    Measure *n/a*   Given by _____   Date _____

    Follow-up required *no*   Reason *Vision adequate.*

    Ophthalmologist/Optometrist: Name _____

                                                Address _____

    _____

    (Enclose copy)   Phone _____

    Recommendation *Follow-up is not necessary at this time. Distance vision appears*
    to be within the normal range in both eyes.

    _____

2. Hearing screening

    Auditory acuity results   Left ear *Pass*   Right ear *Pass*

    Measure *Conversational speech*   Given by *Ms. Parkens (nurse)*

    Date *Oct. 22, 1989*   Follow-up required *no* Reason _____

    Audiologist   Name _____

                                Address *Hearing (conversational speech) adequate.*

    _____

    (Enclose copy)   Phone _____

    Recommendation *Follow-up is not necessary at this time. Both ears responded to*
    stimuli (given conversational speech).

    _____

FIGURE 7.6   Lindsay's health/sensory screening results.

3. Speech/language screening

Clinician *Jan Jenkins*   Date *Oct. 14, 1989–Oct. 22, 1989*

Test name	Results	Recommendation
Articulation TOLD; VCS	*Passed*	
Voice TLD	*Passed*	*No follow-up*
Fluency TOLD; VCS; PSLT	*Passed*	*necessary at*
Language PSLT	*Passed*	*this time*

Goldman Fristoe-Woodcock Test of Auditory Discrimination Vocabulary Comprehension Scale; Test of Language Development; Picture Story Language Test

Follow-up required? *No*

Reason for speech/language placement option:
At this time, speech and language training not recommended. Lindsay's articulation, voice, fluency, and language skills appear to be within the normal range.

4. Overall health

Physician's name *Dr. Joseph Charles*
Address *1608 Fairway Circle*
Phone number *451-3928*
Date of last physical *March 9, 1990*
Comments: *Lindsay appears to be in excellent health*

5. Sensory/health screening comments: *No notable sensory and/or health deviations to report at this time.*

Ms. Parkens (Nurse)
Jan Jenkins (Clinician)

FIGURE 7.6   *(continued)*

BOX 7.7

Examples of Tests in a Battery

ABILITY MEASURES
- Kaufman Assessment Battery for Children (K-ABC)
- Standford-Binet Intelligence Scale
- Wechsler Adult Intelligence Scale (WAIS)
- Wechsler Intelligence Scale for Children — Revised (WISC-R).

ACHIEVEMENT MEASURES
- Brigance Diagnostic Inventories
- Gates-McKillop Reading Diagnostic Test
- Gray Oral Reading Test
- Inventory of Elementary Reading Skills
- Key Math
- Metropolitan Achievement Test
- Peabody Individual Achievement Test
- Wide Range Achievement Test
- Woodcock Johnson Psychoeducational Battery

PROCESS MEASURES
- Auditory Discrimination Test
- Auditory Sequential Memory Test
- Bruininks-Oseretsky Test of Motor Proficiency
- Developmental Test of Visual Perception
- Frostig Test of Visual Motor Integration
- Purdue Perceptual-Motor Survey
- Wepman Auditory

SOCIAL-EMOTIONAL MEASURES
- Achenbach Behavioral Scales
- Burke's Behavior Rating

ADAPTIVE BEHAVIOR SCALES
- American Association on Mental Deficiency (AAMD) Adaptive Behavior Scales
- Adaptive Behavior Inventory for Children
- System of Multi-Cultural Pluralistic Assessment
- Vineland Social Maturity Scale

SELF-REPORT TECHNIQUES
- Bower-Lambert Screening Scales
- California Test of Personality
- Children's Apperception Test
- Piers-Harris Self-Concept Scale

SOURCE   Based on Salvia, J., & Ysseldyke, J. E. (1984). *Assessment in special education* (3rd ed.). Boston: Houghton Mifflin.

be given solely by the educational diagnostician or school psychologist. Many various assessment devices are used by personnel in different school systems. Box 7.7 is a partial listing of assessment devices used by psychologists and educational diagnosticians.

Explanation and Interpretation of Formal Testing

When testing is completed, all data are condensed in a written, psychological report, which is to be shared with parents and professionals. Testing results must be interpreted and explained by the evaluator. Implications for instruction are generated from results, and assessment should link the student's present abilities to teaching strategies and procedures used by regular class or special class teachers. An example of Lindsay's psychological report is included in Box 7.8. On this report, the psychologist provided evidence of Lindsay's above average intelligence and her lack of severe behavioral and sensory problems. Data support the claim that while she displays learning problems, her difficulties are not severe enough to remove her from the regular-class setting. Data from the present education setting and the formal testing completed by Dr. Weiss, the school psychologist, have been summarized on the written psychological report. All information is explained and interpreted to parents and professionals by evaluators.

Eligibility Meeting

After completion of all formal testing, parents and professionals decide whether the student qualifies for specialized help. This decision occurs at an eligibility meeting.

An eligibility meeting to determine an appropriate placement and discuss the results of all written data must be held (EHA, 1975; Federal Register, 1977). All data generated to date are compiled and synthesized during the eligibility meeting. For many students, the explanation and interpretation of the psychological report are completed during the eligibility meeting.

The purpose of the meeting is to match the needs of the student to the most appropriate setting available. If an appropriate setting is unavailable, the school district may contract for the needed services. In all cases, a placement must be found for the student. (Chapter 1 describes all placement options.) A representative of the assessment team, often the school psychologist or educational diagnostician who conducted the assessment, is a member of the eligibility meeting. Other members include a school administrator, the referring teachers, the special education teacher, parents or guardians, and if warranted, the student. An example of the paperwork used in Lindsay's eligibility meeting is included in Figure 7.7.

BOX 7.8

Psychological Report on Lindsay Christopher

Name: Lindsay Christopher
Birthdate: May 14, 1982
Parents: John and Mary Christopher
School: Howard Elementary School
Grade: 3
Teacher: Ms. Mary Marshall
Evaluator: Betty Weiss, Certified School Psychologist
Date: 6/8/90

Background Information: Lindsay has been reported by her teacher, Ms. Marshall, to be a well-mannered, attractive youngster attending third grade at Howard Elementary School. Lindsay recently transferred from Pelton School, Bowersville, another school district in the state. At the time of her entry into Howard, few prior school records on her were available. School officials from Pelton did send an incomplete cumulative record of her kindergarten experience. Former professionals indicated her normal progress in kindergarten. However, no data were received describing her school progress during the last 2 years when she attended grades 1 and 2.

During the current school year, Lindsay has been experiencing problems in reading comprehension and study skills. On the Cromer Achievement Test, given by Ms. Marshall on September 22, 1989, Lindsay performed at 3.7 in mathematics, 1.9 in reading, and 3.3 in spelling. Chapter tests from the Universal Reading Series, Level 3, were provided by her teacher. Lindsay had not mastered the first group of objectives from Chapter 1 of this reading series, suggesting to Ms. Marshall some of her difficulties in reading comprehension. Mr. and Mrs. Christopher have reported also that Lindsay has problems reading homework assignments and completing household chores and family responsibilities at home. The parents indicated, however, she does not seem to have any difficulties in making and keeping friends in and around the neighborhood. She appears to get along well with her younger brother, Larry, age 4.

Ms. Marshall reported, also, Lindsay's near-perfect handwriting and her love of drawing. Lindsay's motor development is adequate for a child in the third grade. She is able to run, jump, skip, and hop as most children her age. She competes satisfactorily in physical education with her classmates and performs excep-

BOX 7.8 (continued)

tionally well in swimming. Lindsay's medical history is unnotable.

Lindsay's speech and language development appear to be adequate for a child of her age. She was screened by the school nurse, Mrs. Parkens, on October 2, 1989 for vision and hearing. Both vision and hearing screenings were unremarkable. Mrs. Jenkins, the speech and language clinician at Howard, screened Lindsay on October 14, 1989, in areas of articulation, voice, fluency, and language using the Test of Language Development, Goldman-Fristoe-Woodcock Test of Auditory Discrimination, Vocabulary Comprehension Test, and Picture Story Language Test (refer to the completed screening report, dated October 22, 1989). Based on the results of these speech and language assessments, no speech/language training appears necessary at this time.

In the classroom, Ms. Marshall reported Lindsay's difficulty to begin on time and complete assignments in reading. Other subject area requirements do not appear to pose problems to her. She continues to perform well in mathematics and spelling, although assignments in social skills and science are beginning to contain more required reading skills than assignments previously. Ms. Marshall reported her fears of Lindsay falling further and further behind her classmates as the school year continues. Due to these reasons, prereferral strategies were proposed by an educational planning team on March 9, 1990. Teaching modifications applied in the regular classroom were suggested and implemented by Ms. Marshall. The school's counselor, Mr. Thompson, special education teacher, Ms. New, and I, psychologist, participated in prereferral strategies. After completion of 6 weeks, however, peer tutoring with a classmate during reading comprehension time was not successful. Lowering the amount of work required for her was also reported to be an unsuccessful strategy. For a majority of the time, Lindsay continues to display problems in completing her work and in comprehending the assignments. Her papers continue to contain many errors (62% accuracy was the highest reported score). Observations by Ms. Marshall, Mr. Thompson, Ms. New, and myself included an analysis of: Lindsay's **work samples** (during a 6-week period, work samples were turned in 10 out of 64 times; problems in reading comprehension were noted); **anecdotal records** (Ms. Marshall's daily log continued to verify problems specific to reading comprehension), and a **frequency count** of observable behavior during reading instruction (relative to peers, Lindsay was on task during independent reading instruction only 4 out of 14 times; Lindsay was off task for 73% of reading instruction and off task for 90% of seatwork during two inde-

(continued)

BOX 7.8 (continued)

pendent observations by the counselor and psychologist). She appears to respond well to direct-instruction strategies when working one-on-one with her teacher. When she was provided direct-instruction strategies geared to her level of learning (e.g., acquisition stage for reading comprehension), she improved in reading attention and level.

Testing: On May 12, 1990, Lindsay was given the following tests and obtained these scores:

- Wechsler Intelligence Scale for Children—Revised: Lindsay obtained a full scale of 114 (Verbal: 110, Performance: 116) on the WISC-R including raw scores on picture completion, picture arrangement, block design, object assembly, coding, and mazes. All are within the average or above raw-score range.
- Woodcock Johnson Psychoeducational Battery: Only the educational component was given to Lindsay, and she scored 2.5 in reading, 3.7 in math, 3.2 in language.
- Gates-McKillop Reading Diagnostic Test: On this measure she obtained a score of reading comprehension grade level 2.4.
- Brigance Diagnostic Inventories: This measure was given to determine more specific information about Lindsay's reading abilities. An overall score of 2.3 was obtained with the breakdown of the subsets as follows:

Word Recognition	3.1
Oral Reading	2.7
Reading Comprehension	2.3
Functional Word Recognition	2.4
Word Analysis	2.4
Reference Skills	2.0
Writing	2.1
Spelling	2.1
Forms	2.4

- Achenbach Behavioral Scales: The ABS was completed by both Lindsay's parents and Ms. Marshall, her classroom teacher, with no significant behaviors reported in any areas of the behavior-rating scale. Her social-emotional development appears to be adequate for a child of her age.
- Developmental Test of Visual Perception: To determine whether Lindsay displays problems in visual processing, the DTVP was given. Lindsay appears to have adequate functioning in all areas of the DTVP.

BOX 7.8 (continued)

Summary of Data: Lindsay was given testing in areas of ability, achievement, social-emotional development, processing, and reading-diagnostic skills. Classroom strategies and observations of her progress in Ms. Marshall's class were conducted prior to testing. Peer tutoring and lowered rates of homework/seatwork requirements (teaching modifications) did not appear to aid Lindsay in skills in which she needs to succeed in the regular class.

On the present testing, Lindsay performs at the above average range of intelligence (ability results of the WISC-R are one standard deviation above the norm). Reading scores range from a low of 2.1 to 3.1 on reading diagnostic testing. Overall reading comprehension is reported currently at the 2.3 level. There is no discrepancy between achievement and ability. Processing and social-emotional ratings are unnotable for a child of her age. Tentative strategies that may prove to be helpful to Lindsay are suggested by Ms. New, Ms. Marshall, Mr. Thompson, and I:

1. Have Lindsay repeat directions to assignments prior to the initiation of independent work problems.
2. Cue Lindsay orally to read for facts before she starts reading comprehension assignments.
3. Work with Lindsay to use underlining strategies (important details of assignments).
4. Teach Lindsay self-questioning strategies so she can ask herself whether she comprehends tasks.
5. Paraphrase important details to her in a variety of ways (e.g., orally say directions in two different ways).
6. Highlight assignments (color-code important information in each paragraph she is to read).
7. Set time limits on and monitor her completion of tasks.
8. Reward Lindsay with tangibles, special class privileges, and so forth, when she hands assignments in on time and follows classroom suggestions.
9. Post a record of her accomplishments for assignments and for successful completion of reading comprehension tasks (chart or graph).
10. Consider her stage of learning and plan instructional methods accordingly. If in the acquisition stage, consider direct instruction methods. Use independent and practice activities only when she demonstrates mastery or near mastery of the skills.
11. Continue to use, over time, peer tutors, student interns, and volunteers/paraprofessionals as warranted to assist her.
12. Plan for consultation time among her parents, the special education teacher, and the regular class teacher to consider Lindsay's individual progress.

Student's name _Lindsay Christopher_   Teacher _Ms. Marshall_   Class _3_

Problem area defined _Lindsay appears to lack motivation. Her reading_
comprehension and study skills are reported as low.

Reason for referral _She was referred for testing because preferral strategies of_
regular class were not successful. Multi-observations provided evidence of off-task
behaviors and low accuracy rates in performance.

Prereferral strategies _Peer tutoring and lower rates of homework/seatwork_
requirements have not aided Lindsay in completion of tasks and reading comprehension.

Results _Assignments over a 6 week period continue to be incomplete and to have_
low accuracy rates.

Observation _4 completed_   **Name(s)** _Thompson_   **Date(s)** _5/2/90_
                                          Thompson   _5/3/90_
                                          New   _5/6/90_
                                          Weiss   _5/14/90_

Results _Off-task in group reading 73% of the time. 4/17 times off task. Does not keep up_
with others (28/35 minutes off task 70% of time).

Test results _Lindsay's test results include: WISC-R (verbal 110; performance, 116;_
full scale, 114); Woodcock Johnson (reading, 2.5; math, 3.7; language, 3.2); Gates, 2.4
(reading comprehension); Achenbach (no significant problem behaviors); DTVP: adequate
in all areas; Brigance reading (2.3). Although her reading comprehension appears to be low
(2.3 level), results of testing indicate she is beginning to comprehend grade appropriate material
but is not ready for independent assignments at this time. Motivation may be a problem.

Recommendation for placement _Continue in regular class._

Reason _Lindsay does not meet the requirements for special education. Teachers should con-_
tinue to provide small group and tutorial help on a one-to-one basis in the acquisition of reading
comprehension skills. Tentative strategies as listed on the psychological report of 6/2/90 should
be implemented. Team meeting should reconvene to update regular class strategies on 8/20/90
to provide direction for the coming school year. Continue to emphasize direct instruction.

	Participants' signatures	Date
LEA	_Thomas Smart, Principal_	_6/20/90_
Evaluator	_Betty Weiss, School Psychologist_	_6/20/90_
Teachers	_Jane Marshall, Teacher_	_6/20/90_
Others	_Betsy New, Special Education_	_6/20/90_
	Terri Thompson, Counselor	_6/20/90_
Parent/Guardian	_Mary/John Christopher, Parents_	_6/20/90_

FIGURE 7.7   Lindsay's eligibility meeting.

The results of the eligibility meeting for Lindsay are used to determine the LRE for her. Lindsay will remain in the regular class. She is not a candidate for special education because her formal test results, along with prereferral information and formal observation data, were found to confirm the appropriateness of the regular class for her. Lindsay does display learning problems, but she is not a student with severe problems to necessitate her removal from her present educational setting. She responds well to small groups, direct instruction techniques, and some modifications in the regular curriculum. Her achievement levels are low to moderate and not severe enough to require special education. An important recommendation by her eligibility team members is that a team meeting reconvene at the start of the school year to update potential regular-class strategies. At this point, the special education teacher may continue to be a consultant to Lindsay's regular classroom teachers.

Pertinent Questions of Formal Testing Results

If the purpose of formal testing is a change in placement, a number of important questions developing and beginning teachers should ask during the eligibility meeting might include:

- What other information is relevant about the student's functioning that test results may not provide?
- Does the written report present a complete and accurate picture of the student's ability in cognitive, language, social, motor, or other forms of development?
- Do test results conflict with previous data collected?
- What are the implications for instruction and management based on the test results? That is, do the results provide a framework to instruct or manage the student in the special education situation?
- If a change in placement is not warranted, do test results imply other strategies, materials, or evaluation systems that may help the student in the regular education setting? (Cartwright et al., 1981)

Box 7.9 demonstrates the types of responses professionals at Lindsay's school gave in answering these questions. One key element not to be overlooked is Lindsay's opportunity to remain in the regular education class and be provided consultive services by a team, including her school's special education teacher. Even after formal testing is completed, many students may continue to display problems in the regular curriculum but not be candidates for specialized programming. When this happens, the role of the special education teacher continues to be as consultant to the regular classroom teacher. However, all students with individual differences in learning or behavioral needs are not removed from instruction with normally functioning peers. As in Lindsay's case, many students can remain in the mainstream when professionals are provided comprehensive data and work as a team to facilitate the LRE.

BOX 7.9

Pertinent Questions and Answers on Lindsay Christopher

These questions were answered by Ms. Marshall, the regular classroom teacher.

- **What other information is relevant about the student's functioning that test results may not provide?**

Other information that may be helpful for us to consider include readability level of the classroom material; distractions from peers, paraprofessionals, or volunteers; and expectations of parents and professionals. More emphasis on direct instruction techniques and less requirements on independent assignments (for Lindsay's learning stage) are important.

- **Does the written report present a complete and accurate picture of the student's ability in cognitive, language, social, motor, or other forms of development?**

The written report provides data about Lindsay's functioning in the domains listed above but the question still remains, How do we best instruct Lindsay? No matter what the psychologist and educational diagnostician diagnose, we still must find strategies and techniques to teach and help Lindsay succeed.

- **Do test results conflict with previous data collected?**

Lindsay's parents have reported her lack of initiation to study independently at home and to complete home chores, so there is some reliability across individuals and settings concerning the data. However, I really believed Lindsay's reading scores would have been much lower than she actually obtained on the formal achievement test given by our school psychologist.

- **What are the implications for instruction and management based on the test results? That is, do the results provide a framework to instruct or manage the student in the classroom situation?**

How can we teach Lindsay best if she remains in the regular class? Should we change her reading assignments? Should we provide another formal reading program? Should we allow her to attend reading class with second graders?

BOX 7.9 *(continued)*

- **If a change in placement is not warranted, do test results imply other strategies, materials, or evaluation systems that may help the student in the present education setting?**
(Cartwright et al., 1981).

Other strategies may include a change in her reading curriculum, more time alone with the teacher, additional small-group instruction, direct instruction for reading comprehension and study skills.

Summary of the Formalized Testing Situation

After securing parents' permission to test and obtain all sensory information, a complete battery of testing is given. Each educational decision for students should be based on comprehensive information. Because data have been collected by many professionals over time and in a variety of settings, much is now known about the student. An objective decision is more likely to be made on how best to offer instruction and management. Some students, like Lindsay, may have undergone the formal testing situation but are ineligible for special education and related services. These students may be provided remedial help through general mainstream education courses with consulting help by the special educator. An emphasis by professionals on teaching behaviors (e.g., use of modified materials, direct instruction techniques, management using tokens and rewards) will allow many students opportunities to remain in the mainstream. Other students, however, may have undergone the formal testing situation and are eligible for special education and related services. The special education teacher's role for the student requiring formal special education (i.e., removal from the regular classroom placement for at least part of the school day) is the direct service model.

Individualized Education Plans

Prior to a new educational placement the Individualized Education Plan (IEP) must be developed for every student entering special education and related services (EHA, 1975; Federal Register, 1977). All paperwork collected to date can be very useful in determining goals and objectives of the new educational setting. All data are linked to the student's IEP.

Students' IEPs are the most important documents that teachers, school officials, and parents develop cooperatively. Important aspects of the IEP process that developing and beginning teachers should recognize include: (a) the necessity of parents' consent for placement; (b) requirements of initial placements; (c) requirements of annual updated IEPs; and (d) results and implications of reevaluations.

Consent for Placement by Parents

All students placed into special education programs are provided with
an IEP. Plans must be current and in effect at the initiation of every
school year or within 30 calender days from eligibility meetings specifying the special education and related services provided (EHA, 1975;
Federal Register, 1977). Prior to placement, parents or guardians must
give and date their written permission for their child's program. If
parents refuse, mediation and hearing procedures (as described in Chapter 2) are initiated.

Also, consenting parents or guardians are given the opportunity to
attend the IEP meeting at a time and place convenient for them. Federal
authorities have mandated school officials to give parents two notices of
the upcoming IEP meeting. One notice must be written and a copy
saved for school records. The other notice may be a written request,
personal correspondence, phone call, or other means. Figure 7.8 illustrates the paperwork used in securing parents' permission to place their
child. Lindsay's example is a reminder that she will continue in her
regular education program. While an IEP is not required for her, an
IEP is required for all students who receive special education and related
services.

Requirements of Initial Placement IEPs

Federal requirements are very specific for students entering special education and related services for the first time. Documentation must be
provided by school personnel in two major areas: the legal participants
at IEP meetings and the required components of the IEP written document. Because developing and beginning teachers must demonstrate
knowledge of the IEP from the first day of school, it is very important
to be familiar with all requirements during preservice training.

IEP PARTICIPANTS   Federal requirements specify the presence of
various individuals when an IEP meeting commences. Box 7.10 describes
the title and function of required participants. An IEP should never be
written prior to the actual meeting but must be developed during the
meeting with all participants providing insights to meet the student's
needs best. Each participant should be given the opportunity to: (a)
provide information on the student, (b) suggest IEP goals and objectives,
(c) question interpretations and explanations, (d) examine educational
alternatives, and (e) disagree with proposed actions.

SPECIFIC COMPONENTS OF THE IEP   EHA (1975) has mandated
specific IEP sections. Seven areas must be specified in writing for each
student including: (a) documentation of the student's current level of
educational performance; (b) annual goals or the attainments expected
by the end of the school year; (c) short-term objectives, stated in instruc-

Student's name *Lindsay Christopher*   Class   *3*
Present setting *Sandling Howard Elementary*   Teacher *Ms. Marshall*
Type of setting *Regular classroom*   Date *June 20, 1990*

Results of tests *Results of ability, achievement, processing, and social-emotional testing were discussed by the eligibility team. Motivation appears to be a major problem for Lindsay. Learning, ability, achievement, social-emotional, and processing appear to be in at least the average range.*

Recommended program name *Regular classroom placement.*

Reason for recommendation *Lindsay meets the criteria for regular classroom placement continuation. Lindsay does display learning problems (she appears to be at the three-level acquisition stage of reading comprehension — rather than generalization as most of her peers). She appears to need extrinsic, tangible motivation and small-group instruction to help her succeed. Direct instruction in a small-group format should be highlighted.*

Delivery service provided *Lindsay will continue to receive her educational placement in the regular classroom with consulting help provided by the special education specialist at the start of the new school year.*

Recommended school name *Continue in Sandling Howard Elementary*
Address *230 Haystack Court Road, Maimlee, Florida*
Continue in regular class, summer school, June 24, 1990–July 23, 1990 J.C. M.C.

Placement to begin on *August 15*   19 *90*   (thirty calendar days from eligibility determination).

_____√_____ I have been given a copy of "Procedural Due Process"

_____√_____ I give permission to place my child *Lindsay*
               in the recommended program.

_____ I do not give permission to place my child
               _____ in the recommended program.

_____ I request another meeting prior to making a decision.

Parent/guardian's name *John Christopher/Mary Christopher*

LEA representative *Thomas Smart, Principal*

Date: *6/20/90*   Evaluator: *Betty Weiss, Psychologist*

Teacher: *Jane Marshall (Regular Classroom)*

Others *Betsy New (Special Education Certified)*

FIGURE 7.8 Lindsay's parents' permission to place.

BOX 7.10

Required IEP Participants and Their Functions

1. *LEA representative:* The local education agency (LEA) representative provides meeting participants with pertinent data about
   available programs of the local area. The individual must be
   available to discuss service delivery options, transportation
   methods, and district procedures of program implementation.
   The LEA representative is usually a district administrator of
   special education or the principal of the local school attended
   by the student.
2. *Member of the evaluation team:* Someone knowledgeable about
   psychological and educational testing must be available to discuss, interpret, and explain all test results to those in attendance at the meeting. Usually this person is the school psychologist or educational diagnostician who has provided the testing
   to the student.
3. *Teacher:* A professional who is knowledgeable about the special
   education program to be provided to the student must be present. This may include the regular class teacher or the special
   class teacher. The individual answers questions of group participants and guides the writing of student-oriented goals and
   objectives on the written document.
4. *Other participants* of the IEP meeting may include the parent,
   guardian, or surrogate parent, and, when appropriate, the
   student. Also, any other person the student, parent, guardian,
   or surrogate parent wishes may attend. Lawyers, therapists,
   physicians, or other advocates may represent parents or school
   officials at meetings. Their functions are to provide input and
   feedback on goals and objectives proposed for the IEP.

tional terms, which are the intermediate steps leading to mastery of
annual goals; (d) documentation of the particular special education and
related services that will be provided to the student; (e) indication of
the extent of time a student will participate in the regular education
program; (f) projected dates for initiating services and the anticipated
duration of services; and (g) appropriate objective criteria, evaluation
procedures, and schedules for determining mastery of short-term objectives, at least on an annual basis. Box 7.11 details information IEP
planning meeting participants would analyze and discuss in the development of the written plan.

Figure 7.9 illustrates the component parts of IEPs (starting with prereferral strategies, observations, and formalized testing results). Written

BOX 7.11

Development of the Written Plan

1. *Present education levels.* This is a statement of the strengths and weaknesses of current levels of functioning. The present education levels may be derived from teachers' informal or formal observations, classroom assessments, prereferral strategy analysis, or case studies. Present education levels are the bases for annual goals.
2. *Annual goals.* These are broad statements of students' anticipated educational outcomes and behavioral outcomes for the year. Annual goals may include generic statements of subject or performance areas students will encounter during the year. Annual goals should be linked to both the present education levels and the short-term objectives.
3. *Short-term objectives.* Short-term objectives are very specific statements of students' educational areas and behavioral programs anticipated for the year. Short-term objectives should be written concisely and clearly in concrete terminology. It is best to use behavioral terminology observed easily by objective observers. Short-term objectives are statements teachers and parents anticipate students will master within the year. All short-term objectives specify conditions (i.e., circumstances under which objectives are presented to students) and behavior (specifically what students must do or how students are to act or behave).
4. *Statement of special services needed.* This statement must reflect the specific special education program and related services provided for students. Usually this is written in the form of the category assigned to students (e.g., specific learning disabilities, physical impairment, etc., to designate special education programs; or specialized transportation, specific counseling, social services to designate related services). The special services noted should be based on the results of assessment reports and data collected from case studies during prereferral or referral. All information can be reported to the multidisciplinary team at the eligibility meeting or continuation placement meeting.
5. *Programs to be followed.* Participants of the IEP meeting must agree to all educational programs provided to special students. This component specifies the degree to which students are integrated with regular students. Writers of IEPs must specify the amount of regular education (basic education), special education, and, in some areas, vocational education. The need for adaptive physical education or regular physical education should be determined for each student.

(continued)

BOX 7.11 (continued)

6. *Initiation date and expected duration.* These dates must specify when programs are to take place and how long they will last. Most expected duration dates run 1 year from the date of the initation of programs when parents first give written consent. However, IEPs can be updated and rewritten any time during the school year.

7. *Criteria to assess objectives.* Every short-term objective written for students should be assessed continually to monitor progress made toward goals and objectives. Mastery levels for objectives should be specified. Specification is done usually in terms of duration (e.g., for 2 minutes), trials to criterion (e.g., 4 out of 5 trials), or percentages (e.g., 80% mastery level for acceptable performance). All materials, evaluation procedures, and schedules used to monitor should be specified. When students have obtained the duration, criterion level, or reached the number of trials specified, the person responsible for implementing the program area should write the date of mastery by the objective. If objectives are not mastered by the ending duration date of the IEP, objectives may be eliminated or revised for continuation on the next IEP. During periodic monitoring of the IEP, teachers may write progress reports on students' completion of objectives (e.g., On January 24, 1991, Sara mastered 3 out of 5 trials for decoding skills. On March 16, 1991, Sara mastered 4 out of 5 trials for decoding skills).

examples of required components also are illustrated. Beginning and developing treachers may be involved in every step of Figure 7.9, either as a consultant to some students (e.g., Lindsay) in the regular class placement, or as a direct service provider to others requiring specialized programming.

The IEP As a Working Document

As described earlier, specific written statements provide (a) a destination for teachers, parents, and students to strive for and (b) the basis for evaluating the effectiveness of the instructional activities and materials in aiding students to arrive at some prescribed skill level. An IEP helps parents and teachers to describe annual plans for students with special needs. Some teachers may view the IEP process as a dreaded chore. The IEP is a true opportunity to plan with parents and other professionals. The IEP is the focal point for planning the student's program and coordinating services received in order to provide for the student's needs. Developing and beginning teachers are wise to recognize

ASSESSMENT RESULTS

A. Prereferral strategies
B. Observations
C. Data of classroom teachers
D. Psychological testing using battery of tests

PRESENT EDUCATION LEVELS

A. Academic strengths and weaknesses
B. Social–behavioral strengths and weaknesses

ANNUAL GOALS

A. Yearly academic outcomes
B. Social–behavioral expectations

SHORT-TERM OBJECTIVES

A. Conditions
B. Behavior
C. Criteria

ANNUAL UPDATE

Reevaluation for program continuation

EXAMPLES OF ASSESSMENT RESULTS

A. Tim completed 3/5 chapters in the Global Reading Series at Level 6. He was observed by his reading teacher to be struggling with oral reading skills. He could not answer any comprehension questions after reading a paragraph out loud.

B. Ruby was assessed by the school psychologist with the WISC-R and received 98 verbal, 109 performance, and 104 full scale. Her behavior ratings by the classroom teacher and parent yielded no significant problems. She received a 4.0 in reading, a 3.6 in mathematics, and a 4.1 in spelling, revealing average achievement for a student of her age.

FIGURE 7.9   Individualized education plans.   *(continued)*

EXAMPLES OF PRESENT EDUCATION LEVELS

A. John displays letter–sound association for all consonants and for the vowels "a" and "o."
B. Mary demonstrates legible cursive handwriting strokes. She cannot use the margins of paper and often writes letters too large for the size of space.
C. Tom adds two digit numbers and has begun to demonstrate carrying into higher columns.

EXAMPLES OF ANNUAL GOALS

A. Karen will increase her ability to comprehend four- to five-sentence paragraphs.
B. Jane will increase independent study skills during social studies.
C. Bob will maintain good personal hygiene skills.

EXAMPLES OF SHORT-TERM OBJECTIVES

A. Given 20 spelling wordcards, Marsha will spell words correctly with 80% mastery.
B. During recess Sarah will play cooperatively with her peers, initiating two social contacts in the first 3 minutes of play.
C. While reciting the Pledge of Allegiance, Bill will stand at attention with his hand over his heart with eyes focused for 4 days per week.

FIGURE 7.9 *(continued)*

that the IEP will only be as useful as the individuals employing them in schools. Employability of IEPs is a concept significant to every teacher. Only by actually devising, monitoring, and revising continually IEPs for students requiring special education and related services can the true intent of federal and state laws be implemented.

Effective IEP Meetings

Professionals and parents who work together and can agree on a common set of objectives can share in the decisions regarding the nature of the student's programs. As indicated by Schulz and Turnbull (1984), the legal intent was for parents to be equal partners in decision making; unfortunately, several researchers have painted a rather bleak picture of parental participation (Goldstein et al., 1980; Lynch & Stein, 1982;

Morgan, 1982). Regular classroom teachers, too, may have concerns over their involvement in the IEP process and the guarantee they will receive the assistance they need to instruct special needs students. The thinking is if classroom teachers are required to provide specially designed instruction to students with learning or behavioral problems, they have both the right as well as the responsibility to share in decisions regarding the nature of the student's program (Schulz & Turnbull, 1984). Ms. Marshall, Lindsay's regular classroom teacher, expressed legitimate concerns about instructing Lindsay effectively after the formal testing situation (as represented from her statements in Box 7.8). Special educators and regular classroom teachers must continue to work on teaming ideas for all students requiring support from school personnel. Special educators of the 1990s must reaffirm that parents' and regular classroom teachers' input is valued and that their concerns for the student and his or her educational programming are legitimate. Effective special educators continue to offer consulting services when students exit from the referral process and/or exit from placement in special classes.

RIGHTS AND RESPONSIBILITIES OF ALL IEP PARTICIPANTS   IEP members share a number of rights and responsibilities. Every member must believe that he or she can contribute to the written product and should work to reach a consensual agreement of what is in the best interests of students. Participants should be able to provide input into determining responsibility for instruction, curriculum planning, scheduling, roles in implementing the IEP, and specifying reasonable expectations for students to master goals and objectives. Rights of IEP participants that developing and beginning teachers will share with all other team members include: (a) the opportunity to attend all IEP meetings, (b) a chance to determine appropriate goals and objectives for the students they serve, (c) access to all specialized materials, equipment, and curricula, (d) input and feedback related to all learning and behavioral management strategies devised for the student, (e) the opportunity to call additional IEP meetings as indicated by the student's mastery of goals and objectives, and (f) assistance in implementing individualized instruction from other multidisciplinary team members.

Responsibilities of IEP participants are also pertinent and include: (a) demonstrated preparedness for all meetings, (b) display of professionalism during every meeting, (c) demonstrated organization and timeliness for every meeting, (d) display of empathy, positive regard, and nonjudgmental statements of other team members, (e) concerted effort to actually implement the written IEP, (f) continual attempts to evaluate the appropriateness of the IEP, and (g) ongoing consultation efforts underscoring the importance of parents and other professionals.

If personnel new to school systems take the rights and responsibilities of IEP team members seriously, IEPs can remain vital documents to ensure the appropriateness of the student's education in the LRE.

BEHAVIORS OF SPECIAL EDUCATION TEACHERS   There are behaviors that new teachers should focus on to facilitate the involvement
of others in the IEP process. These behaviors, listed below, occur prior
to, during, and after the IEP meeting. Many of these behaviors are vital
to students who continue to receive a majority of their educational services in the regular class after formal testing and/or exit from specialized
programs, as well as students pinpointed for special education and related services.

PRIOR TO THE IEP MEETING
- Observe confidentiality, report objectively, and qualify subjective judgments whenever possible. Always demonstrate this attitude when working with others.
- Be sensitive to the attitudes of other professionals involved with the
  student. Try to display empathy for their situation while still seeking
  appropriate solutions for the student with special needs.
- Try to anticipate potential problems that could arise during the meeting. Write down possible solutions prior to the meeting's initiation.

DURING THE IEP MEETING
- Be sure a leader is present to organize the meeting.
- Make sure introductions are completed prior to starting the formal
  meeting. Participants should sign and identify their relationship to the
  student.
- Determine in advance the length of the meeting. The leader should
  state the purpose of the meeting, provide a brief outline of the expectations of the meeting, and guide the meeting according to appropriate
  timelines.
- Encourage the administration to keep the number of professional participants to the fewest possible. Consider the professional/parent ratio
  and the special education/regular education ratio. Realize some may
  feel awkward when outnumbered.
- In speech and all written statements, avoid the use of teacher jargon
  that may be confusing or too technical for some participants' use.
  Speak and write in a clear, understandable level of discourse but never
  miscalculate any participants' ability to understand and use data.
- Ensure that the evaluator summarizes all testing done and parents are
  provided a copy of the evaluation.
- If disagreements arise over any components of the evaluation, ensure
  that the leader asks participants to specify their disagreements in writing. Secure a copy of the disagreements for administrators not in
  attendance.
- Ensure that the leader states the placement-delivery system most appro-

priate for the student's needs (e.g., resource room, special class). Be sure parents understand placement options by asking questions and encouraging their questions.

- Develop and write the IEP during the meeting. Never have a completed form for participants merely to sign.
- Develop complete IEPs before requesting participants' signatures and dates.
- Select and specify in writing goals, objectives, and instructional procedures appropriate to the student based on identified strengths and weaknesses.
- Link interventions to assessments. Ensure that the present education levels are tied to the psychological report and other pertinent classroom data. Link present education levels to annual goals, annual goals to short-term objectives, and so forth.
- Write verifiable objectives for students in all areas of concern specifying conditions, behaviors, and criteria.
- Solicit input from parents and all participants during the meeting. Actively encourage others' input and feedback through display of visual cues, communication, and appropriate questioning and responses as warranted. Use empathy, positive regard, and nonjudgmental statements in all communication efforts.
- Encourage the leader to summarize the meeting and to plan for follow-up strategies during future meetings. The leader should write down all follow-up plans and promise all participants a copy of the plans.
- Discuss the tentative date for the next IEP meeting. Ensure participants it is at least within one year's time.

AFTER THE IEP MEETING
- Implement all goals and objectives devised at the meeting.
- Strive to match the written plan to actual programming for the student.
- Monitor goals and objectives consistently. Date all monitoring efforts.
- If changes need to be made, hold another IEP meeting to revise.
- Continue to solicit input and feedback from all participants including parents and regular classroom teachers. Demonstrate a team approach.
- Continue to keep written records and reports affecting students, parents, other professionals, and all educational decisions made about the student.

Specific behaviors of teachers before, during, and after the meeting are included to represent the continuing process of a useful IEP. Effective IEPs are implemented by concerned teachers who know their students well, who will continually collect and maintain useful written data on students, and who respect and implement their rights and responsibilities in the IEP process.

Student's name Jenny Wain

Date 4/3/90   Level —   Grade 6   School Fiddler Middle

Subject area/class ESE (English/Math)   Teacher Mr. Metan

Dates of observation April 1, 1990 to April 4, 1990 (3rd period)

Number of students present 12   Teaching format used Small group; independent self-management

Target student's behavior (description prior to observation) During functional English and math classes, Jenny continues to be on-task for 95% of total allocated time.

Important antecedents Observation of 90% to 100% on-task compliant behavior reported by Mr. Metan for 6 weeks during the last 3 months.

√ = mastery
× = absent

Comments

1. 100% compliance (except 1 day due to absence)

2. Met criterion level for every day (except due to absence).

Behavior

Describe:

1. Functional English: Followed teacher's directions 90% of time after given oral instructions.

√	√	√	√	√	√	×	√	√	√

2. Functional math: Completed math assignment with 80% accuracy in self-instructional format.

√	√	√	√	√	√	×	√	√	√

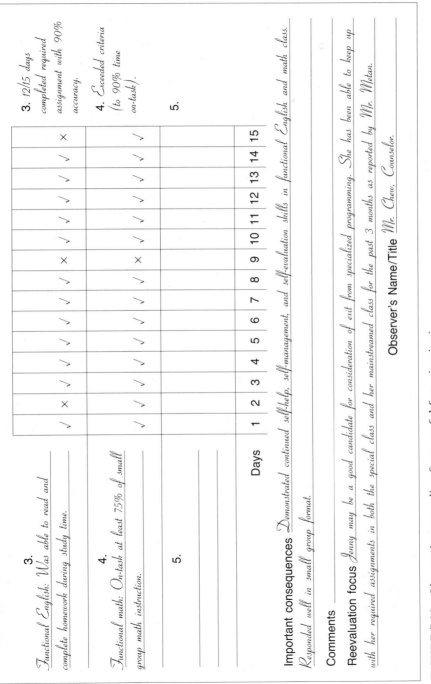

Objective	1	2	3	4	5	6	7	8	9	10	11	12	13	14	15	Result
3. *Functional English: Was able to read and complete homework during study time.*	√	×	√	√	√	√	√	√	×	√	√	√	√	√	×	3. *12/15 days completed required assignment with 90% accuracy.*
4. *Functional math: On-task at least 75% of small group math instruction.*	√	√	√	√	√	√	√	√	×	√	√	√	√	√	√	4. *Exceeded criteria (to 90% time on-task).*
5.																5.
Days	1	2	3	4	5	6	7	8	9	10	11	12	13	14	15	

Important consequences *Demonstrated continued self-help, self-management, and self-evaluation skills in functional English and math class. Responded well in small group format.*

Comments

Reevaluation focus *Jenny may be a good candidate for consideration of exit from specialized programming. She has been able to keep up with her required assignments in both the special class and her mainstreamed class for the past 3 months as reported by Mr. Metan.*

Observer's Name/Title *Mr. Chew, Counselor.*

FIGURE 7.10 Observation recording form useful for exit criteria.

Requirements of Annual Updated IEPs

IEPs must be updated yearly for students in special education and related services (EHA, 1975). This means that school professionals must ask parents to attend an annual IEP meeting to reconsider all goals and objectives. Again, parents must be notified twice. One notice must be in writing and a copy saved for school records. Attempts for a mutual time and place should be set. However, if the parents then refuse to attend the updated IEP meeting, school officials may continue with the meeting as planned without the parents (EHA, 1975; Federal Register, 1977). It is the responsibility of multidisciplinary team members to initiate additional meetings when the student's IEP no longer matches needs as the school year progresses.

Results and Implications of Reevaluations

It is a professional responsibility to reevaluate students every three years (EHA, 1975; Federal Register, 1977). Just as eligibility meetings are held to determine whether students meet entrance criteria into programs, a decision for exit criteria is also important (Ysseldyke & Algozzine, 1984). Figure 7.10 is an example of an observation-recording form that may be used to help verify a student's exit from specialized programming.

Reevaluations determine whether the student's program should change. Developing and beginning teachers should become familiar with local and state procedures for exit requirements when a change in educational placement is warranted for the student. Box 7.12 is provided to demonstrate four phases of an exit process to remove a student from special education. These steps are important aspects of placing students back into the regular classroom. Many data are required to verify the regular classroom as the LRE for the student. Again, the role of the special educator is as consultant to the regular classroom teacher when the student exits from special education. Professionals continue to team together to implement the exit process steps of Box 7.12.

Writing Reports to Parents and Other Professionals

Reports to parents and other professionals should be a continuous process all teachers undertake. Developing and beginning teachers must realize the importance of communication. Special educators, regular educators, other professionals, and parents need a continual communication process — more than can be provided through yearly IEP meetings or case conferences and school-based committees. Reports may be formal

BOX 7.12

Four Phases of an Exit Process

PHASE I: Plan (prior to reevaluation/exit conference)

- Identify a systematic data collection procedure for exit from special education programming.
- Identify pertinent strategies based on the student's needs.
- Determine how information is to be observed and collected.
- Identify data gatherers in the special education class and, as necessary, the mainstream class.
- Develop a time frame and schedule for data collection.

PHASE II: Data collection (prior to reevaluation/exit conference)

- Identify student demographic attributes.
- Collect background data on mastery of mainstream goals/objectives.
- Provide observational data including teacher-made tests and behavioral ratings in the regular class and special class.
- Compare and contrast past standardized test results with past and present criterion-referenced tests.
- Collect work samples from the regular class and special class.
- Analyze personal health and sensory data.
- Compare past prereferral strategies with present strategies.
- Collect individual interest surveys and goals.

PHASE III: Data analysis (prior to/during exit meeting)

- Provide comparison with norms after individualized re-evaluation.
- Analyze strengths and weaknesses within the individual.
- Note patterns of behaviors and changes across time.
- Determine goals and objectives for the mainstream class.
- Determine timelines for mainstream transition.
- Develop consultation teaming strategies and schedules of observation to implement during mainstream transition.

PHASE IV: Mainstream implementation (student returns to regular programming)

- Continue to observe and modify practices as needed.
- Collaborate with other professionals.
- Consult with parents.
- Implement goals and objectives in the mainstream class.
- Monitor progress and continue to collect data.
- Evaluate continually appropriateness of the new LRE.

statements of the student's progress, or they may be informal notes on the day's events or the student's reactions to them. Teachers may do simple tasks to complete the communication process with parents and other team members. Such things as writing down expectations, teacher's roles, and anticipated study units to share with parents and professionals is a good method to implement at the start of the school year. Special education teachers may try, also, to elicit from others how they perceive their role in the student's development. In an informal planning session, teachers may write down ways of working together. A suggestion to establish and maintain a continual positive rapport with the student's family is to initiate the first written contact with the parents or guardians during the beginning of the school year. Sharing responses intermittently will establish a positive rapport with others.

Also, a plan could be devised at the IEP meeting to maintain communication throughout the year. Such a plan could schedule updated review meetings for parents and teachers to discuss the student's progress, or set up a notebook the student could take back and forth from the regular classroom teacher to the special education teacher (Schulz & Turnbull, 1984). Getting together on a consistent basis with parents and other teachers may help the novice teacher understand the importance of continual communication with all significant individuals to the student.

Developing and beginning teachers should work to send written data home to parents on an informal basis. For example, the teacher may send home periodic newsletters or class happenings to keep parents informed of units of instruction, to target special activities, to announce special events, or to request inexpensive resources or household items from home. It's a good idea to send a copy of all newsletters and class happenings to the regular classroom teachers updated as well. Another example is sending home notes of progress and specific praise for tasks accomplished. (Try to accent the positive rather than contacting parents only when negative behaviors occur. Again, do the same positive correspondence with the regular classroom teachers to alert them when students have had a particularly productive day.) Still another idea is to have a suggestion box available for parents' and professionals' use to demonstrate active solicitation of their written feedback.

In all written correspondence with parents and other professionals, special educators should remember to translate all technical information. Write notes, letters and information sheets in short, clear, uncluttered language. In all contacts with parents, consider the discourse used. Try to communicate respect for the family's values, ideas, cultural background, and needs in all written correspondence.

Finally, all teachers should strive to establish and maintain a positive rapport with parents and other professionals by meeting formally and informally throughout the year. Providing a written invitation to all get-togethers and following up with a letter of thanks for their attendance at functions coordinated by the teacher are effective ways to help maintain positive communication throughout the year.

Who Can Help the Novice Teacher Understand the Ins and Outs of Paperwork?

This chapter stresses the importance of paperwork in the special education process. After reading it, developing and beginning teachers should recognize the link between updated, accurate paperwork and effectiveness in teaching.

Teachers must understand the crucial role paperwork plays in the communication process and in assuring an appropriate education to the student with special needs. Effective paperwork will pinpoint those students who need to be removed from regular-class programming and those who can function adequately in the regular class. Professionals should strive to implement effective teaming ideals. Developing and beginning teachers must not view either the vast amount of documentation needed for prereferral, referral, and the IEP process, or the less formal means of communication with parents and other professionals as busy work.

Just as it is important to recognize the value of paperwork and be aware of potential strategies to alleviate pitfalls of stress and conflict associated with paperwork, teachers new to the profession must also realize they are not alone in generating, collecting, and maintaining quality paperwork and instruction for their students. Colleagues can help. Peer teachers can answer many questions about the realities of paperwork. Regular educators and special educators can share documentation ideas, as well as effective teaching strategies. Administrators may provide critical feedback about the proper procedures of using paperwork efficaciously. Parents and students can provide valuable clues to the content and types of data teachers will find necessary on forms or other documentations. The teacher's own experience during meetings can help to make more sense of the necessity of and logic behind paperwork requirements. The novice teacher will function best by asking many questions. By using some of the strategies and teaming suggestions offered throughout this textbook, developing and beginning teachers may begin even to like using paperwork and value the utility of well-written documentation.

In Lindsay's case example, a well-documented set of data were vital in continuing her in the appropriate LRE—the regular class. The special education teacher can provide assistance to her regular class teacher through continual teaming efforts and support. Teachers of the 1990s can continue to team together to ensure all students the best educational opportunities available in the public school setting.

Summary

This chapter provides developing and beginning teachers with an overview of data collection involved in special education. The theme of the chapter, paperwork, is central to the role of the special educator. Initially, a rationale for the importance of writing tasks was provided as was comprehensive documentation required for referral and communication tasks. Additionally, IEPs and IEP meetings were discussed. Specific behaviors of classroom teachers before, during, and after the IEP meeting were listed. Finally, the chapter ended with suggestions to help teachers in writing reports and informing parents and regular class teachers of classroom activities and student progress. The role of teachers maintaining effective paperwork is to facilitate teaming efforts to ensure the most appropriate educational setting for all students.

References

ALGOZZINE, B., YSSELDYKE, J., & CHRISTENSON, S. L. (1983). An analysis of the incidence of special class placement. The masses are burgeoning. *Journal of Special Education, 17,* 141–147.

BARNER, A. (1982). Do teachers like to teach? *Pointer, 27,* 1, 5–7.

BRAATEN, S., KAUFFMAN, J. M., BRAATEN, B., POLSGROVE, L., & NELSON, C. M. (1988). The regular education initiative: Patent medicine for behavioral disorders. *Exceptional Children, 55,* 21–28.

CARTWRIGHT, P., CARTWRIGHT C. A., & WARD, M. (1981). *Educating special learners.* Belmont, CA: Wadsworth.

EDUCATION FOR ALL HANDICAPPED CHILDREN'S ACT (EHA) (Public Law 94–142). (1975). Washington, D.C.: Office of Special Education and Rehabilitation Services.

FEDERAL REGISTER (1977, August). Washington, D.C.: U.S. Government Printing Office.

GLOECKLER, T., & SIMPSON, C. (1988). *Exceptional students in regular classrooms: Challenges, services, and methods.* Mountain View, CA: Mayfield.

GOLDSTEIN, S., STRICKLAND B., TURNBULL, A. P., & CURRY, L. (1980). An observational analysis of the IEP conference. *Exceptional Children, 46,* 278–286.

GRADEN, J. L., CASEY, A., & BONSTROM, O. (1985). Implementing a prereferral intervention system: Part 2. The data. *Exceptional Children, 51,* 487–496.

GRADEN J. L., CASEY, A., & CHRISTENSON, S. L. (1985). Implementing a prereferral intervention system: Part 1. The model. *Exceptional Children, 51,* 377–387.

LYNCH, E., & STEIN, R. (1982). Perspectives on parent participation in special education. *Exceptional Education Quarterly, 3*(2), 73–84.

MAHEADY, L. (1988). An opportunity for developing instructional diversity. *Special Services Digest, 2,* 4–6.

MORGAN, D. P. (1982). Parent participation in the IEP process: Does it enhance appropriate education? *Exceptional Education Quarterly, 3*(2), 33–40.

MORSINK, C.V. (1982). Changes in the role of special educators: Public perceptions and demands. *Exceptional Education Quarterly,* (The Special Educator as a Professional Person), 2(4), 15–25.

SCHULZ, J. B., & TURNBULL, A. P. (1984). *Mainstreaming handicapped students: A guide for classroom teachers* (2nd ed.). Boston: Allyn & Bacon.

YSSELDYKE, J., & ALGOZZINE, B. (1984). *Introduction to special education.* Boston: Houghton Mifflin.

CHAPTER 8

Collaborative Programming and Consultation

One area often overlooked or given only superficial attention in teacher-training programs is professional interaction. Effectively communicating with other professionals in a school system embodies a set of critical skills that will enable developing teachers to better use the resources available in a school. Developing teachers new to a school are given greater than normal attention. Other professionals, paraprofessionals, parents, and children observe and begin to make decisions about the kind of persons new teachers are, whether or not they believe they will be effective teachers, helpful associates, or even personal friends. Consequently, there is a need to be cognizant of how individuals come across to others.

By verbal and nonverbal actions, developing teachers can manipulate others' perceptions. If they want to be viewed as aggressive, they can make demands about what they will and will not do, and what resources they expect to be available. On the other hand, they may act passively, by being very acquiescent and giving in to the demands of everyone else. And, of course, there are myriad degrees of aggressive/passive behavior between these extremes. The point is that developing teachers have a degree of control over how they are perceived by others within this continuum. Consequently, the perceptions of others are going to determine how cooperative they will be and what human and other resources will be made available.

Developing and beginning teachers take on a variety of roles in professional relationships with other school staff (see Figure 8.1). Obviously, they will take on the role of a beginning teacher and therefore be the **consultee** (recipient of consultative services) from supervisory personnel (e.g., principal, program supervisor, or consulting teacher). On the other hand, it is likely they will have paraprofessionals in their classroom whom they will manage (e.g., assign instructional tasks, train in different teaching techniques, and so forth), thus their role will be that of a **consultant** (provider of supervisory services). In addition, they may be asked to take on the role of an educational consultant for other teaching staff in their school as well as consult with parents.

To assist in taking on these diverse roles, the discussion that follows is a description of the roles that developing teachers will take on at some point. The first section of the chapter contains common-sense ideas about interacting with consultants (i.e., consulting teachers, supervisors, or principals). The next section contains more technical information regarding interpersonal communication skills and procedures for conferring with others. It is important to remember that developing and beginning teachers have to be well versed in playing the roles of recipient and provider of consultative or supervisory services. Therefore, they need to look at the discussion from both points of view and envision how they would apply principles of interpersonal communication and collaborative problem solving from any one of the roles they may play at any given time. Their ability to function effectively in these roles will help shape the perceptions of others toward them.

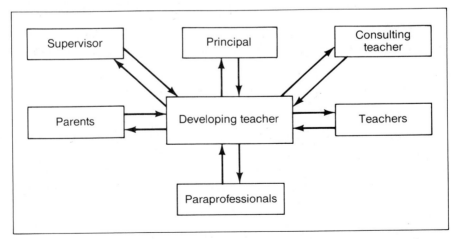

FIGURE 8.1 Relationship of developing teacher to other education professionals in the consultant and consultee roles.

The Beginning Teacher as the Recipient of Consulting Services

Preservice teacher trainees and developing teachers are invariably the recipient of consulting services. Consulting services are activities or interactions provided by other professionals to help novice teachers improve their teaching performance. They may include a consulting teacher or supervisor formally assisting with setting up a classroom program on an ongoing basis, another teacher informally taking on the role of mentor and assisting as needed, or a principal evaluating teaching performance and providing corrective feedback.

More experienced teaching personnel can help with problem solving in more efficient ways by helping new teachers avoid mistakes and bureaucracy. They have gone through the process and have more than likely learned a lot that can be passed on. For instance, teaching materials that would be of interest may be tucked away in some remote closet, or the school system may have a library of video tapes that require reserving far in advance. Often asking the right person may better ensure receipt of some needed materials. More experienced teachers know how the school system really works and ways of getting around potential roadblocks.

Interactions with consulting teachers, supervisors, or principals can give developing teachers insights as to what is important in the eyes of key school personnel. Accordingly, new teachers can learn where to focus their time and attention. Administrators, for instance, may place more emphasis on classroom management and presentation of content than on having attractive bulletin boards. They may implicitly indicate hidden agenda, like the expectation that teachers handle discipline problems in their rooms and not send students to the principal for reprimanding.

Appreciating the Competence of Other Professionals

A large part of learning from experienced teachers and administrators is accepting that others are skillful and willing to be helpful when asked. Other teachers have refined their teaching skills so well that they make the act of teaching and classroom management look simple. They have developed styles that may or may not be congruent with the style of teaching that developing and beginning teachers wish to emulate. Nonetheless, developing and beginning teachers can learn a great deal about why specific teachers use certain styles and may find that what experienced teachers do can be modified to fit their conception of teaching and management. For example, a new teacher may observe that a teacher has excellent control of her students, but seems to be verbally rough with them. This may not be appealing, but beyond the surface the new teacher may notice that this teacher is very consistent in reinforcing appropriate behavior and in punishing inappropriate behavior. For the new teacher's own development, the rough tone may be dispensed and the consistency incorporated into his approach to student-behavior management.

Another point to consider is developing and beginning teachers' evaluation of and interaction with those individuals of authority. Supervisory and administrative personnel are granted a degree of authority simply by the position they hold. New teachers are expected, if nothing else, to respect the position of such individuals in the organizational hierarchy. On the other hand, developing and beginning teachers will make judgments about the competence of supervisory and administrative personnel and accordingly afford them varying degrees of respect for their professional competence. In either case, developing and beginning teachers will have to subordinate their views in order to survive in a hierarchical organizational system. If they find that the individuals with whom they work warrant respect for their competence, they can acquiesce to the dominant views with little or no resentment. However, if they only respect an individual for the position that individual holds, it may at times be exceedingly difficult to subordinate their own views. Developing and beginning teachers then have to make judgments for themselves based on their level of confidence and whether their views will be perceived by others as having more merit. They also must depend on their willingness to jeopardize their continued employment in the system, on their perceptions of another individual's power, and on the degree of support they believe they have among others in positions of power. An analysis of these variables is difficult especially for teacher trainees or developing teachers who have not been a part of the system for long enough to know its intricacies or to have established friends in high places who will look after them.

Obviously, the safest strategy for developing teachers is to concede to authority in the early stages of induction into the school system unless such a concession entails committing an immoral, unethical, or illegal act. As developing and beginning teachers become more familiar with the system and demonstrate their own professional competence, they may become more assertive and challenge the system. Also, it should be remembered that new teachers are not necessarily alone — professional organizations and teachers' unions may be of great help especially when an issue at hand is a very serious one.

Often developing and beginning teachers find that the consulting teachers, supervisors, and principals with whom they work have a different training background or teach different types of students or subject matter. Ideally, those professionals who are assisting with a developing teacher's growth have direct experience teaching in the same content area, material, and category of students. But, that may be a luxury that new teachers will not experience. Accordingly, they may be inclined to underestimate the quality and relevance of the assistance teaching professionals in other areas can lend.

The fact remains, however, that the principles of effective instruction and behavior management used by skilled teachers are, by definition, generalizable rules that guide teacher behavior (Box 8.1). They are appropriate for most populations and content. (Albeit, there needs to be modifications to the application of those principles to different populations and content.) Teachers unfamiliar with the specific content of instruction, however, may not be able to assist with issues of content accuracy and structure. But teachers in other content areas with different types of students and age groups can demonstrate techniques or help developing and beginning teachers recognize effective or ineffective techniques that they are using in their instruction. Nonetheless, developing and beginning teachers must be able to apply principles and good examples in their own classrooms.

Making the Most of Consultative Services

If the supervision process is viewed as a service being provided to developing and beginning teachers by their employer, then they can view their role in the process as that of a consumer receiving a service. Consequently, they should take advantage of supervision by making full use of the process. The consultative service should entail a systematic approach to the supervision process whereby conferences and observations are conducted on a regularly scheduled basis. Conferences and observations target specific performance objectives. Critiques of developing teachers' instructional or management behaviors are presented in conjunction with constructive suggestions for alternative teaching behaviors. Novice teachers should also be given increasing responsibility for identifying their own strengths and weaknesses and devising prescriptions for their improvement.

If developing and beginning teachers tactfully indicate to supervisory personnel that these are their expectations for the consultation process, then they communicate to others that they are knowledgeable about the process, are serious about developing their skills as a teacher, and want some control over their own professional development.

Accepting Constructive Criticism

The most difficult aspect of consultation is being critiqued. When partaking in a collaborative consultation conference, the first priority for the developing and beginning teacher is to maintain objectivity to the greatest extent possible. They need to suppress their desires to defend

BOX 8.1

Effective Instructional and Behavior Management Principles

INSTRUCTIONAL ORGANIZATION AND DEVELOPMENT

- Efficiently uses instructional time.
- Reviews of subject matter are provided frequently.
- Signals the initiation of lesson and lesson transitions.
- Levels of questioning are varied.
- Numerous opportunities to respond are provided.
- Question presentation and signal to respond are mediated by wait time.
- Acknowledges and elaborates student responses.
- Provides specific academic feedback.
- Provides and monitors guided and independent practice.

PRESENTATION OF SUBJECT MATTER

- Defines, gives examples and nonexamples of concepts.
- States cause and effect for laws and law-like principles.
- States and applies academic rules.
- Establishes criteria and assembles facts to make value judgments.

MANAGEMENT OF STUDENT CONDUCT

- Sets, monitors, and enforces classroom rules.
- Is aware of student behavior.
- Manages multiple activities simultaneously.
- Uses positive reinforcement.
- Uses contingent punishment.

COMMUNICATION: VERBAL AND NONVERBAL

- Clearly and logically presents discourse.
- Emphasizes important information.
- Makes academic tasks attractive and challenging.

SOURCE Adapted from the Florida Coalition for the Development of a Performance Measurement System (no date). Domains: Concepts and indicators of effective teaching—Florida Performance Measurement System. Tallahassee, FL: Department of Education.

their performance, listen to what is being conveyed, and objectively present their rationale for their actions. If developing teachers are experiencing such a strong emotional response that they are on the verge of going out of control, they should say as little as possible and allow the supervisor to finish, then indicate the need to think over the points that were made and schedule another conference. This will provide the new teacher with a cooling-down period during which they can vent any anger and then spend time carefully analyzing the supervisor's or consulting teacher's comments. In most cases, they will find that the feedback is not as terrible as first thought and that it is valid.

Before reconvening with the consulting teacher or supervisor, they should reflect on how they could have approached instruction in a different, more effective way. Making some notes about what they think went wrong and how they can avoid making the same mistakes in the future can be a helpful strategy. On the other hand, if they believe that the feedback was invalid, then they need to reflect on what occurred during instruction and build a case to defend their performance. Again, they need to make notes that can be taken to the next conference. (The conference planning guide, Figure 8.5, may be helpful to record notes).

Regardless, keep in mind that effective teachers are made, not born, and that no one should expect developing and beginning teachers, and that includes themselves, to walk into a classroom and do a flawless job of managing classroom behavior and providing instruction. Developing effective teaching skills takes years of practice and conscious effort. Developing and beginning teachers should be patient and work toward the goal of becoming an effective teacher.

The Developing and Beginning Teacher as the Provider of Consulting Services

Now that these great expectations have been built up for exemplary consultative services to be provided to the developing and beginning teacher, consideration needs to be given to how these teachers can do the same for other teachers and paraprofessionals. When they have to be the consultant, developing and beginning teachers quickly realize how much work, frustration, and skill is involved. The kinds of skills needed are outlined in the next section and are categorized as interpersonal communication and problem-solving skills. A description of these skills is provided in some detail, but before reading about that, the developing teacher needs to consider a few simple concepts when acting as a consultant.

Novice teachers have a great deal of potential to become an effective teacher and consultant, but they have to accumulate a great deal of experience in both roles before becoming effective in either. In working with others during the early stages of their career, developing and beginning teachers need to accept that they know some things but they have a great deal more to learn. They need to consider the sensitivity of others to constructive criticism. Again, they need to use the skills outlined below, always being aware that the feedback they provide may not be the information that others want to hear. They need to tune into the verbal and nonverbal reactions to what is being said.

Collaborative Model for Consultative Processes

As recipients of consultative services (consultees), or as providers of consultative services (consultants), new teachers are active participants in a **collaborative consultation process**.

As consultees, developing and beginning teachers need to assist in scheduling conferences and observations. They have to prepare lesson plans and present them to their supervisor in advance. They are expected to reflect on their own teaching performance and analyze their strengths and weaknesses. During conferences, they are asked to communicate their perceptions of their own teaching in an honest and uninhibited way and assist in devising strategies for improving their teaching. Follow-up responsibilities are devised, and they are required to complete tasks before the next conference (e.g., practicing new techniques, observing other teachers demonstrating alternative teaching behaviors, reading reference texts).

As the consultant to other teachers, paraprofessionals, or parents, the developing and beginning teacher has to schedule conferences, direct the conferences toward achieving some set of goals, analyze information related to the situation at hand, determine a strategy for resolving target problems, and determine the procedures and responsibilities for consultant and consultee (Warger & Aldinger, 1984).

Consensual Decision Making

The overall goal of collaboration is agreement on what is to be accomplished and how it is to be accomplished. Individuals working on a problem need to feel a part of the problem-solving process. To accomplish this, the consultant and consultee in a working group need to participate actively in the process. This concept of active participation to achieve group consensus is referred to as **consensual decision making.** Consensual decision making requires a commitment of individuals within a working group to three principles (Chandler, 1982):

1. A belief that others understand their point of view.
2. A belief that they understand others' points of view.
3. Committed support for decisions made, whether or not they prefer the decisions, because they were arrived at in an open and fair manner.

Consensual decision making relies on individuals working as a cohesive group, perceiving the process as fair and worthwhile, and committing to the outcome of the efforts made. As consultees, developing and beginning teachers want to know they have contributed to the problem-solving process, instead of being criticized on how they should improve their teaching skills. As consultants, they will want to help others (e.g., teachers, paraprofessionals, parents) to develop ownership and commitment to the decisions.

Balance of Control

In successful collaborative consultation, there typically is a balance of control that moves away from the consultant and toward the consultee. Early in the consulting relationship, consultees tend to be more reliant on others to provide them with information and directions on how to complete job-related activities. They do a lot of asking and a lot of listening. On the other hand, consultants usually have a great deal of information about the school and views as to how the system should work. In the early stages of the process, consultants typically do a lot of telling and directing. Researchers like Blumberg (1980) refer to this as a **directive** style of behavior. Conversely, as the consultees become more knowledgeable and confident in what they are doing, they ask fewer questions and seek less direction. They begin to do more talking in a conference and asking consultants to confirm their suspicions about a situation. Consultants do more listening and ask leading questions to guide consultees in analyzing their own teaching performance. This style of consultive behavior is referred to as **indirective** (Fig. 8.2).

The directness or indirectness of a consultant's style is related to the degree of emphasis given to the task at hand (i.e., improving consultee's performance) or to the interpersonal relationship between the consultant and consultee. Directive consultants *tell* developing consultees what their strengths and weaknesses are and how to improve their performance. Telling is usually a more efficient means of identifying problem areas and strategies to remediate them. With direct consultation, however, little attention is given to the consultee's self-esteem or the development of his self-evaluation skills. Indirective consultation, on the other hand, entails consultants asking the developing consultee questions in order to lead them to recognizing problem areas and deducing possible solutions. Under this indirect style, consultees tend to feel more in control of their performance, accept ownership for the diagnosis and intervention strategies, and develop self-evaluation skills.

Productive interpersonal work seems to be achieved best by maintaining an overall balance between energy directed toward the task of improving consultees' teaching and energy directed toward establishing a good interpersonal relationship among team members. Effective consultation is a combination of both direct and indirect approaches. The results of at least one study (Copeland, 1982) indicate that teachers (consultees) positively evaluate their supervisory interpersonal relations when they

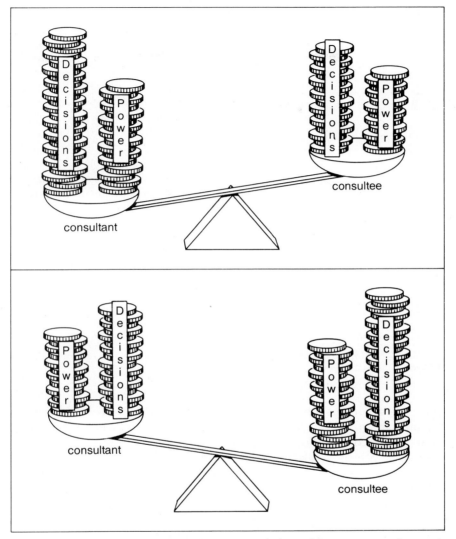

FIGURE 8.2   Decision making and power are balanced between consultee and consultant, although at different points in the process the consultant or consultee may have more or less of each.

perceive their supervisor's (consultant's) behavior as being high direct, high indirect (style A) or low direct, high indirect (style C) (Table 8.1).

In sum, the collaborative model for consultative processes involves the consultant and consultee actively participating in decision making and problem solving. There is an understanding that the purpose of the process is to improve instruction and an understanding of the need to

TABLE 8.1   Styles of Behavior Applicable to Consulting

Style A	High direct, high indirect	The consultee (teacher) sees the consultant (supervisor) emphasizing both direct and indirect behavior — he tells and criticizes, but he also asks and listens.
Style B	High direct, low indirect	The consultee perceives the consultant as doing a great deal of telling and criticizing but very little asking or listening.
Style C	Low direct, high direct	The consultant's behavior is rarely direct (telling, criticizing, and so forth); instead, he puts a lot of emphasis on asking questions, listening, and reflecting back the consultee's ideas and feelings.
Style D	Low direct, low indirect	The consultee sees the consultant as passive, not doing much of anything. Some consultants, may appear passive as they try to engage in a rather misguided democratic role.

SOURCE   From Blumberg, A. (1980). *Supervisors and teachers: A private cold war.*
Berkeley, CA: McCutchen.

come to agreement about the goals of consultation and the means for attaining them. Consensual decision making helps to facilitate a commitment to the consultation process and ownership of the responsibilities associated with the goals and strategies agreed on by the team. In order for there to be a true consensus, there needs to be a balance of control in the process. That is not to say that at each conference there will be an equal distribution of control between consultant and consultee, but that over the course of a series of conferences, each will equally contribute to the decision-making process. Early in the process, the consultant will usually dominate, but this will shift to the consultee as the relationship develops.

Interpersonal Communication Skills

Some constructs taken from the work of Carl Rogers (1965) may be helpful to developing and beginning teachers in building a cooperative rapport with those with whom they work. Developing and beginning teachers need to keep in mind that they will apply these constructs primarily in their role as a consultant, but they are also applicable to their role as consultee. There will be differences in how they are operationalized depending on whether they are acting as a consultant or consultee.

The first construct is that of **positive regard** for others. This is the ability to maintain a degree of respect for others simply because they are fellow human beings. Although developing and beginning teachers may respect others as individuals, this does not mean they necessarily agree with or condone their actions. In essence, the person is separated from their actions. For instance, a fellow teacher may photocopy copyrighted material in a way that violates the law and a new teacher's own moral values. The new teacher does not condone this behavior but can still maintain a degree of respect for the individual as a skilled teacher. The benefit of developing a positive regard for others is that greater objectivity is gained in dealings with others.

Positive regard for others can be shown by providing **honest feedback** and offering **encouragement**. Honest feedback describes frankly what the target behavior is, the perceptions that the speaker has of the listener's attitudes and behaviors, and the response that the speaker has to the listener's behavior. For example, rather than saying to their classroom paraprofessional who was obviously not prepared, "Well, I thought the tutoring went fairly well . . . considering," the developing teacher might provide honest feedback by saying, "This lesson did not go well because you were not fully prepared. You didn't have any visuals ready, and you weren't organized. Can we talk about why you weren't prepared?"

Encouragement is the acknowledgment that another person has the skills and behavioral repertoire to overcome problems and to extend existing skills to higher performance levels. Behaviors that express encouragement help to build and maintain self-esteem and should increase the probability that similar positive behaviors will be demonstrated in the future. Importantly, statements of encouragement need to include specific, descriptive praises. Such statements describe the observed behavior and the observer's response to it. When a consultant observes that a consultee has displayed an effective behavior and comments on the behavior and his impressions of its effect, then descriptive praise is being used. For instance, the consultant might say, "I thought it was very effective when you stopped the talking by walking over to the student, yet continued to discuss regrouping of numbers without a moment's interruption."

A second construct is **empathy**. Empathic responses indicate an understanding about what another person is going through. In everyday life, individuals often make empathic statements regarding both the positive and negative experience of others. For instance, in acknowledging a colleague's successful instruction of a student, a new teacher might say,

"Oh, you must have been thrilled to see that Sara finally was able to conquer regrouping." When unpleasant experiences occur, teachers often console friends or colleagues with empathic statements such as, "Getting a parking ticket first thing in the morning is aggravating." Being empathic toward the experiences of others often helps to convey the fact that individuals are concerned and can appreciate the emotional responses of others to situations or events.

Burke (1984) describes **responding behaviors** as skilled expressions reflecting an empathic attitude for another person. Empathy for another person as described by Rogers (1965) is not an overt behavior. The attitude of empathy, however, can be expressed through outward behavior in the form of active listening. Active listening entails

1. Using **open-ended** responses that focus on the other person, are nonjudgmental, seek further information and are uncomplicated utterances.

   Example: "How do you feel the lesson went today?"

2. Using **paraphrasing/clarifying** responses to help the other person hear his/her own words, help the listener understand what the speaker's concerns are, and relate back to the speaker that the listener has carefully considered his statements.

   Example: "You said they didn't understand the concept very well. Do you mean they had difficulty with the follow-up activity?"

3. Focusing on emotions so that the component of a person's message is **objectively and openly acknowledged** as existing and not ignored.

   Example: "I can see you're upset with this situation. Let's talk it over."

The third concept, **congruence**, refers to the degree of accuracy between individuals' perceptions of their behaviors or experiences and the actual pattern of behaviors and experiences. Developing and beginning teachers in a state of congruence are psychologically well-adjusted (i.e., comfortable about what they do and about their experiences). Consultants and consultees in a state of congruence are genuine and sincere when interacting with each other. They project the impression that they are honest and express their true impressions of a targeted problem area. Burke (1984) refers to statements with these characteristics as **attending skills**, which involve the use of **self-disclosure statements**. Such statements are characterized by three criteria (O'Shea & Hoover, 1986):

1. Taking responsibility for thoughts, behaviors, and emotions.

   Example: "If I had planned that transition a little better, we wouldn't have lost so much time."

2. Making concrete rather than vague or abstract statements.

   Example: "I find my school day goes so much better if I get a good night's sleep, eat a full breakfast, and arrive half an hour before the students."

3. Referring to conditions in the immediate environment.

   Example: "I plan the math lesson for late morning before the music teacher comes in. After she leaves, the children are so excited, that spelling is more easily accomplished."

   Statements with these characteristics objectively convey the position of the consultant or consultee, specify what exactly the subject of the statement is, and puts the subject into the immediate context. One subset of self-disclosure statements is that of "I statements" (Gordon, 1974). These statements involve three components (O'Shea & Hoover, 1986):

1. Description of consultee's target behavior is in nonjudgmental terms.

   Example: "I heard you ask 12 literal-level recall questions and 2 evaluation questions."

2. The effect of the target behavior on the speaker is described in concrete terms.

   Example: "I can't keep my roll book up to date when you fail to give me the weekly test results for your students on time."

3. The emotional response of the speaker to the other person's behavior is specified.

   Example: "I feel delighted to have a developing teacher who is as interested and as willing to put forth effort as you are."

These kinds of statements convey that the speaker is a clear, honest, and sincere communicator.

Again, these interpersonal communication skills are applicable to both consultant and consultee. When individuals in both roles use positive regard, empathy, and congruence, communication is clearer and more effective. Without clear communication, collaborative consultation used for problem solving will be muddled by ineffective attempts to communicate ideas, instead of attempts to resolve targeted instructional problems (Fig. 8.3).

General Procedures for Collaborative Consultation

The focal point of interpersonal relations in collaborative consultation is the series of conferences among members of the consultation team (i.e., consultee, consulting teacher, supervisor, or principal) that occur throughout the consultation process. In addition to spending energy and attention on the interpersonal relationships between consultant and consultee, an equal amount of energy needs to be directed at identifying and resolving instructional problems. The second facet of collaborative consultation, therefore, is the systematic implementation of procedures for conducting conferences. While interpersonal communication skills aid in establishing a positive relationship among members of the collaborative consultation team, the procedures for conducting conferences focus on the activities that need to be accomplished. Initially, the procedures for conferences involve discussing team members' roles, scheduling conferences and observations, and identifying important classroom variables (i.e., types of students, classroom rules and schedules, and so forth). After the first few weeks, however, conferences focus on diagnosing problems and testing strategies to resolve them (Garland, 1982; Goldhammer, Anderson, & Krajewski, 1980).

Three Basic Procedures

Many of the procedures incorporated into the collaborative consultation process are derived from behavioral principles and decision-making systems. These general procedures are designed to help developing teachers to define roles, functions, and goals of the collaborative consultation team. The three general procedures outlined below underlie the entire conference process and are designed for use by both consultant and consultee in collaboratively solving instructional problems.

First, a system for formulating **behaviorally descriptive statements** related to the targeted instructional problem area needs to be established. Behaviorally descriptive statements are those that operationally identify

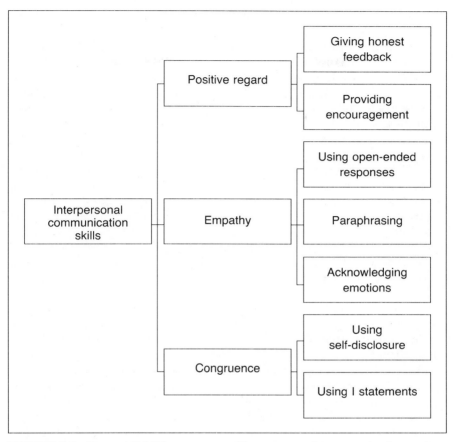

FIGURE 8.3   Rogers' (1965) constructs of interpersonal communication and the overt behavior used to exhibit them.

a behavior in specific, accurate, and concise terms. They refer to quantities or frequencies of behavior occurrences. Behavioral statements do not contain subjective descriptions that imply a judgment of the behavior. A statement like, "The developing teacher is not enthusiastic" is imprecise and may lead to poor communication. Vague statements should be avoided or backed-up with a more objective statement of observable behaviors in order to indicate clearly the basis for the statement.

In addition to behaviors, the **conditions** of behaviors need to be stated. These elements provide a clear reflection of the context in which behaviors occur. For instance, it may have been agreed on by the consultation team that the consultee should praise students each time they provide an accurate response to a question (condition) and not when they simply respond with any answer (non-condition). When a change in a specific teaching behavior is targeted, the desired level (i.e., greater or lesser) or direction (i.e., increase or decrease) of the change should be made clear. Behaviors must be referenced in clear, quantifiable, and observable terms. In this way, documentation and monitoring of changes in behavior are made easier and more objective (Piper & Elgert, 1979).

Second, **scheduling and maintaining schedules** are necessary for consistency and to routinize collaborative consultation procedures. In addition to their roles as consultants, developing and beginning teachers often have their own classroom responsibilities. Direct instructional services to students take a priority over consultations with other teachers. As a result, they fail to make time available for conferences with consultees, be they other teachers, paraprofessionals, or parents. Unless consultants and consultees make the time by setting goals and scheduling observations and conferences, they are likely to defer these activities in favor of others. Following through with schedules establishes, over time, distributed practice of the procedures for various collaborative activities, which in turn better ensures that consultation activities take place.

To ensure that schedules are maintained, it is important not only to write down the series of activities to be completed, but also to set a time and date to engage in each of the activities. Each subsequent conference should end with the confirmation of the next interaction as well as projected meetings that are to follow in the near future. Following this strategy ensures that the schedule is constantly used, reviewed, and modified throughout the consultation program.

The third general procedure involves the **problem-solving process**. During collaborative consultations, the principal activity is that of identifying relevant classroom variables, identifying instructional program strengths and weaknesses, and formulating alternative strategies to improve student performance. These steps are delineated by the diagnostic teaching model (Cartwright & Cartwright, 1972) discussed in Chapter 4. The steps in the model include (a) identify attributes, (b) specify objectives, (c) select strategies and materials, and (d) test strategies and materials.

The first step, as applied to consultation, involves the collection of information about the classroom setting, the behavior and learning attributes of students, teaching style and behaviors of the teacher, and any other relevant variables. Consultants and/or consultees collect baseline data prior to any systematic intervention, allowing team members to form a picture of what is occurring in the classroom. Next, the team must determine what it is they want to maintain or modify by specifying clear and behaviorally stated objectives that reflect the desired outcomes of the instructional program (step 2). Team members then select alternative strategies for accomplishing the stated objectives (step 3). Once implemented by the consultee, the strategies and materials are tested through subsequent observations and data collection (step 4). Based on the information gathered, team members analyze the feedback and determine whether or not the objectives have been reached. Accordingly, the sequence is repeated in either one of two ways. If objectives have been reached, the team forms new ones (step 2) and continues through the other steps as described. On the other hand, if objectives are not reached, then the team reexamines the accuracy and appropriateness of the baseline data, stated objectives, strategies, and materials. If modifications in any one of these areas are necessary, the team makes the changes and the sequence is continued. When all steps seem to be accurate and appropriate, then the clinical team implements the strategies and materials again and retests.

Behaviorally descriptive statements, schedules, and problem-solving procedures are used in conferences to identify and remediate instructional problems (Fig. 8.4).

Operationalizing Conference Procedures

During the **preobservation conference** that occurs at the beginning of the consultation experience, the consultant and consultee focus on obtaining a **baseline measure of salient situational variables** involving the

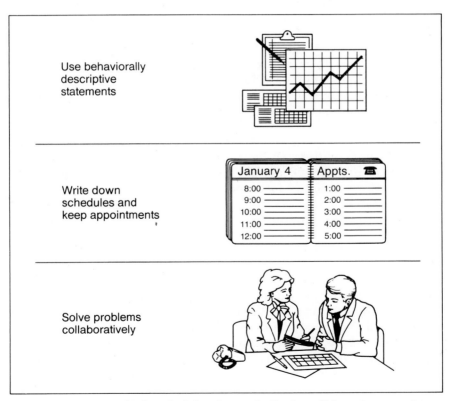

FIGURE 8.4 Three basic principles that underlie the collaborative consultation process.

students, teacher aides, or a new teacher. At this point, the team members will discuss anecdotal observations of the members, most importantly those of the consultee. Areas of possible concern to the consultee may set the agenda for the initial observation by the consultant. Any additional areas dealing with planning, student conduct, management of classroom procedures, presentation of instructional material, building rapport, and so forth, that the observer will be attending to should be overviewed with the consultee.

Next, the means for **collecting data** on these areas need to be devised or selected. In systematic observation models, some form of data recording is used to monitor behavior and to provide feedback. Recordings of teacher behavior can take a variety of forms: (a) continuous event recording, (b) time sampling, and (c) interval recording.

Judgments about the situation and type of information sought from an observation dictate the type of recording system used. In any case, the recorded data provide the basis for discussion between the observer and the new teacher.

Used in conjunction with specific operational definitions of behaviors, **observation records** effectively communicate by providing a clear, quantifiable picture of the consultees' and/or students' behaviors. Observation records also serve as a prompt in follow-up conferences. For instance, after having observed and conducted a postobservation conference using a systematic observation record, consulting teachers can use the record in the subsequent preobservation conference to remind consultees of behavior patterns in order to guide them to vary the pattern during the upcoming observation.

If a predesigned recording instrument is to be used (e.g., FPMS, COKER, Flanders Interaction Analysis), then the team members should simply review the target behaviors on the instrument and the recording method to be used (e.g., continuous-event recording, time sampling, and so forth). If an informal instrument is to be designed and used, the team should design the form and recording method together, incorporating the principles of interpersonal communication and participative decision making outlined in previous sections.

During the **postobservation conference**, feedback on earlier observations is provided. This critical step involves providing consultees with objective data reflecting environmental variables including student and teacher behavior in the classroom. Observers should present the data and explain how they were collected but should avoid making any value judgments about the student's, teacher aide's or developing teacher's performances. Both the consultant and the consultee should then discuss the data and analyze it to discern any **recognizable patterns** that reflect when a specific behavior occurs in the context of any antecedent or consequent events. For instance, every time a new teacher sits at her desk during seatwork assignments, the noise level may begin to rise.

This may become evident to the consultant and consultee when a recurring pattern is noted on the data record.

As consultees become more skilled at analyzing data, more responsibility should be shifted to them for identifying patterns with increasingly less direction from the consultant. This gradual fading process will help consultees develop **self-evaluation skills**. In addition, by analyzing the data with consultees and helping them to identify salient patterns, consultants create an atmosphere that is less defensive and more productive in locating problems and devising solutions.

Once patterns of behaviors have been identified, team members need to **specify those student, teacher aide, or new teacher behaviors** to maintain or increase and those to reduce or eliminate. Here, again, the emphasis is on behaviorally stated target behaviors that the consultant and consultee will focus on in the future. In addition, the team members should determine **alternative strategies** for modifying the behavior of the students, teacher or aide. These strategies may also involve modifications to the classroom setting (e.g., rearranging the physical space) or the curriculum (e.g., moving students to more appropriate points in the curriculum or changing curricula).

Finally, the responsibilities of each member for the next observation and conference should be documented. For instance, if the strategies for changing the consultee's behavior include the consultant modeling a specific teaching technique, then arrangements for the consultee to observe the consultant should be made. If the consultees are to review some reference books, then arrangements for getting those books to them need to be made. This documentation helps to ensure that the activities identified by the team are carried out. Included within this step is the scheduling of the next observation and conference. The conference planning guide (Fig. 8.5) can be used to document the decision made in the postobservation conference and provide a permanent record of the process.

Summary

Developing and beginning teachers are involved in the consultation process in two ways: as recipients and providers of consultative services. In the first case, as consultees, their role is to assist in the process of developing their own teaching and classroom-management skills. They need to accept the consultant's assistance and, to some extent, acquiesce to their control and authority. In the latter case, as consultant, developing and beginning teachers will be required to direct others carefully in their development. This will entail being humble and sensitive to the perceptions of those with whom they work. For both of these roles, the following principles and procedures of a collaborative consultation model have been suggested.

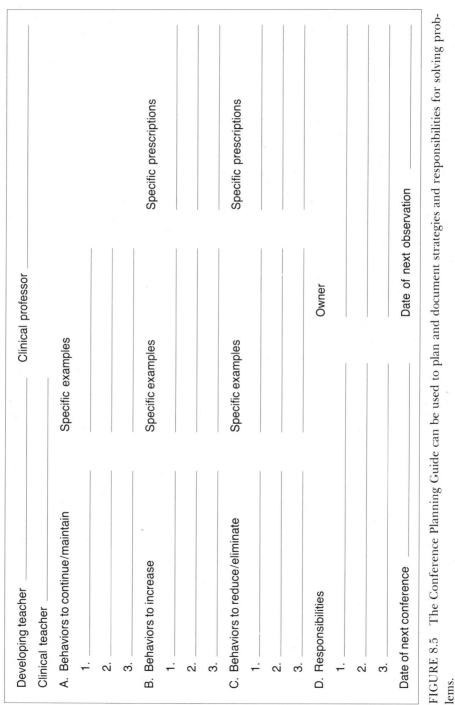

FIGURE 8.5 The Conference Planning Guide can be used to plan and document strategies and responsibilities for solving problems.

The first critical facet of collaborative consultation is the establishment and maintenance of productive interpersonal relationships between consultants and consultees. This can be accomplished through the application of the constructs of positive regard, empathy, and congruence. These constructs are displayed through verbal and nonverbal communication techniques. Consultants and consultees can operationalize these constructs through facilitating, responding, and attending. By facilitating, team members provide honest feedback regarding instructional variables, but encourage continued professional development as well. Consultants respond to consultees' concerns by recognizing the affective elements of the learning process and by exploring and clarifying consultees' perceptions of their situation. Team members attend to the situation at hand by making concrete, nonjudgmental statements about the behaviors and emotions of the people within the instructional environment (e.g., teachers, paraprofessionals, or students).

Facilitating, responding, and attending are the elements of the indirect style whereby consultants ask questions of consultees and attentively listen to their responses. Although under a direct consultation style active listening is replaced by telling and criticizing, facilitating and attending still can be employed. There is a time and place for both an indirect or direct approach as long as team members are aware and strive to maintain a complementary mix.

An important element that appears to influence consultees' responses to varying styles is their level of skill and confidence. During the early stages of consultation, more directive approaches by consultants may be necessary. As skills and confidence grow, consultees are better prepared to participate in the decision-making processes during conferences. Under these circumstances, consultees are able to self-evaluate more objectively and to commit themselves to decisions made by the consultation team.

References

BLUMBERG, A. (1980). *Supervisors and teachers: A private cold war.* Berkley, CA: McCutchen.

BURKE, J. B. (1984). Interpersonal communication. In J. M. Cooper (Ed.), *Developing skills for instructional supervision.* New York: Longman.

CARTWRIGHT, G. P., & CARTWRIGHT, C. A. (1972). Gilding the lily: Comments on the training based model for special education. *Exceptional Children, 39,* 231–234.

CHANDLER, T. A. (1982). Can Theory Z be applied to the public schools? *Education, 104,* 343–345.

COPELAND, W. D. (1982). Student teachers' preference for supervisory approach. *Journal of Teacher Education, 33,* 32–36.

GARLAND, G. (1982) *Guiding experiences in teacher education.* New York: Longman.

GOLDHAMMER, R., ANDERSON, R. H. & KRAJEWSKI, R. J. (1980). *Clinical supervision: Special methods for the supervision of teachers* (2nd ed.). New York: Holt, Rinehart & Winston.

GORDON, T. (1974). *T.E.T.: Teacher effectiveness training.* New York: Peter H. Wyden.

O'SHEA, L. J., & HOOVER, N. L. (1986). *Conferring with teachers about teacher performance.* Tallahassee, FL: Florida Department of Education.

PIPER, T. J., & ELGERT, D. B. (1979). *Teacher supervision through behavioral objectives: An operationally described system.* Baltimore: Brokes.

ROGERS, C. (1965). *Client-centered therapy.* Boston: Houghton Mifflin.

WARGER, C. L., & ALDINGER, L. E. (1984). Improving student teacher supervision: The preservice consultation model. *TEASE, 7,* 155–163.

CHAPTER 9

The Master Teacher

This chapter is written to provide direction to developing teachers who are determined to make the field of special education a long-term career. The goal is to increase developing and beginning teachers' awarenesses of the necessity of continual professional growth and active involvement in the field. Professional development and active involvement are vital steps in becoming and remaining master teachers. The chapter opens with a discussion on the need for teaming, consultation, and observing colleagues to share strategies and techniques. Practical strategies of incorporating elements of collaborative teaming (Chapter 8) are highlighted. The next portion of the chapter is devoted to teaming approach strategies for dealing with paraprofessionals — classroom aides or volunteers.

All special educators must be able to recognize and deal with stress and burnout, factors that impede the master teaching process. A discussion is provided on sources, signs and signals of stress and burnout in teachers, and strategies to lessen negative effects.

Finally, techniques to facilitate the master teacher process are reviewed, highlighting advancements within the field of special education. Strategies that help to invigorate special education teachers to remain committed to their field are provided. By being involved in professional organizations, obtaining advanced degrees, and renewing teacher certifications, master teachers help to promote appropriate education for all students with special needs.

Teaming in Special Education

Team approaches are being used increasingly in American schools. Classrooms are no longer the exclusive domain of teachers. Peer teachers, related services providers, student teachers, teacher aides, and volunteers are becoming members of the instructional and management team (Algozzine, 1986; O'Shea & Hoover, 1986). In today's schools, teachers will work very closely with each other and with other adults during school activities or extracurricular functions. The close proximity of working together has much influence on what happens to teachers, students, and the classroom environment. As pointed out in Chapter 8, new teachers of special education assume the role of consultee or consultant in most teaming models. Developing and beginning teachers will benefit from teaming models but need to be aware of additional stress and conflicts teaming may create.

Team Approach

In team teaching, two or more individuals share a common classroom environment, curriculum, or set of students. To be effective, teaming must include collaborative programming and consultation with individuals. When a teacher makes a commitment to work from a team approach, this implies a willingness on the teacher's part to partake in group decisions and to function willingly as a team member. The advantages of teaming include collaborative problem solving, consensual decision making, and shared ownership and responsibilities for team activities by members who partake in team decisions (O'Shea & Hoover, 1987).

The team is composed of adults and students working together and sharing common activities and experiences. Drury (1986) highlighted attributes of a team as highly involved people who are committed to achieving common objectives, who work well together and enjoy doing so, and who produce high quality results. Box 9.1 is based on Drury's work of differentiating a team from a collection of individuals.

Teaming can influence teachers' abilities to work in an integrative and flexible manner with each other. Also, with a common theoretical and clinical base, each team member shares certain areas of expertise with the other and can frequently substitute or provide additional services when needed (Ysseldyke & Algozzine, 1984). Developing teachers who work with mildly to moderately handicapped students will be exposed to teaming through mainstreaming efforts. As elaborated on in Chapters 7 & 8, effective teaming requires the new teacher to demonstrate listening skills and empathy. Communication skills and constructive problem-solving ability are also important. Effective interpersonal skills with parents and

BOX 9.1

Developing and Beginning Teachers Who Operate as a Team Versus Those Who Operate as a Collection of Individuals

A TEAM

Developing teachers who
• Listen and try to understand.
• Share common visions.
• Share in decision making by consensus.
• Use clear communication within and outside the team.
• Display ability to talk through conflicts and problems in a constructive way.
• Display openness, honesty, mutual respect, and trust.
• Focus on the task.
• Make use of all team resources including parents and professionals from other disciplines.

A COLLECTION OF INDIVIDUALS

Developing teachers who
• Fight for their own views.
• Use little effective listening.
• Operate on right or wrong premises.
• Have no clear group vision.
• Operate on negative assumptions and hidden agendas.
• Display suspicion, distrust, and competition.
• Often are sidetracked.

SOURCE   Adapted from Drury, S.S. (1986). *Team effectiveness.* Newark: University of Delaware.

other professionals are vital, as are the abilities to be task-oriented and resource-oriented. Mainstreaming students with mild to moderate handicaps successfully requires shared responsibility involving special educators working cooperatively with regular classroom teachers and parents to provide quality educational programs to their students (Schulz & Turnbull, 1984). Teaming involves appropriate management and efforts by all teachers. Developing and beginning teachers should remember also that teaming is not easy and conflicts can arise often. Many problems with team approaches may not be observed readily, but can be stumbling blocks in new teachers' efforts to work cooperatively with those around them.

Problems

Problems with team approaches have been identified by Gloeckler and Simpson (1988) who suggested teaming can be counterproductive at times because some professionals identify particular activities or skills as their exclusive domain. Differing theoretical orientations and vocabulary also may interfere with communication. Occasionally, professionals are unwilling to share knowledge with others. Schulz and Turnbull (1984) caution that uncoordinated shared responsibility is self-defeating. If all team members have different goals with no knowledge of what others are doing, progress will be minimal and students may suffer. Because team members work closely, it is vital that each understands the roles and functions of other members. Role conflict and ambiguity within teams are important sources of stress to special educators who provide consulting services to students in the mainstream and must work cooperatively with others daily. Role conflict and ambiguity can be very stressful to first-year and preservice-level teachers (Crane & Iwanicki, 1986; Fimian & Blanton, 1986). To make teaming work, new teachers should be mindful of the pitfalls of teaming and should strive to make teaming work whether they assume the role of consultant or consultee.

Making Teaming Work

The effectiveness and proficiency of teaming may be influenced heavily by the teacher's attitude toward having another adult present in the class or by working with others on joint projects within the school. For example, in the classroom, there may be shifting of attention by the students to the other adult to some degree, a factor to which the teacher may react. During schoolwide projects, teachers may have to share recognition for success rather than being singled out for individual accomplishments. Special education teachers must work effectively with others in order to make IEPs work well for students. The teacher's attitude and style are important in that they may encourage or sabotage other adults' abilities to interact effectively with students or to succeed in schoolwide projects.

Individual attributes of the teacher may be especially important to the interplay of individuals and team effectiveness. These skills and abilities are listed in Box 9.2.

One way new teachers can initiate the teaming process is to interact with more experienced colleagues through peer reviews and observations. New teachers need to observe experienced peers and ask questions in order to clear up role conflict and ambiguities. In this way, new teachers may sharpen their own personal teaching styles and be able to function more proficiently in teaming models. They should strive for and imitate best practices. It is important to keep realistic expectations; initial mistakes are bound to occur until experience accumulates.

BOX 9.2

Important Teacher Attributes Influencing Teaming Effectiveness

- Skills in organizing and planning for students, adults, and activities.
- Leadership ability.
- Observational skills.
- Ability to communicate needs and wants to all present in the group.
- Experience in training, managing, and monitoring students and adults.
- Skills in taking and following directions from others.
- The teacher's educational background and experiences.
- An awareness of others' educational background and experiences.
- The teacher's philosophy of education.

SOURCE   Adapted from Lombardo, V. (1980). *Paraprofessionals in special education.* Springfield, IL: Charles C Thomas.

Peer Reviews and Observations

Peer reviews and observations may encourage a teacher's professional development and skills in teaming. By observing others and sharing information either through formal or informal methods, teachers are implementing a collaborative approach (O'Shea & Hoover, 1986). Teachers can share the benefits of teaching that makes the field rewarding and challenging. Many teaming benefits of a give and take approach may result.

1. Observation of similar activities by peers can confirm in the developing and beginning teacher's mind the appropriateness of the strategies, materials, procedures, and techniques used in his classroom.
2. New approaches and techniques may be generated by observing experienced peers who model best practices.
3. Patterns of students' behaviors in various class settings can be recorded and analyzed to compare across settings.
4. Teachers can share observations during team meetings and conferences with peers or supervisors.
5. Factors influencing the success of peer teachers' behaviors may be analyzed by the developing and beginning teacher.
6. Peer teachers may aid in the communication process and corrective feedback. Developing and beginning teachers may discuss behaviors of concern during peer reviews as a reference for change.

Developing and beginning teachers who want to acquire pertinent and practical information concerning teaming and consultation in a data-based model should see McKenzie (1972). Those who want practical information on how to consult with teachers should see Lippitt and Lippitt (1978) and Wiederholt, Hammill, and Brown (1983). Finally, those interested in observation, teaming, and consultation with peers and preservice teachers should see O'Shea and Hoover (1986). While tenacity and skill are required for successful peer reviews, observing and team consulting with others effectively must be considered major steps to becoming master teachers today.

Paraprofessionals

The vast majority of teachers serving children with mild to moderate problems will have responsibilities supervising teacher aides and/or adult volunteers in the classroom. These other individuals are referred to as paraprofessionals. Paraprofessionals (i.e., aides, teacher aides, classroom aides, or auxiliaries as used interchangeably here) are all nonprofessionals who relieve teachers of some nonteaching duties, whether they are paid or volunteer their time (Beach, 1973). In this team model, the developing and beginning teacher is a consultant to paraprofessionals and must supervise, manage, and evaluate their ability to interact in the classroom. Teachers function as leaders to classroom aides.

The role of teacher's aide is especially important to personnel in special education because students with special needs often require the assistance of more than one adult for a majority of the day. Teacher's aides make a noticeable, positive impact in school systems if they are used effectively in a team format (Clough & Clough, 1978). Paraprofessionals (a) lessen the adult/student ratio in the classroom; (b) facilitate the implementation of the curriculum; (c) enable the teacher to develop more effective programs based on the individual or small group needs of students; (d) make it possible for teachers to use more variety in structured classroom activities; (e) enable the teacher to use more instructional media and materials; (f) provide increased teacher time for evaluating learning situations, using behavioral management techniques, and counseling or guiding students; and (g) relieve teachers of the numerous semi- and nonprofessional tasks that consume a disproportionate amount of the teacher's time and energy. However, developing teachers may be asked to manage a paraprofessional who has been in the class for many years prior to the new teacher's arrival. The new teacher may be assigned to work with an aide who displays an inappropriate attitude or whose personal goals and aspirations conflict with those of the teacher's. Without proper management and insight into these sources of difficulty, new teachers may develop a negative working relationship with aides, which will affect classroom interactions. Stress and conflict may arise from the difficult situation, and effective teaming may come to a halt. Awareness of management techniques to facilitate teaming with paraprofessionals may help the new teacher to encourage a smooth transition in class supervision and operations.

Teaming Techniques Useful with Paraprofessionals

Drury (1986) discussed teaming techniques pertinent to developing teachers in their management of teacher aides and volunteers. As a team consultant and leader in the classroom, the new teacher should consider

1. **Major decisions are made by the team with a team consultant or leader facilitating the decision-making process.** New teachers should consider differences in their roles as group consultees for some teams (e.g., observing peers or consultations with supervisors) or group consultant-leaders for other teams (e.g., supervising students and paraprofessionals). New teachers must take the lead in determining classroom decisions — no matter how long the aide has been working.

2. **Goal setting and action plans are based on team analyses of problems**. Developing and beginning teachers should set goals and objectives for classroom happenings and follow up with action plans designed to implement team decisions. Problem solving often can be accomplished faster when many individuals share strategies. Teacher aides are a good source of information particularly pertaining to their classroom. New teachers can use the suggestions of teacher aides as an additional source of input into goals and objectives. Teachers, however, have the major say in goal setting and action plans.

3. **Team members have input into team decisions**. All members of the educational team can make special contributions to the team. Determining that special role and degree of input is important in effective teaming. New teachers will benefit from appropriate suggestions of other adults.

4. **Team members need access to all data relevant to decisions**. Sharing information in written form promotes team cohesiveness and effective team functioning. Sharing data with paraprofessionals working with particular children will encourage effective communication for all classroom members. (Teachers should remember to safeguard confidentiality of pertinent data).

5. **Communication is encouraged for all team members.** Being part of a team entails listening to and receiving messages from all other members of the team. By being open with the paraprofessional, the new teacher is encouraging a healthy, working rapport.

Working with Paraprofessionals

Working with paraprofessionals is one area in which the new teacher may be required to lead the team. The aide can perform any task not requiring professional training or judgment but should not assume nor be assigned the responsibilities reserved for teachers (Beach, 1973; Clough & Clough, 1978). Aides should not be given independent responsibility for classroom teaching, management, or organization. The aide should function in the classroom only if a trained teacher is available for direction and guidance, albeit, a new teacher can work within the context of a team model to use teacher's aides to supplement professional instruction and management. The teacher functions as the team consultant and must facilitate major classroom decision making. Under the special education teacher's direction and support, aides can assist in classroom management, supplemental teaching, housekeeping chores, and extracurricular activities.

Box 9.3 provides tips to help paraprofessionals get oriented to the special education situation. Orientation inservice conducted by the teacher is a rapport-building technique new teachers can use to help establish a team model.

O'Shea and Hendrickson (1987) offered these suggestions to classroom teachers to encourage teaming with paraprofessionals.

1. Treat the paraprofessional with respect in all dealings.
2. From day one, capitalize on the personal strengths of the aide. Point out these strengths whenever possible in a written fashion and share them with the paraprofessional, administration, and other teachers or aides.
3. Give the aide plenty of compliments on work that is well done.
4. Maintain high performance standards and encourage the aide to do the same.
5. Make the communication process as optimal as possible. Be willing to listen and respond with empathy as necessary to the aide's concerns.
6. Strive for consistency in the working relationship with the aide. Don't tell the aide one thing one day and something different the next day.
7. Organize the classroom in a manner that promotes good order and a sense of forward movement. Tell the aide specifically how the class is to operate. Discuss directly with the aide what, where, why, when, and how duties are to be done. Demonstrate the correct procedures as well. Elicit feedback and input from the aide on the success of classroom procedures.
8. Distribute duties in a fair and equitable manner. Get continual feedback from the aide to assess reasonableness of the type and amount of assigned work. Ask questions and encourage the aide to do the same.

BOX 9.3

Tips to Orient the Paraprofessional in the Special Education Setting

Introduce the aide to other adults and the students with whom she will be working. The intent is to plan for early interactions with the aide. Help the aide acquire as much information about each student as quickly as possible.

Expose the aide to written guidelines and review these materials (e.g., classroom or board of education policies, teacher's handbook, aide's handbook, and so forth) with which the aide should become familiar.

Tour the school with the aide if the principal has not already done so. Provide a tour of the classroom and where the following necessities are kept: supplies, books, games, charts, desks, curriculum guides, district course of study, picture files, and audiovisual collection.

Have the aide become familiar with the following during her first days of work:

- *Personnel names and location within the school:* Principal, assistant principal, dean, other supervisors, psychologist, social worker, speech clinician, therapists, librarian, other ancillary personnel, custodian, nurse, cafeteria director, cooks and lunchroom personnel, teachers, other classroom aides, other aides (playground, lunch, bus, special education, and so forth).
- *Location of important school areas:* Special education classrooms, library, supply room, storage areas, workroom, bookstore, cafeteria, auditorium, gymnasium, faculty lounge.
- *Location of things within the school:* Audio-visual equipment, storage cabinets, copying machine, art supplies, other machines.

Provide the aide with a job description that outlines the functions of the position. Spell out specifically all clerical, housekeeping, technical, and supervised instructional tasks assigned. Also point out tentative activities that might occur irregularly (e.g., field trips, school projects).

Help the aide to devise her own weekly schhedule to be filled out each week.

SOURCE   Adapted from O'Shea, D. J., & Hendrickson, J. M. (1987). *Tips for using teacher aides effectively.* Monograph No. 16. Gainesville: University of Florida Diagnostic and Teaching Clinic.

9. Within a structured conference, explain to the aide the importance of increasing the quality and quantity of the duties as her expertise grows.
10. Help the aide to observe and follow the disciplinary measures used by the teacher; make adjustments only after a conference together.
11. Try to encourage the aide to handle her own disciplinary problems, but if serious problems occur, the advice and help from the teacher should be sought.
12. Do not correct the aide in front of others, especially in front of students. (If you must provide corrective feedback, do it privately at a scheduled conference.)
13. Provide constructive criticism by telling the aide what can be improved and how it is to be improved. Aim criticism with the goal of improved performance.
14. Encourage the aide to keep a sense of humor whenever possible.

All teachers should remember, too, that paraprofessionals have lives outside of school. Effective teachers should get to know and respect the personal side of the people with whom they work so closely. It is important to show interest, when appropriate, in the aide's personal stories.

Finally, Box 9.4 describes tasks in which paraprofessionals may assist special education teachers in order to provide the teacher more quality time with students. Some of these tasks are supplemental instructional activities, while others are housekeeping chores of the classroom. All of these tasks can be accomplished by paraprofessionals with direction and guidance from the classroom teacher using the team model. The key to completion is good management skills, organization, and supervision by teachers. As new teachers will discover, managing, organizing, and supervising teacher's aides and volunteers effectively are necessary steps toward becoming master teachers.

Managing Stress and Burnout

While some researchers have suggested teaming may help to reduce teacher stress and burnout, especially through a teacher's involvement in functional and daily decision making (Dunham, 1983; Fimian & Blanton, 1986; Taylor & Salend, 1983), others have noted the potential ineffectiveness of some teaming models (Gloeckler & Simpson, 1988; Schulz & Turnbull, 1984; Zabel & Zabel, 1980). Stress and burnout are variables influencing the master teaching process whether new teachers perceive conflict from paraprofessionals, from role conflicts and role ambiguities with other professionals, or from ineffective working conditions and environmental factors. As teachers continue to instruct and manage students with special needs, stress and burnout are important

BOX 9.4

Teaming Tasks Aides Can Do to Assist Special Education Teachers

- Assist students in academic subject areas in which the teacher feels tutoring is necessary.
- Circulate around the room to check students' progress.
- Provide individualized assistance, such as flash card drill or listening to oral reading.
- Prepare charts, graphs, or teaching bulletin boards.
- Correct written assignments from the teacher's key or model.
- Work with those students who were absent to review or summarize lessons or activities.
- Collect assignments from the regular classroom teacher for completion in the resource classroom.
- Assist students with written compositions, especially with spelling, punctuation, and grammar.
- Correct homework and workbooks; note and report weak areas.
- Call the class to order.
- Collect money for lunch, class pictures, field trips, or special items.
- Care for bulletin board appearance and the overall appearance of the room.
- Help students move from one activity to another.
- Assist students in the lavatory.
- File correspondence and other reports in students' records.
- Keep inventory of classroom stock: equipment, books, and instructional supplies.

SOURCE Adapted from Clough, D. B., & Clough, B. M. (1978). *A handbook of effective techniques for teacher aides.* Springfield, IL: Charles C Thomas.

factors influencing many teachers' desire to stay with special education as a chosen career.

Stress is part of everyday life and, in manageable doses, can motivate individuals to improve and grow. Too much stress, however, may cause serious repercussions for an otherwise healthy individual (Epanchin, 1987). Many educators have observed changes over the past two decades that make teaching, especially special education, a more stressful profession (Barner, 1982; Crane & Iwanicki, 1986; Dunham, 1983; Iwanicki, 1983; Morsink, 1982; Pattavina, 1980). The composition of today's schools represents the makeup of society. As society gets more complicated and stressful, it follows that so, too, do schools. Schools are, in essence, mini-societies and among others, can reflect: (a) the growing and diverse population of students and their needs; (b) changing social, ethical, and moral values of society; and (c) increased external pressures on teachers (e.g., parents' and administrators' desires for educators' accountability in instruction and management).

Stress is a very real dilemma for educators that cannot be overlooked by new teachers. As reported in Chapter 3, Doyle's (1980) conceptualization of complex organizational pressures portrays the classroom as a public forum requiring frequent and immediate actions by the teacher in the face of almost overwhelming and, often, unpredictable environmental variables. Developing and beginning teachers who deal with intense pressures on a daily basis, due to the often unpredictable nature of students with special needs, added responsibilities of working from team models, difficult parents and the management and supervision of paraprofessionals, may be hit hardest by the pressures of school and classroom stress. Self or others' expectations of what they can accomplish may be problems (Retish, 1986). Additionally, the changing roles of special educators are reflected by public demands and increased public expectations making the job of the special educator very difficult (Morsink, 1982).

Stress and the Special Educator

Morsink (1982) examined trends in the roles of special educators and reported potential sources of stress to professionals. The effects of social change on schools and the ways teachers perceive these changes as affecting them personally may be an impediment to their development as master teachers. Public perceptions and demands on teachers and teachers' self-perceptions of what they believe is expected may be related to the successful completion of their roles. Increased legal responsibilities of teachers to implement federal, state, and local laws and regulations within required timelines are often pertinent sources of their conflict.

Barner (1982) also commented on increased legal responsibilities of special educators as a source of their conflict. He found that many teachers consider too much red tape in their jobs as a major source of their discontent. An additional problem pertinent to developing teachers is lack of time-management skills that may impede the new teacher (Algozzine, 1986). Time-management skills may influence teaming models and opportunities to work with peers, paraprofessionals, and students. Pervasive feelings for teachers overwhelmed by changing legal, behavioral, and social responsibilities include: a special educator's perceived sense of failure and impotence to do a job well; daily confrontation with problems of students, parents, peers, paraprofessionals, and administrators; complex and vast paperwork connected with IEPs; and feelings of loneliness and helplessness, especially in the first year of teaching (Fimian

& Blanton, 1986; Pattavina, 1980). When added together, all of these factors help to make special education a demanding profession.

Figure 9.1 illustrates potential sources of stress to special educators, factors which new teachers should examine closely. Awareness of stress factors is a first step in lessening the negative effects of stress that may impede a new teacher's desire to remain in the field. For a comprehensive picture on major sources of conflict and stress to special educators, see Barner (1982), Fimian and Blanton (1986), Holland (1982), and Weiskopf (1980).

Signs and Signals

Many professionals do not agree on common definitions or strategies for remediation of stress, although most agree on the variable ways stress and conflict manifest on teachers: loss of productivity, work refusal, physiological disorders that are psychologically based, loss of quality teachers (i.e., burnout—the desire to leave the field because of emotional overload associated with teaching, schools, students, or the entire educational process, see Algozzine, 1986; Bradfield & Fones, 1985; Crane &

STRESS FACTORS

Effects of social changes
Increased legal responsibilities
Lack of administrative support
Career stagnation
Lack of training
Teaching competencies
Vast paperwork
Poor salaries/benefits
Public perceptions
Unrealistic expectations
Lack of time management skills
High teaching loads
Low self-perceptions
Daily confrontations with students
Uncooperative/uninvolved parents
Feelings of loneliness
Feelings of lack of control
Lack of recognition
Little planning time
Lack of input into school policies/procedures

FIGURE 9.1   Potential sources of stress to special educators.

BOX 9.5

Signs and Signals of Stress

- Avoidance of school through many absences, continual tardiness, or an intense desire to leave the building before the school day is over.
- Apathy to students, parents, and teachers.
- Lower productivity in teaching, especially in teachers who at one time were highly productive.
- Continual negative self-statements concerning teacher effectiveness.
- Physical signs including prolonged headaches, stomach pains, or voice problems.
- Real or imagined mental fatigue over time.
- Blatant refusal to comply with school policies and rules.
- Prolonged crying and depression.
- Deep feelings of loss of control over career, personal life, or business matters.
- Continual complaints to loved ones.

Iwanicki, 1986; Fimian, 1983; Morsink, 1982; Retish, 1986; Smith & Cline, 1980). Many quality teachers may be lost to the profession because they do not heed warning signals.

Signs and signals of stress are provided in Box 9.5. If a teacher recognizes many of these signs frequently, over time, and to such an intensity that coming to school becomes a daily chore, it is time to reevaluate and redefine personal priorities and strategies of coping. Even teachers new to the field may experience some of these after a few short weeks in school. It is vital to target strategies to alleviate these sources of conflict as soon as they are recognized.

Strategies of Coping

Strategies to reduce stress and burnout are listed in Box 9.6. Some of these strategies are implemented by the external control of others (e.g., administrative support to reduce class size) or by self-control of teachers (e.g., commitment to exercise, adequate sleep). It is important to note that administrators can recognize the need for strategies to help teachers cope better with their jobs, but not necessarily have personal control to change policies (e.g., the recognition for increased teacher pay but lack of power to change school financial policies). Administrators also can have a direct influence in their own schools on coping interventions for teachers by enforcing their personal policies to lessen a teacher's stress

BOX 9.6

Strategies to Reduce Stress and Burnout

EXTERNALLY CONTROLLED STRATEGIES

Administrative support (recognized/supported by administrators)

- Access to counseling
- Reduced class size
- Reduced teacher loads
- Adequate resources/materials
- Adequate paraprofessional and volunteer help
- Tangible incentives for successful teaching
- Increased pay
- Increased job benefits
- Environmental variables (lighting, acoustics, and so forth)
- Opportunities for teacher advancement

Administrative interventions (controlled by administrators)

- Increased planning time
- Increased responsibility for job performance
- Teacher's lounge discussion sessions
- Organized personnel social functions
- Functioning feedback mechanisms in school (e.g., school suggestion box)
- Teacher input into curriculum and scheduling
- Increased involvement of teachers in faculty decision making
- Analysis of school-classroom expectations

SELF-CONTROL STRATEGIES

Physical strategies

- Relaxation training
- Adequate diet
- Adequate sleep
- Regular exercise
- Self-verbalization of positive attitudes

Development of personal activities
- Hobbies
- Clubs/organizations
- Family
- Sports/leisure
- Community support systems
- Increased networking
- Increased professional skills and training

(continued)

> BOX 9.6 (continued)
>
> *Time-management strategies*
> • Plan for stress
> • Plan time for priority tasks
> • Plan quality time for activities requiring high cognitive levels
> • Realize individual limits
> • Make the most of individual strengths

and burnout (e.g., principals may structure weekly sessions in the faculty lounge so that teachers can discuss concerns or exchange ideas to reduce tensions). Thus, in Box 9.6, external controls may be an administrator's support (i.e., the administrator recognizes the need for the strategy but may or may not have personal control over the strategy) or administrator interventions (i.e., the administrator has personal control within his own school to implement the strategy). Self-control strategies for teachers include physical controls (i.e., related to body function) or interpersonal controls (i.e., related to commitment of family or community involvement). Self-control strategies can be continually implemented directly by new teachers.

Time management strategies also may be useful sources of stress reducers to developing teachers (Youngs, 1986).

1. Be proactive, not reactive. Learn to anticipate and plan for stress. By being prepared, new teachers can learn to avoid sources of difficulty.
2. Plan time. Try not to be controlled by events and persons around you beyond your own personal limits. Assert yourself so that others do not push you beyond these limits. Communicate to others and yourself what your limits are.
3. Identify and plan for quality time. This is a time during the day where you can focus your awareness on a specific task without interruption. Avoid doing more than one thing at a time.
4. Don't place demands on yourself that you can't meet. Be honest with yourself and with others. Demanding too much of yourself causes stress and may create failure. Special education teachers should know when to say no as well as yes.
5. Know where your time goes. If necessary, make a list of what you did during a day and evaluate whether you spent your time wisely. Developing and beginning teachers should self-evaluate continually.
6. Build your strengths and not your weaknesses. Concentrate on what you can do rather than what you cannot do. As with special needs students, new teachers should be kind to themselves.
7. Be aware that, in general, poor time management includes:
     a. Excess time spent in crisis situations.

    b. More time spent on trivia than is necessary.

    c. Frequent interruptions that destroy planning incentive and momentum.

    d. Less time spent on high-priority items than low-priority ones.

    e. Little quality time spent on items requiring creativity and productivity.

8. Set long-term life career goals as well as short-term goals.

9. Reward yourself for what you do well. Put what you don't do well in proper perspective. Time management strategies can help to reduce stress and can help to facilitate the master teacher process. New teachers can help reduce their feelings of lack of control over their teaching careers and advance within their profession.

Facilitating the Master Teacher Process

Peer reviews, observing colleagues working effectively with paraprofessionals, parents, and students, and responding to stress factors are important components to becoming master teachers. However, what is it about teaching special education that is rewarding and that stays challenging over the years? Why are some teachers fulfilled by teaching students with special needs, while others are not? While there are no simple answers to these questions, there are steps teachers can follow in order to increase self-fulfillment and realize positive expectations from teaching. Successive approximations toward a desired goal are important: teaching is a process that takes time, trial and error learning, tenacity, and resiliency. By continually upgrading teachers' commitments to the field, individuals in special education may be closer to fulfillment as master teachers. Recognition of advancements within teaching, involvement in professional organizations, obtainment of higher degrees, and renewed certifications in areas of specializations all help to inform, reinforce, and challenge teachers. These steps will help to encourage professionalism and continual active involvement through the years. As teachers begin to feel confident of their abilities and develop a prolonged commitment to the field, master teachers evolve.

Advancement within the Field

There are ways other than direct contact with students to affect changes in the field of special education and to advance personally within the field. Many teachers change with their jobs and still provide services to their field. Other services that make a noticeable difference include involvement in research, administration, teacher training, service organizations and advocacy groups, curriculum planning and development, parent training, and support services and counseling. Work in every one of these areas helps to increase benefits to teachers and to all students with special needs, including their parents and peers. Teachers who are committed to these other areas may also become master teachers by making a difference in the field. By expanding services and professional memberships, committed teachers remain in the field but specialize in areas outside of direct contact with students.

Involvement in Professional Organizations

Developing and beginning teachers will be able to maintain knowledge of current strategies and best teaching practices through active participation in professional organizations. Many professional organizations provide and promote conferences, workshops, inservices, or continuing education classes. Working actively in local, state, or national professional groups may widen the contacts teachers have and may aid in professional awareness. By actively participating in professional organizations, new teachers are executing some control over their teaching careers. Increasing professional awareness helps to maintain master teachers and invigorate and challenge developing and beginning teachers.

Higher Degrees

Many teacher-training colleges and universities offer courses leading to advanced degrees in education. Often local school districts provide inservice training modules that can be exchanged for college credit or advanced standing, leading toward additional degrees for teachers. Obtaining higher degrees increases teachers' competency levels and mastery of teaching objectives—all relevant to feelings of success and confidence in teaching. When teachers feel successful and confident, teaching abilities increase.

Certifications

Many current special educators are renewing certifications to teach. They are adding on areas of specialization in order to broaden their base to instruct and manage students with special needs. Certification provides a mechanism for establishing regulations to carry out the intent of PL 94–142. It is often the foundation for the establishment of minimum training and experience levels expected of teachers. In a sense, certification provides to teachers and administrators confidence that certified employees are trained, competent, and able to carry out the responsibilities they have been assigned. Teachers with varied and/or updated certification have obtained more than the minimum necessary to survive in teaching and maintain their stance as master teachers.

What Can Teachers Do to Remain Invigorated and Committed to Their Careers?

Teachers with advanced degrees and additional certification are in an excellent position to affect changes in their individual classrooms and the total school system. Armed with updated information on current research and teaching practices, these teachers help to ensure students with mild to moderate handicaps a free and appropriate public education. They remain invigorated and committed over time. Teachers who respect the teaming model and who actively target strategies against stress are enhancing their own professionalism. As these teachers develop and change in conjunction with the needs of the students they teach, they are on the road to becoming master teachers. These teachers continually observe students and discuss ways of meeting students' needs with their peer teachers. They implement learning strategies and behavior management strategies consistently. They work well on team models with parents, professionals, and paraprofessionals. They recognize stress factors and ways of reducing stress when they begin to feel burnout. These teachers are committed to the field of special education through active professional involvement, additional training and inservices, and continued commitment to specialized areas of expertise. These teachers have made the transition from student teacher to master teacher. They have found that teaching special education is rewarding and stays a challenging career over the years.

Summary

The chapter opened with a discussion on the need for teaming, peer reviews, and observing fellow educators in other settings. Observation and continual professional discussion lead to positive changes as teachers collaborate and share successful teaching techniques and strategies.

A portion of the chapter was devoted to strategies for dealing with paraprofessionals. In addition to working with peers, many teachers will work in close proximity to other adults, either with classroom aides or volunteers. A team approach was advocated for a successful teacher–paraprofessional relationship.

All special educators must be able to recognize and deal with stress and burnout, factors that impede the master-teaching process. A discussion was provided on potential sources, signs and signals of stress and burnout in teachers, and strategies to lessen negative effects that may result when warning signs are not heeded immediately.

Finally, techniques to facilitate the master teacher process were reviewed including advancement within the field of special education, involvement in professional organizations, obtainment of higher degrees, and renewal of teacher certifications. Master teachers are committed to the field and change in accordance to the needs of their students.

References

ALGOZZINE, B. (1986). *Problem behavior management. Educator's resource guide.* Rockville, MD: Aspen.

BARNER, A. (1982). Do teachers like to teach? *Pointer, 27(1),* 5–7.

BEACH, R. G. (1973). *Help in the school: Establishment of a paraprofessional program.* Philadelphia: Dorrance.

BRADFIELD, R. H., & FONES, D. M. (1985). Special teacher stress: Its product and prevention. Special report. *Academic Therapy, 21,* 91–94.

CLOUGH, D. B., & CLOUGH, B. M. (1978). *A handbook of effective techniques for teacher aides.* Springfield, IL: Charles C Thomas.

CRANE, S. J., & IWANICKI, E. F. (1986). Perceived role conflict, role ambiguity, and burnout among special education teachers. *Remedial and Special Education, 7(2),* 24–31.

DOYLE, W. (1980). *Classroom management.* West Lafayette, IN: Kappa Delta Pi.

DRURY, S. S. (1986). *Team effectiveness.* Newark: University of Delaware.

DUNHAM, J. (1983). Coping with stress in schools. *Special Education: Forward Trends, 10,* 2–6.

EPANCHIN, B. C. (1987). Anxiety and stress-related disorders. In B. C. Epanchin & J. L. Paul (Eds.) *Emotional problems of childhood and adolescence. A multidisciplinary perspective.* Columbus, OH: Merrill.

FIMIAN, M. J. (1983). A comparison of occupational stress correlates as reported by teachers of mentally retarded and nonmentally retarded handicapped students. *Education and Training of the Mentally Retarded, 18,* 62–68.

FIMIAN, M. J. & BLANTON, L. P. (1986). Variables related to stress and burnout in special education teacher trainees and first-year teachers. *Teacher Education and Special Education, 9,* 9–21.

GLOECKLER, T., & SIMPSON, C. (1988). *Exceptional students in regular classrooms. Challenges, services, and methods.* Mountain View, CA: Mayfield.

HOLLAND, R. P. (1982). Special educator burnout. *Educational Horizons, 60(2),* 58–64.

IWANICKI, E. F. (1983). Toward understanding and alleviating teacher burnout. *Theory into Practice, 22,* 27–32.

LIPPITT, B., & LIPPITT, R. (1978). *The consulting process in action.* San Diego: University Associates.

McKENZIE, H. S. (1972). Special education and consulting teacher. In F. W. Clark, D. R. Evans, & L. A. Hamerlynck (Eds.), *Implementing behavioral programs for schools and clinics.* Champaign, IL: Research Press.

MORSINK, C. V. (1982). Changes in the role of special educators: Public perceptions and demands. *Exceptional Education Quarterly, (The Special Educator as a Professional Person), 2(4),* 15–25.

O'SHEA, D. J., & HENDRICKSON, J. M. (1987). *Tips for using teacher aides effectively. Monograph No. 16.* Gainesville: University of Florida Diagnostic and Teaching Clinic.

O'SHEA, L. J., & HOOVER, N. L. (1986). *Conferring with teachers about teacher performance.* Tallahassee, FL: Florida Department of Education.

PATTAVINA, P. (1980). Bridging the gap between stress and support for public school teachers: A conversation with Dr. William C. Morse about teacher burnout. *Pointer, 24(2),* 88–94.

RETISH, P. (1986). Burnout and stress among special educators and others. B.C. *Journal of Special Education, 10(3),* 267–270.

SCHULZ J. B., & TURNBULL, A. P. (1984). *Mainstreaming handicapped students. A guide for classroom teachers* (2nd ed.). Boston: Allyn & Bacon.

SMITH, J., & CLINE, D. (1980). Quality programs. *Pointer, 24(2),* 80–87.

TAYLOR, L., & SALEND, S. J. (1983). Reducing stress-related burnout through a network support system. *Pointer, 27(4),* 5–9.

WEISKOPF, P. E. (1980). Burnout among teachers of exceptional children. *Exceptional Children, 47,* 18–23.

WIEDERHOLT, J. L., HAMMILL, D. D., & BROWN, V. L. (1983). *The resource teacher: A guide to effective practices.* Boston: Allyn & Bacon.

YOUNGS, B. B. (1986). *Stress in children: How to recognize, avoid, and overcome it.* Melbourne, Victoria: Nelson Publishers.

YSSELDYKE, J., & ALGOZZINE, B. (1984). *Introduction to special education.* Boston: Houghton Mifflin.

ZABEL, R. H., & ZABEL, M. K. (1980). Burnout: A critical issue for educators. *Language Unlimited, 2,* 23–25.

Council for Exceptional Children's Standards for Professional Practice

1. Professionals in Relation to Exceptional Persons and Their Families

1.1 Instructional Responsibilities

1.1.1 Special education personnel are committed to the application of professional expertise to ensure the provision of quality education for all exceptional individuals. Professionals strive to:

1.1.1.1 Identify and use instructional methods and curricula that are appropriate to their area of professional practice and effective in meeting the needs of exceptional persons.

1.1.1.2 Participate in the selection of and use appropriate instructional materials, equipment, supplies, and other resources needed in the effective practice of their profession.

1.1.1.3 Create safe and effective learning environments which contribute to fulfillment of needs, stimulation of learning and of self-concept.

1.1.1.4 Maintain class size and caseloads which are conducive to meeting the individual instructional needs of exceptional persons.

1.1.1.5 Use assessment instruments and procedures that do not discriminate against exceptional persons on the basis of race, color, creed, sex, national origin, age, political practices, family or social background, sexual orientation, or exceptionality.

1.1.1.6 Base grading, promotion, graduation, and/or movement out of the program on the individual goals and objectives for the exceptional individual.

1.1.1.7 Provide accurate program data to administrators, colleagues, and parents, based on efficient and objective record-keeping practices, for the purpose of decision making.

1.1.1.8 Maintain confidentiality of information except where information is released under specific conditions of written consent and statutory confidentiality requirements.

1.2 Management of Behavior

1.2.1 Special education professionals participate with other professionals and with parents in an interdisciplinary effort in the management of behavior. Professionals:

1.2.1.1 Apply only those disciplinary methods and behavioral procedures which they have been instructed to use and which do not undermine the dignity of the individual or the basic human rights of exceptional persons (such as corporal punishment).

1.2.1.2 Clearly specify the goals and objectives for behavior management practices in the exceptional person's Individualized Education Program.

1.2.1.3 Conform to policies, statutes, and rules established by state/provincial and local agencies relating to judicious application of disciplinary methods and behavioral procedures.

1.2.1.4 Take adequate measures to discourage, prevent, and intervene when a colleague's behavior is perceived as being detrimental to exceptional persons.

1.2.1.5 Refrain from aversive techniques unless repeated trials of other methods have failed and then only after consultation with parents and appropriate agency officials.

1.3 Support Procedures

1.3.1 Adequate instruction and supervision shall be provided to professionals before they are required to perform support services for which they have not been previously prepared.

1.3.2 Professionals may administer medication, where state/provincial policies do not preclude such action, if qualified to do so or if written instructions are on file which state the purpose of the medication, the conditions under which it may be administered, possible side effects, the physician's name and phone number, and the professional liability if a mistake is made. The professional will not be required to administer medication.

1.3.3 Professionals note and report to those concerned whenever changes in behavior occur in conjunction with the administration of medication or at any other time.

1.4 Parent Relationships

1.4.1 Professionals seek to develop relationships with parents based on mutual respect for their roles in achieving benefits for the exceptional person. Special education professionals:

1.4.1.1 Develop effective communication with parents, avoiding technical terminology, using the primary language of the home, and other modes of communication when appropriate.

1.4.1.2 Seek and use parents' knowledge and expertise in planning, conducting, and evaluating special education and related services for exceptional persons.

1.4.1.3 Maintain communications between parents and professionals with appropriate respect for privacy and confidentiality.

1.4.1.4 Extend opportunities for parent education, utilizing accurate information and professional methods.

1.4.1.5 Inform parents of the educational rights of their children and of any proposed or actual practices which violate those rights.

1.4.1.6 Recognize and respect cultural diversities which exist in some families with exceptional persons.

1.4.1.7 Recognize that the relationship of home and community environmental conditions affects the behavior and outlook of the exceptional person.

1.5 Advocacy

1.5.1 Special education professionals serve as advocates for exceptional persons by speaking, writing, and acting in a variety of situations on their behalf. Professionals:

1.5.1.1 Continually seek to improve government provisions for the education of exceptional persons while ensuring that public statements by professionals as individuals are not construed to represent official policy statements of the agency by which they are employed.

1.5.1.2   Work cooperatively with and encourage other professionals to improve the provision of special education and related services to exceptional persons.

1.5.1.3   Document and objectively report to their supervisors or administrators inadequacies in resources and promote appropriate corrective action.

1.5.1.4   Monitor for inappropriate placements in special education and intervene at the appropriate level to correct the condition when such inappropriate placements exist.

1.5.1.5   Follow local, state/provincial, and federal laws and regulations which mandate a free appropriate public education to exceptional students and the protection of the rights of exceptional persons to equal opportunities in our society.

2. Professional Employment

2.1   Certification and Qualification

2.1.1   Professionals ensure that only persons deemed qualified by having met state/provincial minimal standards are employed as teachers, administrators, and related-service providers for persons with exceptionalities.

2.2   Employment

2.2.1   Professionals do not discriminate in hiring on the basis of race, color, creed, sex, national origin, age, political practices, family or social background, sexual orientation, or exceptionality.

2.2.2   Professionals represent themselves in an ethical and legal manner in regard to their training and experience when seeking new employment.

2.2.3   Professionals give notice consistent with local education agency policies when intending to leave employment.

2.2.4   Professionals adhere to the conditions of a contract or terms of an appointment in the setting where they practice.

2.2.5   Professionals released from employment are entitled to a written explanation of the reasons for termination and to fair and impartial due process procedures.

2.2.6 Special education professionals share equitably the opportunities and benefits (salary, working conditions, facilities, and other resources) of other professionals in the school system.

2.2.7 Professionals seek assistance, including the services of other professionals, in instances where personal problems threaten to interfere with their job performance.

2.2.8 Professionals respond objectively when requested to evaluate applicants seeking employment.

2.2.9 Professionals have the right and responsibility to resolve professional problems by utilizing established procedures, including grievance procedures when appropriate.

2.3   Assignment and Role

2.3.1 Professionals should receive clear written communication of all duties and responsibilities, including those which are prescribed as conditions of their employment.

2.3.2 Professionals promote educational quality and intra- and interprofessional cooperation through active participation in the planning, policy development, management, and evaluation of the special education program and the education program at large so that programs remain responsive to the changing needs of exceptional persons.

2.3.3 Professionals practice only in areas of exceptionality, at age levels, and in program models for which they are prepared by reason of training and/or experience.

2.3.4 Adequate supervision of and support for special education professionals is provided by other professionals qualified by reason of training and experience in the area of concern.

2.3.5 The administration and supervision of special education professionals provide for clear lines of accountability.

2.3.6 The unavailability of substitute teacher or support personnel, including aides, must not result in the denial of special education services to a greater degree than to that of other educational programs.

2.4   Professional Development

2.4.1 Special education professionals systematically advance their knowledge and skills in order to maintain a high level of competence and response to the changing needs of exceptional persons by pursuing a program of continuing education including but not limited to participation in such activities as inservice training, professional conferences/

workshops, professional meetings, continuing education courses, and the reading of professional literature.

2.4.2   Professionals participate in the objective and systematic evaluation of themselves, colleagues, services, and programs for the purpose of continuous improvement of professional performance.

2.4.3   Professionals in administrative positions support and facilitate professional development.

3. Professionals in Relation to the Profession and to Other Professionals

3.1   To the Profession

3.1.1   Special education professionals assume responsibility for participating in professional organizations and adherence to the standards and codes of ethics of those organizations.

3.1.2   Special education professionals have a responsibility to provide varied and exemplary supervised field experiences for persons in undergraduate and graduate preparation programs.

3.1.3   Special education professionals refrain from using professional relationships with students and parents for personal advantage.

3.1.4   Special education professionals take an active position in the regulation of the profession through use of appropriate procedures for bringing about changes.

3.1.5   Special education professionals initiate support and/or participate in research related to the education of exceptional persons with the aim of improving the quality of educational services, increasing the accountability of programs, and generally benefiting exceptional persons. Professionals:

3.1.5.1   Adopt procedures that protect the rights and welfare of subjects participating in research.

3.1.5.2   Interpret and publish research results with accuracy and a high quality of scholarship.

3.1.5.3   Support a cessation of the use of any research procedure which may result in undesirable consequences for the participant.

3.1.5.4   Exercise all possible precautions to prevent misapplication or misuse of a research effort, by oneself or others.

3.2   To Other Professionals

3.2.1.   Special education professionals function as members of interdisciplinary teams and the reputation of the profession resides with them. Professionals:

3.2.1.1.   Recognize and acknowledge the competencies and expertise of members representing other disciplines as well as those of members in their own disciplines.

3.2.1.2   Strive to develop positive attitudes among other professionals toward exceptional persons, representing them with an objective regard for their possibilities and their limitations as persons in a democratic society.

3.2.1.3   Cooperate with other agencies involved in serving exceptional persons through such activities as the planning and coordination of information exchanges, service delivery, and evaluation and training, so that no duplication or loss in quality of services may occur.

3.2.1.4.   Provide consultation and assistance, where appropriate, to both regular and special education as well as other school personnel serving exceptional persons.

3.2.1.5   Provide consultation and assistance, where appropriate, to professionals in non-school settings serving exceptional persons.

3.2.1.6   Maintain effective interpersonal relations with colleagues and other professionals, helping them to develop and maintain positive and accurate perceptions about the special education profession.

State Departments of Education

Individuals can receive information regarding specific certification requirements from the following:

Alabama
Teacher Certification Office
State Department of Education
349 State Office Building
Montgomery, AL 36130-3901
(205) 261-5060

Alaska
Teacher Certification
Educational Finance &
    Support Services
P.O. Box F
Juneau, AK 99811
(907) 465-2831

Arizona
Teacher Certification Unit
Department of Education
1535 W. Jefferson
Phoenix, AZ 85306
(602) 255-4367

Arkansas
Teacher Education &
    Certification
Department of Education
State Capitol Mall
Room 107B
Little Rock, AR 72201-1021
(501) 374-1414

California
Commission on Teaching
    Credentialing
1812 9th St.
P.O. Box 944270
Sacramento, CA 95814
(916) 445-7254

Colorado
Colorado Department of
    Education
Teacher Education &
    Certification
201 E. Colfax Ave.
Denver, CO 80203
(303) 866-6628

Connecticut
State Department of Education
Teacher Certification Unit
165 Capitol Avenue
Hartford, CT 06145
(203) 566-5201

Delaware
Department of Public Instruction
Certification & Personnel
  Division
P.O. Box 1402
Dover, DE 19903
(302) 736-4688

Florida
Florida Department of Education
Teacher Certification Section
Collins Building
Tallahassee, Fl 32399
(800) 445-6739

Georgia
Department of Education
Teacher Certification
1452 Twin Towers–East
Atlanta, GA 30334
(404) 656-2406

Hawaii
Department of Education
Office of Personnel Services
Teacher Certification
P.O. Box 2360
Honolulu, HI 96804
(808) 548-5217

Idaho
State Department of Education
Teacher Education &
Certification
Jordan Office Building
Boise, ID 83720
(208) 334-3475

Illinois
State Teacher Certification
  Board
100 N. First Street
Springfield, IL 62777
(217) 782-2805

Indiana
Indiana Department of Education
Teacher Education &
  Certification
State House, Room 229
Indianapolis, IN 46204-2798
(317) 232-6636

Iowa
Department of Public Instruction
Teacher Education &
  Certification Division
Grimes State Office Building
Des Moines, IA 50319
(515) 281-3245

Kansas
Department of Education
Certification, Teacher Education
  and Accreditation
120 E. 10th Street
Topeka, KS 66612
(913) 296-2288

Kentucky
Department of Education
Division of Teacher Education &
  Certification
1823 Capitol Plaza Tower
Frankfort, KY 40601
(502) 564-4606

Louisiana
Teacher Certification
Department of Education
P.O. Box 44064
Baton Rouge, LA 70804
(504) 342-3490

Maine
Division of Teacher Certification
State Street Station No. 23
Augusta, ME 04333
(207) 289-5944

Maryland
Maryland Department of
  Education
Teacher Certification
  Division
200 W. Baltimore St.
Baltimore, MD 21201
(301) 333-2142

Massachusetts
Teacher Certification Bureau
Department of Education
1385 Hancock Street
Quincy, MA 02184
(617) 770-7517

Michigan
Michigan Department of
  Education
Teacher Preparation &
  Certification Services
Box 30008
Lansing, MI 48909
(517) 373-1924

Minnesota
Department of Education
Teacher Certification &
  Placement
616 Capitol Square Building
550 Cedar St.
St. Paul, MN 55101
(612) 296-2046

Mississippi
Division of Instruction
Teacher Education &
  Certification
P.O. Box 771
Jackson, MS 39205
(601) 359-3483

Missouri
Department of Elementary &
  Secondary Education
P.O. Box 480
Jefferson City, MO 65102
(314) 751-3486

Montana
Office of Public Instruction
Certification Services
State Capitol
Helena, MT 59620

Nebraska
Department of Education
Teacher Certification
301 Centennial Mall South
Box 94987
Lincoln, NE 68509
(402) 471-2496

Nevada
Teacher Certification
Department of Education
State Mail Room
215 E. Bonanza
Las Vegas, NV
(702) 486-6467

New Hampshire
Office of Teacher Education
State Department of Education
101 Pleasant Street
Concord, NH 03301
(603) 271-2407

New Jersey
Department of Education
Teacher Certification
3535 Quakerbridge Rd
CN 503
Trenton, NJ 08625-8276
(609) 292-8276

New Mexico
Educator Preparation &
  Licensure
N. M. Department of Education
Santa Fe, NM 87501-2786
(505) 827-6587

New York
Teacher Certification
State Education Department
Room 5A11, Cultural Education
  Center
Albany, NY 12230

North Carolina
Public Instruction
Division of Certification
Salisbury & Edenton Streets
Raleigh, NC 27611
(919) 733-4125

North Dakota
Department of Public Instruction
Office of Certification
Capitol Building
Bismark, ND 58505
(701) 224-2264

Ohio
Ohio Department of Education
Division of Teacher Education &
  Certification
65 S. Front Street, RM 1012
Columbus, OH 43215
(614) 466-3592

Oklahoma
Administrator
Teacher Certification
2500 N. Lincoln Boulevard
Oklahoma City, OK 73105
(405) 521-3337

Oregon
State Department of Education
Teacher Standards & Practices
  Commission
730 Twelfth St., S. E.
Salem, OR 97310
(503) 378-3586

Pennsylvania
Department of Education
Teacher Preparation &
  Certification Bureau
333 Market St., 3rd Floor
Harrisburg, PA 17126
(717) 787-2967

Rhode Island
Department of Education
Teacher Certification Office
22 Hayes Street
Providence, RI 02908
(401) 277-2675

South Carolina
Department of Education
Teacher Certification Section
1015 Rutledge Building
Columbia, SC 29201
(803) 734-8464

South Dakota
Office of School Standards
Division of Elementary &
  Secondary Education
700 Governors Drive
Pierre, SD 57501-5086
(605) 773-3553

Tennessee
Tennessee Department of
  Education
Office of Teacher Licensing
125 Cordell Hull Building
Nashville, TN 37219-5338
(615) 741-1644

Texas
State of Texas
Division of Teacher Certification
1701 N. Congress Street
Austin, TX 78701
(512) 463-8976

Utah
Utah Office of Education
Teacher Certification
250 East 500 South
Salt Lake City, UT 84111
(801) 533-5965

Vermont
Department of Education
Education Resources Unit
Certification Office
State Offices Building
120 State Street
Montpelier, VT 05602
(802) 828-2445

Virginia
Department of Education
Division of Teacher Certification
P.O. Box 60
Richmond, VA 23216-2060
(804) 220-2022

Washington
Department of Education
Professional Certification
Old Capitol Building
7th & Franklin
Olympia, WA 98504
(206) 753-6773

West Virginia
Department of Education
Education Personnel
   Development
1900 Washington Street, East
Building 6, Room B-337
Capitol Complex
Charleston, WV 25305
(304) 348-7805

Wisconsin
Bureau of Teacher Education
Certification & Placement
Box 7841
125 S. Webster Street
Madison, WI 53707
(608) 266-1027

Wyoming
Department of Education
Certification/Licensing Unit
Hathaway Building
Cheyenne, WY 82002
(307) 777-7291

District of Columbia
Department of Certification &
   Accreditation
Presidential Bldg. Suite 1004
415 12th St., N. W.
Washington, DC 20004
(202) 724-4230

Publishers and Producers of Instructional Materials for Students with Mild and Moderate Handicaps

Academic Therapy Publishers
20 Commercial Boulevard
Novato, CA 94947-6191

Addison-Wesley Publishing
  Company
2725 Sand Hill Road
Menlo Park, CA 94025

Allied Book
933 Tewa Loop
Los Alamos, NM 87544

Allyn & Bacon
7 Wells Avenue
Newton, MA 02159

American Book Company
450 West 33rd Street
New York, NY 10001

American Education Publications
Education Center
Columbus, OH 43216

American Federation of Teachers
555 New Jersey Avenue, N.W.
Washington, DC 20001

American Guidance Center
Publishers Building
Circle Pines, MN 55014

American Red Cross
17th and D Streets, N.W.
Washington, DC 20006

Ann Arbor Publishers
P.O. Box 7249
Naples, FL 33940

Apple Computer
10260 Brandley Drive
Cupertino, CA 95014

Arista Corporation
P.O. Box 6146
Concord, CA 94524

Aspen Systems Corporation
1600 Research Boulevard
Rockville, MD 20850

Association for Children &
Adults with Learning Disabilities
4156 Library Road
Pittsburgh, PA 15234

Barclay School Supplies
166 Livingston Street
Brooklyn, NY 11201

Parnell Loft, Ltd.
958 Church Street
Baldwin, NY 11510

Basic Educational Books
420 Bell Street
Edmonds, WA 98020-3183

Behavioral Research Laboratories
P.O. Box 577
Palo Alto, CA 94302

Bernell Corporation
750 Lincolnway East
South Bend, IN 46634

Bobbs-Merrill Company
4300 West 62nd Street
Indianapolis, IN 46206

Books on Special Children
P.O. Box 305
Congers, NY 10920

Bowmar/Noble Publishers
P.O. Box 25308
Oklahoma City, OK 73125

C & C Software
5713 Kentford Circle, Dept. A
Wichita, KS 67220

Casteel Innovative Products, Inc.
3879 Lake Street
P.O. Box 2245
Macon, GA 31203

Chaselle-Basic Skill Materials
9645 Gerwig Lane
Columbia, MD 21046

Center for Unique Learners
5705 Arundel Avenue
Rockville, MD 20852

Chronicle Guidance Publications,
   Inc.
Aurora Street Extension
Moravia, NY 13118

Communication Skill Builders
3130 North Dodge Boulevard
P.O. Box 42050-H
Tucson, AZ 85733

Consulting Psychologists Press
577 College Avenue
Palo Alto, CA 94306

Continental Press
520 East Bainbridge Street
Elizabethtown, PA 17022

Coronet Media
65 East South Water Street
Chicago, IL 60601

Council for Exceptional Children
1920 Association Drive
Reston, VA 22091

Counterpoint
14622 Lanark Street
Panorama City, CA 91402

Creative Publications
P.O. Box 10328
Palo Alto, CA 94303

Curriculum Associates
5 Esquire Road
North Billerica, MA 01862

Dallas Educational Services
P.O. Box 831254
Richardson, TX 75083-1254

Davidson Films, Inc.
231 E Street
Davis, CA 95616

Devereux Foundation Press
Devon, PA 19333

Developmental Learning
  Materials
P.O. Box 4000
Allen, TX 75002

Earwig Music Company, Inc.
1818 West Pratt Boulevard
Chicago, IL 60626

Easier to Learn
Box 329
Garden City, NY 11530

Ebsco Curriculum Materials
P.O. Box 11542
Birmingham, AL 35202

Economy Company
P.O. Box 11542
Birmingham, AL 35202

Edmark Associates
P.O. Box 3903
Bellevue, WA 98009

Education Graphics
302 Clinton Avenue
Brooklyn, NY 11205

Educational Resources, Ltd.
109-8475 Ontario Street
Vancouver, BC
Canada V5X 3E8

Educational Teaching Aids
A. Daigger & Company
159 West Kinzie Street
Chicago, IL 60610

Educational Testing Service
Princeton, NJ 08540

Educator's Publishing Service
75 Moulton Street
Cambridge, MA 02238

Entry Publishing Service, Inc.
27 West 96th Street
New York, NY 10025

Fearon Education
Division of Pitman Publishers
19 Davis Drive
Belmont, CA 94002

Field Educational Publications
2725 Sand Hill Road
Menlo Park, CA 94025

Fisher-Price
636 Girard Avenue
East Aurora, NY 14052

Flaghouse, Inc.
150 North MacQuesten Parkway
Mt. Vernon, NY 10550

Follett Publishing Company
Department DM
1010 West Washington Boulevard
Chicago, Il 60607

Foothills Educational Services, Ltd.
13027 Lake Twintree Road, S. E.
Calgary, Alberta
Canada T2J 2X2

Futurcomp
16 Driggs Street
Staten Island, NY 10308

Ginn and Company
P.O. Box 2649
Columbus, OH 43216

Globe Book Company
50 West 23rd Street
New York, NY 10010

Gray's Distribution Company
The Learning Tree
4419 North Ravenswood
Chicago, IL 60640

H&H Publishing Company, Inc.
1231 Knapp Drive
Clearwater, FL 34625

Harcourt Brace Jovanovich
757 Third Avenue
New York, NY 10017

Harding House Publishers
P.O. Box 10029
Southport, NC 28461

Harlan Enterprises
P.O. Box 145
Brownfield, TX 79316

Harper and Row Publishers
Keystone Industrial Park
Scranton, PA 18512

Hartley Courseware
P.O. Box 431
Dimondale, MI 48821

Haworth Press
28 East 22nd Street
New York, NY 10010

Health Publishing Company
P.O. Box 3805
San Francisco, CA 94119

Heath, D.C. and Company
125 Spring Street
Lexington, MA 02173

High Noon Books
20 Commercial Boulevard
Novato, CA 94949-6191

Holt, Rinehart and Winston
CBS
383 Madison Avenue
New York, NY 10017

Houghton Mifflin Company
One Beacon Street
Boston, MA 02107

Human Services Press
P.O. Box 2423
Springfield, IL 62705

Hyperactive Attention Deficit
(HAAD)
Parent/Teacher Support Group
106 South Street, Suite 207
Charlottesville, VA 22901

Incentive Publications
3835 Cleghorn Avenue
Nashville, TN 37215

Incentives for Learning, Inc.
600 West Van Buren Street
Chicago, IL 60607

Institute for Child Behavior
    Research
4182 Adams Avenue
San Diego, CA 92116

Instructional/Communications
    Technology, Inc.
10 Stepar Place
Huntington Station, NY 11746

Instructional Fare
P.O. Box 1650
Grand Rapids, MI 49501

International Reading Association
800 Barksdale Road
Newark, DE 19711

Interstate Printers & Publishers
P.O. Box 50
Danville, Il 61834

Janus Book Publishers
2501 Industrial Parkway West
Department AM 454
Hayward, CA 94545

Jastak Associates
1526 Gilpin Avenue
Wilmington, DE 19806

JIST Works, Inc.
The Job Search People
720 North Park Avenue
Indianapolis, IN 46202

Laidlaw Brothers
Thatcher and Madison
River Forest, Il 60305

Lawren Productions, Inc.
P.O. Box 666
Mendocino, CA 95460

Learning Resources
820 North Broadway
Greenfield, IN 46140

Learning Systems Press
P.O. Box 2999
Lafayette, LA 70502

Libros!Libros!Libros!
6036 North 10th Way
Phoenix, AZ 85014

J. B. Lippincott Company
Educational Company
East Washington Square
Philadelphia, PA 19105

Little, Brown and Company
34 Beacon Street
Boston, MA 02106

Longman
19 West 44th Street
New York, NY 10036

Love Publishing Company
1777 South Bellaire Street
Denver, CO 80222

Macmillan Publishing Company
866 Third Avenue
New York, NY 10022

Mafex Associates
90 Cherry Street
Box 519
Johnstown, PA 15907

McGraw-Hill Book Company
1221 Avenue of the Americas
New York, NY 10020

MECC
Publications
2520 Broadway Drive
Saint Paul, MN 55113

Charles E. Merrill Publishing
   Company
1300 Alum Creek Drive, Box 508
Columbus, OH 43216

Milliken Publishing Company
P.O. Box 21579
Saint Louis, MO 63132

Milton Bradley Company
74 Park Street
Springfield, MA 01101

Mindscape, Inc.
Educational Software Division
3444 Dundee Road
Northbrook, IL 60062

C. V. Mosby Company
11830 Westline Industrial Drive
Saint Louis, MO 63141

Mosier Materials, Inc.
61328 Yakwahtin Court
Bend, OR 97702

National Geographic Society
17th and M Streets, N. W.
Washington, DC 20036

Noble and Noble Publishers
1 Dag Hammarskjold Plaza
New York, NY 10017

Numark Publications
104-20 Queens Boulevard
Forest Hills, NY 11375

Opportunities for Learning, Inc.
20417 Nordhoff Street
Chatsworth, CA 91311

Optometric Extension Program
   Foundation, Inc.
2912 South Daimler Street
Santa Ana, CA 92705

Pacific Drum Company
The Wholearth Ball
P.O. Box 4226
Bellingham, WA 98227

Porter Sargeant Publishers
11 Beacon Street
Boston, MA 02108

Prentice Hall
Educational Books Division
Englewood Cliffs, NJ 07632

Pro Lingua Associates
15 Elm Street
Brattleboro, VT 05301

Pro-Ed
8700 Shoal Creek Boulevard
Austin, TX 78758

Professor Phonics
St. Ursula Academy Phonics
   Department
1339 East McMillan Street
Cincinnati, OH 45206

Project Earth
P.O. Box 31
Sauk Centre, MN 56378

Project P.R.E.S.
Santa Cruz Company
Office of Education
809-H Bay Avenue
Capitola, CA 95010

Psychological Assessment
   Resources, Inc.
16204 North Florida Avenue
Lutz, FL 33549

The Psychological Corporation
555 Academic Road
San Antonio, TX 78204

Publishers Test Service
2500 Garden Road
Monterey, CA 93940

Rand McNally and Company
P.O. Box 7600
Chicago, IL 60680

Random House School Division
400 Hahn Road
Westminister, MD 21157

Reader's Digest Services
Educational Division
Pleasantville, NY 10570

Research Press
Box 31773
Champaign, IL 61821

Resources in Special Education
900 J Street
Sacramento, CA 95814-2703

Rock 'n Learn
Educational Products
P.O. Box 7993
Amarillo, TX 79114

S & S Arts & Crafts
Norwich Avenue
Colchester, CT 06415

Scholastic Book Service
904 Sylvan Avenue
Englewood Cliffs, NJ 07632

Scholastic Magazine and Book
   Services
50 West 44th St
New York, NY 10036

School & Pre-School Supply
   Center
5501 Edmondson Avenue
Baltimore, MD 21229

School-Rite
P.O. Box 12547
Fresno, CA 93778

Science Research Association
155 North Wacker Drive
Chicago, IL 60606

Scott, Foresman and Company
1900 East Lake Avenue
Glenview, IL 60025

Scotty Educators
1525 Saunders Street
Wooster, OH 44691

Silver Burdette Company
250 James Street
Morristown, NJ 07960

Slosson Educational Publications
140 Pine Street
East Aurora, NY 14052

The Smart Alex Press
P.O. Box 7192
Quincy, MA 02169

Special Child Publications
P.O. Box 33548
Seattle, WA 98133

The Speech Bin, Inc.
231 Clarksville Road
Princeton Junction, NJ 08550

Steck-Vaughn Company
P.O. Box 2028
Austin, TX 78768

Stoelting Company
1350 South Kostner Avenue
Chicago, IL 60623

Sunburst Communications
Room VJ 52
39 Washington Avenue
Pleasantville, NY 10570

Syracuse University Press
1011 East Water Street
Syracuse, NY 13210

Teachers College Press
Teachers College
Columbia University
1234 Amsterdam Avenue
New York, NY 10027

Teacher's Pet School Supply
2415 Rand Avenue
Colorado Springs, CO 80906

Therapy Skill Builders
3830 East Bellevue Street
P.O. Box 42050
Tucson, AZ 85733

Tri-Services National
Institute of Dyslexia
3200 Woodbine Street
Chevy Chase, MD 20815

U-R Special
P.O. Box 17104
Milwaukee, WI 53217

United Educational Services, Inc.
P.O. Box 605
East Aurora, NY 14052

University Park Press
233 East Redwood Street
Baltimore, MD 21202

Walker Educational Book
  Corporation
720 Fifth Avenue
New York, NY 10019

Weekly Reader
1250 Fairwood Avenue
P.O. Box 16618
Columbus, OH 43216

Western Psychological Services
12031 Wilshire Boulevard
Los Angeles, CA 90025

Wiff n' Proof Publishers
1490-FV South Boulevard
Ann Arbor, MI 48104-4699

John Wiley and Sons
605 Third Avenue
New York, NY 10016

Write 'Em . . . Notes
1233 Settlebench Lane
Kennesaw, GA 30144

Xerox Educational Publications
P.O. Box 16629
Columbus, OH 43216

Index